BORN IN YOSEMITE

PETER T. HOSS

75 years of personal observations

PASSIONS · POLITICS · TRADITIONS
PERSONALITIES · ADVENTURES AND MISADVENTURES

*with photos from the Ansel Adams Family Collection,
the Tom Frost Climbing Collection, and the Yosemite Research Library
and featuring "Music of Yosemite" by Tom Bopp*

BORN IN YOSEMITE

Peter T. Hoss

First Edition August 2011
Second printing May 2012

© 2011 Peter T. Hoss

Library of Congress Control Number: 2011931948

ISBN 13: 978-1-935530-22-0

Published by
Park Place Publications
P.O. Box 829
Pacific Grove, CA 93950
www.parkplacepublications.com

Edited by Barbara Mountrey
Jacket design by Martino Hoss and Michelle Manos
Interior design by Patricia Hamilton

Photographs: Special thanks to the Adams Family Collection,
the Yosemite Research Library, Tom Frost, Mary FitzGerald Beach,
Nancy and Bob Eckart, Dick Mansfield, and Patricia Hamilton.
All other photos are from the Hoss Family Collection.

www.borninyosemite.com

BORN IN YOSEMITE

PETER T. HOSS

Enjoy

Peter Hoss

Virginia Best (the future Mrs. Ansel Adams). Courtesy of Adams Family Collection.

CONTENTS

Maps xii
Dedication xv
Acknowledgements xvii
Introduction by Michael Adams xx
Preface xxii

PART 1

My Life in Yosemite

CHAPTER 1—YOSEMITE: TIMELESS WONDER AND CHANGE. . 3

Seasons in Yosemite 3
  Winter Shutdown 3
  Springtime Awakening 4
  Summertime Bustle 5
  Autumn Withdrawal 5

CHAPTER 2—YOSEMITE CHILDHOOD (1934–1942) 7

How I Came to Be Born in Yosemite 10
The Old Village 11
Other Infrastructure in Yosemite Valley 11
The Neighborhood Where I Grew Up 14
Growing Up in Paradise 15
School Days in Yosemite 19
Ejected from Eden 20

CHAPTER 3—MY YOUTH IN YOSEMITE (1942-1950) 23

Homecomings 23
First Major High Country Trek 24

CHAPTER 4—HIGH SCHOOL SUMMER IN YOSEMITE (1950-1951). 27

Memorable Summertime Characters 28
Freedom of Wheels 30
Getting the "Glad Tidings" 31

CHAPTER 5—COLLEGE DAYS AND YOSEMITE
(1951-1957) 33
Visiting the Ansel Adams Home 34

CHAPTER 6—THE GRADUATE COMES HOME (1955-1956) . . . 37
What Next? 38
The Great Flood of 1955 40
Cabin Living and Interesting Characters 41
Detour to the Tetons 41

CHAPTER 7—AN EVENTFUL FINAL SUMMER (1957) 43
The Plan 43
Setting up the High Sierra Camps 43
The Plan Altered and Abandoned 44
Destiny at Tuolumne Meadows Lodge 46
Working and Playing and Forging a Relationship 48
Back to Law School 49

CHAPTER 8—AWOL FROM YOSEMITE (1958–1960) 51
AWOL from Yosemite (1958-1960) 51
In the Army Now 51
Back to Yosemite 52

CHAPTER 9—INTRODUCING THE FAMILY (1960–1963) 55
Half Dome Climb with Vince and Boy Scouts 56

CHAPTER 10—LEGAL SERVICES FOR THE CONCESSIONERS
1964 TO 1972 57
Paving the Way for the Shuttles 58
A Hostile Takeover 59
A New Life for Della 60

CHAPTER 11—BECOMING A PRIVILEGED VISITOR
1972 TO PRESENT 63
Board Member 64

PART 2
Yosemite's Passions and Politics

CHAPTER 12—YOSEMITE TRADITIONS. 69
Bears in the Park. 69
The Fire Fall. 71
The Bracebridge Dinner 75
The Story of Badger Pass 80
The Wawona Tree. 82
The Conversation Club 83
Yosemite Cemetery. 84

CHAPTER 13—YOSEMITE SUB-CULTURES 85
The Climbers. 85
Extreme Sports in Yosemite 90

CHAPTER 14— A DIFFERENT KIND OF LAW 91
My Father As Commissioner 91
Life on the Bench with Don Pitts. 91
Don't Trifle with the Magistrate ("How To Turn a $25 Fine
    Into Four Days In Jail") 92
"Teachers" 94
Encounters With a 90-Day Wonder. 95
Following in Footsteps Failed 96
Another Familiar Face Becomes Magistrate. 97

CHAPTER 15—HETCH HETCHY—THE CONTROVERSY
THAT WON'T GO AWAY 99

CHAPTER 16—CHANGING PUBLIC INVOLVEMENT 103
Yosemite Valley is Not (and Never Has Been) a Wilderness 103
95% of Yosemite Nat'l Park Comes Closer to Being Wilderness.105
At the Beginning. 109
The White Man "Discovers" Yosemite. 109
Visitors Begin to Arrive. 110

A Public Trust 111
The Influence of John Muir (1838-1914) 111
Galen Clark, the First Yosemite Guardian (1814–1910) 114
Protecting the Public Trust: The Federal Government Steps In. . 114
The New Deal in Yosemite 116
World War II 117
Post World War II Tourism Boom 118
The Media Blasts Yosemite Management 119
David Brower Defends Yosemite Management 120
Changing Character of the Park Service:
           Rangers Become Policemen 122
Visitors Become the Enemy 122
Emerging Role of nonprofits. 124
A Christian Ministry in the National Parks (ACMNP) 127
Getting Smart About Entrance Fees 129
Getting Dumb About Firearms 130
Current Park Service Responsibilities 130

CHAPTER 17— EVOLUTION OF THE CONCESSIONERS 133

The Innkeepers and Early Automobiles 133
Impact of David A. Curry and the Curry Family on Yosemite . . 134
Consolidation of Competing Concessioners 138
Conflict Between the Government and the Concessioners
           (Postwar To 1963). 141
Affirmative Action in the National Parks—A Brief Effort 143
USNR & Shasta—A Hostile Takeover 144
MCA Era 145
Enter and Exit The Japanese:
           How That Changed Doing Business In Yosemite. 150
The Delaware North Era 152
Healthcare Services in Yosemite Valley. 153
Ansel Adams Gallery
           A Surviving Family Business in the National Parks. 156

CHAPTER 18—MASTER PLANNING .163

    Mission 66—The First Plan. 163
    Acquisition of El Portal Property. 163
    1980 General Management Plan 164
    The Yosemite Valley Plan (YVP) 165
    Campgrounds 167
    Employee Housing 167
    The True Meaning of the Yosemite Valley Plan 171

CHAPTER 19—MERCED RIVER LITIGATION 177

    The Wild and Scenic River that is Only Partly Wild and Scenic .177
    Biography of A River: From Glacial Snow Melt
        to the U.S. Ninth Circuit Court of Appeals. 178
    Enjoying the River 181
    The Park Service Blindsided by the U.S.
        Ninth Circuit Court of Appeals. .183
    A Dubious Compromise 187
    What Next? 188
    A Potential Future Concern 189
    What Will Be the Impact on the Average Visitor?. 190

CHAPTER 20—WHAT IS APPROPRIATE IN YOSEMITE. 193

CHAPTER 21—OFF AND ON RELATIONSHIP
             WITH THE SIERRA CLUB 197

CHAPTER 22—THE MUSE IN YOSEMITE. 203

    Art In Yosemite. 203
    Writers About Yosemite. 205
    Music in Yosemite. 208
        Music and The Yosemite Experience by Tom Bopp. 209

PART 3

Personalities, Adventures and Misadventures

CHAPTER 23—PERSONALITIES 225

Family Members

Herman (1894–1971) & Della Hoss (1900–1997). 225

Patti Hoss (1935–2001) 231

Martino Hoss and Maura Murphy Hoss. 232

Vincent Whitney Hoss and Wendy Thomson Hoss 234

Hil Oehlmann, Sr.(deceased),Hil Oehlmann, Jr. (1928–1951)236

Bob & Chuck Eckart 238

Mary FitzGerald Beach 238

Yosemite Icons

Ansel Adams (1902–1984) 239

Nic Fiore (1921–2009). 244

Red Skelton (1913–1997) 246

Don (1894–1948) & Mary Curry Tresidder (1893–1970) . . .247

Stuart Cross (deceased). 250

Shirley Sargent (1927-2004) 250

Martha Miller 252

Carl Sharsmith 252

Ed Hardy, and Don and Kay Pitts .253

Mike Tollefson 253

Dave Mihalic. 253

Natives and Long-time Friends

Mike and Jeanne Adams 255

Anne Adams Helms and Ken Helms. 256

Dick Otter 257

Gordon, and Louise Hooley,

 Bart and Nancy Hooley 258

Charlie Castro. 259

In and Out of My Life

Meredith Little 261

Rol Summit. 262

George McInnis 263

Harkjoon Paik. 263

John Argue (1932-2002) 263

Bob Righter. 264

Tom Shepherd 264

Sue Mathewson 265

Roger and Ann Hendrickson 265

CHAPTER 24—ADVENTURES AND MISADVENTURES 267

Dick Otter's Icy Interlude 267

Ascents. 267

Backpacking Treks I Have Known 269

Where Are My Friends?. 270

A Close Call for Bart 270

Trans-Sierra Gourmet Ski Trip. 272

River Rats. 277

Martino at Tuolumne Meadows. 278

Boy Scouts and Hells Angels. 279

Vince at Sunrise High Sierra Camp—Family Reunion 280

Family Attempts Mt. Lyell 283

Mountain Men's Mental Lapse 284

PART 4

Perspectives on Preservation and Enjoyment

CHAPTER 25—WHAT IS THE STANDARD? 289

The Academic Answer. 289

Pragmatic Answer 297

My Answer 297

Preservation: What?. 299

Preservation: Why? 301

Preservation: How? 304

User Capacity 306

Visitors Are Not the Complainers 306

Advice to Visitors 307

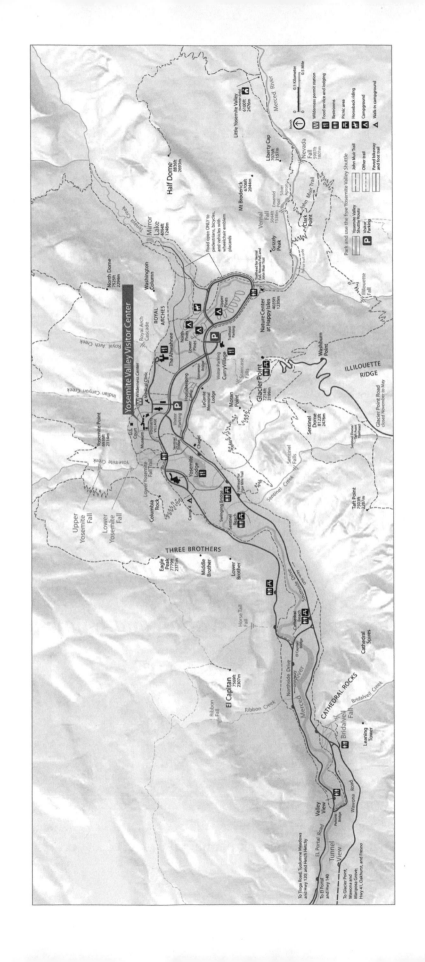

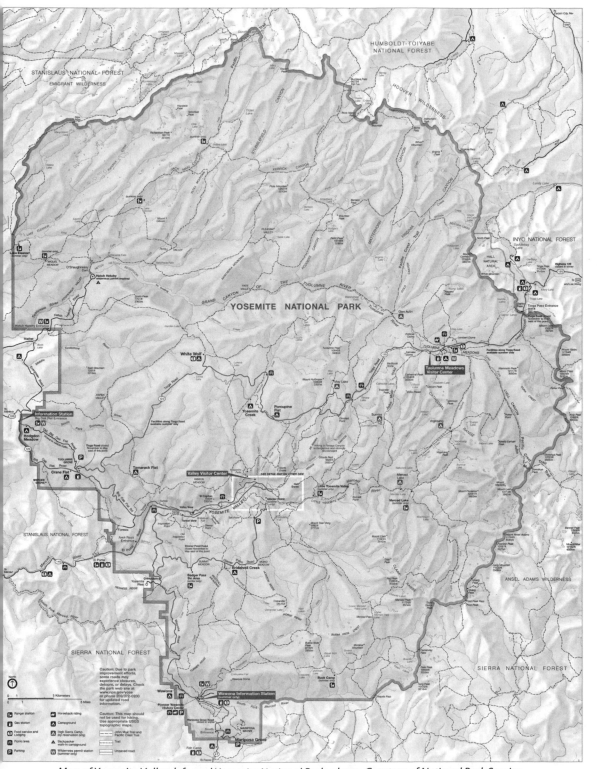

Map of Yosemite Valley, left, and Yosemite National Park, above. Courtesy of National Park Service.

Half Dome. Photo by Patricia Hamilton, 2009.

DEDICATION

Born in Yosemite addresses the Yosemite experience from 75 years of close personal observations and involvement with its inner workings. This book is dedicated to the silent majority of millions who visit Yosemite National Park, especially those who love it and keep coming back for spiritual renewal.

This book is also dedicated to:

Those who, like me, do not like someone dictating in a loud, strident voice how they should enjoy their Yosemite experience.

People who believe that Yosemite is more than a place—it is a state of mind. Individuals who treasure memories of enjoying and interacting with other people in Yosemite, not just ogling the scenery.

Visitors who would not think of defacing or degrading Yosemite; and yet, who believe that Yosemite is so magnificent that it would be very difficult—but not impossible—to ruin it through human intervention.

Individuals who believe that Yosemite's visitors are not the enemy, numerous as they are. Instead, they are the beneficial owners of public property held in trust for them. Like many, I am tired of complaints that Yosemite has been ruined for everyone because something may have ruined Yosemite for the complainer.

This book is also intended to offer reassurance that, despite all the impassioned rhetoric to the contrary, it is still possible for the average visitor to partake of the glad tidings of Yosemite. The term "glad tidings" comes from this famous quote from John Muir: "Climb the mountains and get their glad tidings and nature's peace will fall into you and cares fall off like autumn leaves." For me this best describes the essence of Yosemite. It is a continuing experience every time I visit Yosemite, and that is why I use the term often.

Finally, this book is dedicated to those who recognize that, while not all activities are appropriate for Yosemite, what is appropriate is often in the eye of the beholder.

Yosemite Superintendent's house party, c. 1939. Courtesy of Adams Family Collection.

Acknowledgements

I have been encouraged by several friends over the years to write about my unique experience in Yosemite.

In 1999, after I retired from law practice, I spent three weeks in Yosemite, the longest continuous time there since working there in the 1950s. During this time I decided to write this book.

I was encouraged by my wife, Patti, who died in 2001, and my two sons and their wives, Martino and Maura, and Vince and Wendy. I told my lifelong friend Mike Adams about my idea. He encouraged me, but noted that it was a very ambitious undertaking. Now, 12 years later, I fully understand what he meant.

My first thought was to contact the many people who I knew had firsthand knowledge about Yosemite and ask them to respond to questions and do the writing. I received input from Dave Curry, grandson of David A. Curry. One person, Tom Bopp, leading music historian of Yosemite, graciously contributed a segment, which appears as he wrote it in Chapter 22. It gathered dust in my files for ten years. The late Bill Lane, Jr., son of the founder of *Sunset Magazine*, former ambassador to Australia and a Yosemite enthusiast, expressed interest in publishing it. A retired top management executive of a concessioner operating visitor facilities in Yosemite, Ed Hardy, encouraged me. Don Pitts, retired magistrate, and his wife Kay offered continuing support and information. Many of these folks are prominently mentioned.

I soon determined that I needed to do the writing myself and could not rely on others to do it. I joined a writers group known as "Pebbles," which met in the wonderful Thunderbird Book Store in Carmel Valley under the guidance of its venerable owner, May Waldroup. Our group published a book of short stories called *The Barmaid, the Bean Counter and the Bunjee Jumper*, after a short story I wrote which was a parody on a fairy tale. I started writing sections of the Yosemite book, which were critiqued in a friendly manner by others in the group.

After Pebbles dissolved, when May Waldroup sold the Thunderbird Book Store and ended a tradition, I continued in three other writers groups with former

Pebbles members and some others and continued to write chapters. Of the many who read these chapters I was particularly helped and encouraged by Harold Grice, Marnie Sperry, Martin Dodd, Lisa Merkel, Linda Jardine, Ken Jones, Walter Gourlay, Carol Brown, Pat Matuszweski, Linda Grant, Illia Thompson, Joy Ware, Helen Olson and Georgia Hubley, as well as May Waldroup.

I had been discussing publishing the book with the late Steve Medley, president of the Yosemite Association. Ironically, on the last day I called him about it, I learned he had been tragically killed in an automobile accident in Merced Canyon, only an hour before I called. After learning this, I was somewhat at a loss as to how to proceed. I consulted Patricia Hamilton, a fellow member of the Central Coast Writers, about self-publishing.

Patricia has been extremely helpful and supportive. By the time I contacted Patricia I had written numerous fragments but needed help organizing the material to see how it flowed. Patricia referred me to Don Huntington, a professional writer who helped me organize the material into chapters; Don also assisted me with some of the writing. To give Don and Patricia a flavor of Yosemite, I invited them to stay at The Falcon's Nest, a bed-and-breakfast operated by Don and Kay Pitts, while we all attended a celebration of life for the late legendary Yosemite character Nic Fiore. The event was attended by 850 people, all with Yosemite connections. This afforded Don and me the opportunity to interview several of those in attendance and to generate more stories.

Yosemite is managed by a triad: the National Park Service (NPS), concessioners who operate visitors' services, and the Yosemite Conservancy, a 501(c)(3) corporation, which contributes capital improvements and provides services that the Park Service cannot provide. I needed input from all three entities to provide a balanced perspective. Dave Mihalic, a retired Yosemite Park superintendent, provided much valuable information on recent events from an NPS viewpoint and was very encouraging. Mike Tollefson, who resigned as superintendent to become CEO of the Yosemite Conservancy, was also very helpful and encouraging, as was Kevin Cann, a deputy superintendent under five superintendents, and Don Neubacher, the current superintendent.

Don Huntington left me with a document for review that helped me organize the book. I took this to Patricia, and she directed me to Kedron Bryson, a creative lady who started editing and further organizing what Don Huntington left me. Kedron brought enthusiasm and creative energy to the project. Before she could finish her task, cancer spread rapidly, and she died on January 23, 2011. When Kedron started the project, she gave no hint of illness. She doggedly continued when her illness worsened. B.J. Mountry, a retired McGraw editor, completed the editing. By this time I had a rough draft that could be reviewed by several people interested in the project from various parts of my life for suggestions and to see how it read. For this I am indebted to Mike Adams, Anne Adams Helms, Guy Shoup, Antonia Fiske, Charlotte Bannan, George McInnis, and Michelle Manos.

Finally, I need to acknowledge my friend, travelling companion and the lady of my life for the last seven years, Carol Robles. Carol is a local and internationally recognized expert on the life of John Steinbeck, who is a native of the city in which I have lived since 1962, Salinas, California. She tolerated the many times my mind was off in the book instead of engaged in what we were otherwise doing.

So, as you can see, this book is the product of many minds.

INTRODUCTION
BY MICHAEL ADAMS

Born in Yosemite by Peter Hoss relates his story from the perspective of someone whose parents, when he was born, were already intimately involved in the life of Yosemite. His father, Herman Hoss, was the attorney and personnel director for the Yosemite Park & Curry Company, the major concessioner, and his mother, Della Taylor Hoss, a fine artist whose linoleum and wood block prints of nature are still enjoyed.

Peter and I are each other's oldest friends, having been born a few months apart in the early 1930s, in Yosemite National Park, to parents who were already friends. My parents, Ansel and Virginia Adams, knew Herman and Della in many ways, including the Christmas pageant, the Bracebridge Dinner. Peter's love of Yosemite, its lore, its beauty, its endless fascination, and his sense of fun and spirit of adventure were predestined.

Peter has stated: "I believe that Yosemite is so magnificent that it will be very difficult—but not impossible—to ruin it through human intervention." The dual mandate of both providing access and safeguarding the integrity of nature in national parks is a challenge. Peter, as an avid Yosemite native and attorney, investigates and interviews with background knowledge and fervor. He clarifies the numerous planning efforts over the years, the legal battles, the misclassification of the Merced River as "wild and scenic" as it flows through Yosemite Valley, with the bridges, rip-rap, and roads defining its course. Many devoted citizens are sure that they have the right answers to any planning consideration. Confusion and controversy reign. Perhaps, at rare times of peak visitation, some reservation system for day use might be an option, to not exceed a sense of "carrying capacity."

Personalities and individuals who have worked in Yosemite, in the High Country, or in Yosemite Valley, seasonally or for longer periods, are all influenced by their unique experiences—colorfully described by their friend, Peter Hoss. Peter and his family are and have been friends of the Adams family for generations, with our children knowing each other as well. Martino and Vincent, Peter and Patti's sons, continue the creative genius of the Hoss family. Peter has shared his legal expertise and friendship as a member of the Ansel

Michael Adams and Peter Hoss selecting photos in Ansel Adams' studio, 2010.

Adams Gallery Board of Directors. A true original, Peter provides fresh insight into how the human life in Yosemite National Park benignly fosters nature's self-organizing systems, with people admiring and realizing that the lightest impact of man could well be best.

I am honored to have been invited to introduce *Born in Yosemite*, the record of a lifelong love affair with Yosemite.

— Michael Adams, M.D.
Carmel Highlands, California, 2011

PREFACE

I was born in Yosemite Valley in 1934 and lived there for the first eight years of my life. I returned frequently as a preteen. From high school through college and until graduation from law school, I worked in Yosemite. I have hiked most of its trails. I have done legal work for the concessioner, Yosemite Park & Curry Company. I have brought my family to Yosemite. My two sons have worked in the Yosemite High Country. They have brought my four grandchildren to Yosemite. I am on the Board of the Ansel Adams Gallery and A Christian Ministry in the National Parks (ACMNP). I am a contributing member to the Yosemite Conservancy through the John Muir Heritage Society. I believe I know the territory.

This book is about my personal observations of Yosemite based on actual experience. It is not a guidebook about what to see in Yosemite, nor is it a scholarly history.

The book is divided into four parts. The first, *My Life in Yosemite*, is autobiographical, recounting my personal experience from childhood through seven decades. Hopefully, this will authenticate later observations, since Yosemite is noted for unauthenticated observations.

The second, *Passions and Politics*, explores the management, traditions and subcultures of Yosemite during my lifetime and how ownership of the first scenic area designated for public use has played out and continues to play out.

The third, *Personalities*, identifies people whom I have met in Yosemite and who have come in and out of my life, and recounts adventures and misadventures throughout the years.

The fourth part, *Perspectives on Preservation and Enjoyment*, summarizes my views regarding how Yosemite can be enjoyed by the public (who owns it, after all) and, at the same time, can be conserved for future generations to enjoy without making drastic policy changes. The book will address the most controversial of topics—what is appropriate and what is inappropriate in Yosemite. It will also touch on how one's perception of enjoyment versus the need for preservation changes not only as external conditions change, but also as one matures and becomes better acquainted with Yosemite.

This book is not written to advocate a future agenda for Yosemite. I discuss different viewpoints, render some opinions and discuss both sides of some issues without rendering an opinion. I am neither trying to propose nor sell an approach for the future of Yosemite. I do not believe Yosemite is broken and needs to be fixed.

I start with a mindset based on my experience. I am the son of a management executive for the major concessioner in Yosemite National Park. Since 1925 a single concessioner has operated all of the visitor services in the park, with the exception of The Ansel Adams Gallery, which remains family-owned.

My father was the primary architect of a law designed to protect original concessioners in national parks, who were primarily family-owned businesses based in the national parks in which they operated. The laws he drafted fell out of fashion when concessions came to be operated by conglomerate corporations based outside of the national parks in which they operate.

I have personally known the top management officer of every concession in Yosemite since the 1930s. I grew up with the sons and daughters of National Park Service employees based in Yosemite. Many of my friends are current and retired National Park Service employees. In general, I regard National Park Service personnel as dedicated, underpaid public servants who cherish their proper role as protectors of the national parks. Although I have not agreed with all of their decisions, I do respect the jobs they perform. These are not easy tasks.

I applaud the role of nonprofits in Yosemite. They perform many valuable services and fund capital improvements that the chronically underfunded National Park Service can neither perform nor provide. They are insulated from some of the political pressures facing the National Park Service and the concessioners. I believe that Yosemite's current management system and method of operation work well for the benefit of the visitor.

There is one group of Yosemite spokespersons with whom I do not agree. They are the self-appointed saviors of Yosemite and those who want to dictate how the public, for whom Yosemite is held in trust, must enjoy it. They dogmatically assert by what means we must go about leaving Yosemite unimpaired for future generations to enjoy. The self-appointed saviors are a minority, but they speak with loud and strident voices to anyone who will listen, in a tone of moral superiority. I have heard their rhetoric all my life. Quite frankly, I am tired of it. I am not of their mindset. I do not see Yosemite through their eyes.

The terms "valley" and "high country" are not technically proper names, but they have always been proper names to me and other Yosemite insiders because they describe areas of Yosemite National Park with a distinct history, distinct geographic features and a distinct human footprint.

The Valley refers to Yosemite Valley, inhabited for 1000 years or more by Miwok Indians and a developed recreational area for over 50 years before there was a National Park Service, never a wilderness by any definition (see Chapter 16). The High Country refers to over 95% of the Park added later than the original grant, following lobbying by John Muir, a terrain of granite domes, majestic vistas, soaring peaks, rushing streams and rivers, meadows and forest, and wild animals, snowed in nine months a year, more or less. Most of the High Country is officially classified as wilderness. The High Country is visited only by backpackers and few on horseback trips, and cross country skiers. Even the inhabitants of the Valley enjoy escaping to the High Country when it is accessible in summer and more than a few visitors bypass the Valley during the warm and crowded summer months. The Valley and the High Country are truly different worlds, both referred to by the common name Yosemite.

Born in Yosemite

Peter Hoss at age 3. Photo by Ansel Adams hangs in the Winter Club room in the Ahwahnee Hotel, Yosemite Valley.

PART 1

My Life in Yosemite

Icy winter trees in Yosemite. Photo by Patricia Hamilton, 2009.

CHAPTER 1

YOSEMITE: TIMELESS WONDER AND CHANGE

Yosemite National Park is one of the great wonders of the world. Words cannot adequately express the profound reality of Yosemite Valley, not even the eloquent words of John Muir. Ansel Adams' world famous photographs fall short of conveying the full majesty of Yosemite's towering granite cliffs, rushing waterfalls and verdant Valley floor. First-time visitors may have seen videos of Yosemite, but when they first see Yosemite Valley they are often unprepared for its splendor.

SEASONS IN YOSEMITE

Winter Shutdown

Winter in Yosemite Valley is the season for shutting down, a time of purification. The days are short. In the middle of winter the sheltered Valley floor around Curry Village, nestled between Half Dome and Glacier Point, sees the sunshine only a few hours a day.

At 4000 feet, winter temperatures often hover near freezing or below, chilly but not deadly cold. Snow occasionally falls on the Valley floor, transforming the boulders in the Merced River into giant marshmallows. Snow clings to branches of bare trees and forms kaleidoscopic patterns against a background of blue sky and scudding clouds. Outside Yosemite Valley, the Yosemite High Country is snowbound during winter months, accessible only by cross-country skis or snowshoes.

The flowers in the meadows have died. Ferns have turned brown. Deciduous trees are bare, but evergreen trees remain a vibrant green. The path underfoot is often covered with pine needles and brown leaves, when there is no snow.

Glacier Point Hotel Cafeteria, demolished 1969. Courtesy of Yosemite Research Library.

Springtime Awakening

As winter ends and spring approaches in late March and early April, the falling of freezing water in Yosemite Falls forms a snow cone at the base of the lower falls. Locals used to place bets on when the snow cone would melt. At the same time, ice which has frozen on the cliff next to Yosemite Falls breaks off and plunges into Yosemite Creek beneath the falls, forming what has been named frazil ice. Frazil ice is neither ice nor snow. It forms puffy balls that fall into and float in Yosemite Creek, sometimes giving the appearance that the creek is snow-covered. Frazil ice is interesting to view and dangerous to walk on, because it is not solid. One walking on it is likely to fall into freezing water underneath the frazil ice.

Spring is the season when Yosemite's waterfalls are thundering. It is the time when "the snow is melting into music," in Muir's words. Melting snows from the mountainsides of the nearby High Sierras transform the placid Merced River into a raging torrent, which occasionally overflows its banks.

Spring is the season of new life, with abundant wildflowers blooming. The branches of dogwood trees hang heavy with their rich harvest of white blossoms. It is the time of year when brilliant green appears on the trees and in the meadows.

Summertime Bustle

Summer is the high tourist season, with warm days and mild nights, perfect weather for both hiking and family camping. The roads on the Valley floor are crowded with cars. Stores, snack bars and restaurants are jammed with people.

Summer in Yosemite Valley.

However, a world of secluded natural beauty can be found a short distance beyond the pavement. More than 800 trails twist and turn through the Yosemite High Country, accessible for three to four months. Even in the Valley a day hiker can find solitude just a few yards from the traveled roads.

Yosemite Falls and lesser falls often cease running in midsummer. Nevertheless, in the summertime the Valley is a destination for hikers, river rafters, bikers, climbers and those who just want to drink in the scenery. One of the most popular diversions is peering up at flyspecks, which binoculars reveal to be climbers inching their way up El Capitan's massive wall.

Backpackers interested in greater solitude head for the High Country, which becomes accessible to them in summer.

Autumn Withdrawal

During autumn the pace of life in Yosemite Valley becomes peaceful and serene. The flow of visitors slows. The waterfalls are mostly dry. The trees clothe themselves in fall colors. The weather often provides ideal conditions for the magical experience of noisily tramping through fallen leaves. Early snowfalls in the mountains above the Valley will sometimes awaken waterfalls.

Autumn leaves on the Valley floor.
Photo by Patricia Hamilton, 2009.

INTRODUCING
PETER HOSS

BORN APRIL 10, 1934 -- 7 POUNDS
YOSEMITE NATIONAL PARK

MR. AND MRS. HERMAN H. HOSS

Top, left: Peter with his mother, Della. Top, right: Peter with his father, Herman.
Bottom: Peter's original birth announcement.

CHAPTER 2

YOSEMITE CHILDHOOD (1934–1942)

Ken Burns, who made a definitive documentary on national parks, described his impression on first seeing Yosemite, one that echoes the feelings of many visitors:

> *"There is no preparation for it. A turn in the road and suddenly the Valley unfolds before you. I have never in my life felt the way I felt at that moment. The crisp air and high altitude made the mountains and waterfalls, trees and road look almost like a backdrop you could roll up and store away. But it was something more. Like Muir, though, I was physically outside, I was actually going in, transforming the old generic question once again "Who am I?" The view was an anchor and beacon. It held me gently in its grip. I don't think I have ever completely lost that feeling and it pulled me directly into the heart of the park."*

Burns' passage describes the point at which two highways enter Yosemite Valley from the Merced Canyon. An equally dramatic initial view of Yosemite Valley can be seen from Inspiration Point, just past the tunnel on State Highway 41 coming from Fresno. That is very near to the point from which members of the Mariposa Battalion became the first Caucasians to view Yosemite Valley.

Everyone who drives into Yosemite Valley enters at one of these two points. From either entrance, countless first-time visitors have shared Ken Burns' powerful, spiritual reaction upon first catching sight of the breathtaking majesty of the Valley. The experience of that first glimpse, however, is one that I missed. Having been born in Yosemite Valley, I accepted the sights that Ken Burns and others describe as mysterious and awe-inspiring as ordinary.

Nevertheless, in spite of the fact that I've driven into Yosemite Valley countless times, the first view of the Yosemite Valley still awakens strong emotion. The sight never fails to fill me with powerful feelings of coming home to the place where I belong above all other places on earth. I tell people—only half-jokingly—that I was born in Yosemite and never completely adjusted to the outside world.

At the time of my birth, people were alive who could remember when

Della Taylor Hoss with Peter

Peter with his mother, Della. Courtesy of Adams Family Collection.

Peter with his paternal grandfather.   *Peter as a child .*

Top: Peter with his father, Herman.
Right: Peter at age 6.
Left: Peter with his mother, Della.

Yosemite was first "discovered." Only 60 years had passed since Abraham Lincoln's 1864 declaration that designated the area as a public trust. During those intervening six decades the revolutionary concept of public ownership of scenic areas had transformed Yosemite Valley into a National Park, first under state control, then under federal management.

During the Great Depression, as I was growing up and becoming aware of the world outside Yosemite, visitors to Yosemite swelled to record numbers. This was stimulated in part by the discovery that people from the Central Valley of California who had lost their sources of income could spend the entire summer at the campgrounds. Today there is a seven-day limit.

HOW I CAME TO BE BORN IN YOSEMITE

People ask how I came to live in Yosemite Valley for the first eight years of my life. My father, Herman Hoss, had worked at Camp Curry during his college days, prior to attending Stanford Law School. After a brief clerkship with a Wall Street law firm, Herman decided that life on Wall Street was not for him. He returned to his previous position as chief clerk at Camp Curry to contemplate a different career path. He was soon appointed magistrate judge, a position that at the time carried with it the title of "Commissioner." At that time, his was a part-time position. Herman soon became personnel manager for the Yosemite Park & Curry Company. He was eventually elevated to the position of secretary-treasurer for the company, third in the chain of command.

My mother, Della Taylor Hoss, was a talented artist, whose medium was linoleum block prints , mostly of trees, and also pencil drawings. Her color woodcut "Half Dome, Yosemite, Autumn" is featured on the cover of this book. My parents met in Yosemite and married in 1928.

Most of the Yosemite Valley infrastructure has remained little changed since my earliest memories. Outside of Yosemite, the rest of the State of California has changed in ways unimaginable when I was born. In 1930 the population of California was a little more than 5,000,000 people, which is less than the population of the San Francisco Bay area today. During the succeeding decade, the state added a million more people, raising the population to 6,000,000 in 1940.

During my childhood I was unaffected by the Great Depression which enveloped the nation. Hardships endured by people outside Yosemite had little or no effect upon Yosemite residents. No one in Yosemite was unemployed, because, in order to live in Yosemite, one also had to be employed there.

THE OLD VILLAGE

I remember when the Old Village was a lively gathering place for visitors and locals alike, centered around the chapel, which is the oldest building in Yosemite Valley. Today the chapel is the sole reminder of the Old Village.

Built in 1879, the chapel was originally located near the beginning of the four-mile trail to Glacier Point. It was moved to its location in Old Village in 1901 and has served people at that site ever since.

During my childhood the Old Village was the central shopping area for Yosemite Valley residents. Besides the chapel, the Old Village was the site of several photography studios, Degnan's Bakery and Store, a barber shop, the Sentinel Hotel, a general store, a shoe repair shop, a number of private residences, a movie theater called "The Pavilion," and a small eatery called "The Old Village Fountain," known by locals as "The Greasy Spoon." For most of its history, this small restaurant lacked a sign. A sign showing a picture of a spoon was eventually created. The Greasy Spoon served good food. Ice cream cones were sold at the front window.

One of the buildings in the Old Village was the Sentinel Hotel. Across the street was the Cedar Cottage, which had a tree growing through it. Both have been torn down, but the tree still stands.

The Old Village disappeared when what is now called "The Village Mall'"was built in the late 1950s. The National Park Service (NPS) has restored the Old Village site to its natural appearance, with only plaques remaining.

OTHER INFRASTRUCTURE IN YOSEMITE VALLEY

The old Yosemite Lodge was built by the U.S. Cavalry when they policed Yosemite Valley before the rangers. A new Yosemite Lodge replaced the old structure in the late 1950s.

Across the road from the lodge was the Indian Village, home to about a half-dozen families who were descendants of the original Miwok tribe that had inhabited the Valley. "Ahwahne," which means "deep grassy valley," is the Indian name for Yosemite Valley, and the name of the tribe that lived there was the Ahwahnechee.

The Indian families remaining in Yosemite Valley were relocated several times, as the Park Service wanted the sites where they lived. The Indian Village that I knew as a child and during the years I worked in the Valley was built in 1932 and removed in the late 1960s. Since that time Indian families employed in the Valley have lived where other employees live. As with other employees working in the Valley, only those working in the Valley are entitled to live in the Valley.

At the time of the removal of the Indian Village I knew, the government granted to the Mariposa Native American Indian Council the right to reconstruct homes and other structures occupied by the Indians in earlier days, in order to allow a historical tradition to be perpetuated. In 2010 Leanna Castro, granddaughter of my childhood friend and current friend Charlie Castro (see Personalities, Chapter 23), with the help of others, reconstructed the Umacha, in which the Ahwahnechee lived. These teepee-like, bark-covered structures were reproduced as originally built, with areas for the ceremonial "smudging" ceremony to remove evil spirits. Umachas may also be seen behind the museum.

A short distance across a meadow, near the base of Yosemite Falls, was an area where Park Service employees lived and where the two-room school, serving grades one through eight, was located. Today this area is largely unchanged.

Adjacent to the Park Service housing were the museum and NPS administration offices. Nearby were Best's Studio and Pohono Studio, the post office and a soda fountain known as The Lost Arrow, a gathering place for local kids. Now a visitor center has been added. Best's Studio has been renamed "The Ansel Adams Gallery." The Lost Arrow is no more. Otherwise, the area looks much the same.

The next complex of buildings as one moves up the Valley comprises the hospital where I was born (now a day clinic) and some surrounding housing for concessioner employees. Beyond that is the Ahwahnee Hotel, a luxury hotel built in 1927 that was in full operation when I was a child.

Across the Valley is Curry Village, founded by David A. Curry, which still provides tents and cabins for visitors, some employee housing, an ice rink, a swimming pool, shops, an outdoor stage, a store, a gift shop, a mountaineering center and a restaurant.

Between Curry Village and the Old Village is the tented Housekeeping Camp, where visitors can cook their own meals and sleep in beds.

1. Sentinel Hotel, demolished
2. Wawona Hotel, circa 1885
3. Old Village Store. Courtesy of Yosemite Research Library.
4. Yosemite Valley Chapel

Across from the Housekeeping Camp is Le Conte Lodge, a stone structure containing exhibits built and maintained by the Sierra Club.

Campgrounds are located around the Valley. Their locations and names have changed throughout Yosemite's history.

The infrastructure described above remains. In my childhood there was a fish hatchery in an area known as Happy Isles, where the Merced River enters Yosemite Valley. It is no longer there.

There were three service stations in Yosemite Valley when I was a child. Now there are none. Near one of the stations was a garage and company offices, both of which remain.

This describes most of the infrastructure in Yosemite Valley that existed when I was a child. All of it could be easily reached by walking or by bicycle.

THE NEIGHBORHOOD WHERE I GREW UP

We lived in a row of houses, known as "The Row," together with the other management employees of the Yosemite Park & Curry Company, which we referred to as The Company. Yosemite was a company town. The Company occupied buildings owned by the government. No one could own a home or choose where they would live. Single employees lived in dorms, cabins and sometimes tents. Housing was assigned, and all families paid rent to the company. Rent, groceries, and other expenses were deducted each month from a paycheck.

Peter's childhood home. Photo circa 1930.

Even a car could be purchased this way through the company.

Our house was on the end of The Row and across the road from the Merced River. The house was small, but we had a meadow for our side yard with Half Dome towering above it. The houses are still there, amazingly unchanged by more than 75 years of wind, weather and wear. I walk by them, and my memory resurrects the ghosts of the families and playmates who inhabited those houses in the long-ago days of my childhood. I still remember who lived in most of the houses.

Growing Up in Paradise

Just beyond the borders of our little row of houses lay the wonderful and easily accessible world of the Yosemite Valley. We accepted the towering granite cliffs, waterfalls, meadows, trees and the Merced River that meandered past our homes as ordinary. We were strangers to such things as traffic signals, streetlights and tall buildings that most other children regard as common. Neon lights outside the Park fascinated me as a young child, since they were so unfamiliar. I referred to them by the rather clumsy name of "bwight lights going wound and wound."

Pets were forbidden in the Park. We children became familiar with deer, bear, chipmunks and a variety of birds. We were taught that wild animals are not pets. Even though the Valley had no cattle, we became friends with resident cowboys who led trail rides, complete with cookouts and music, for park visitors. An annual rodeo featured the usual rodeo activities.

Like most kids during that era, we devised our own methods for having fun. We formed a neighborhood club called the Bobcats. We would set off on adventures exploring hidden corners of Yosemite Valley. We fished in the Merced River and played Kick the Can and Andy Over along the alley behind our houses. We built roads and buildings in the small yards beside our houses, which we called "developments."

Children of Yosemite had normal childhood experiences, unchanged in any significant way by the fact that we were living and playing in paradise. The Old Village had a movie theater. The Ahwahnee Hotel had tennis courts and a pitch-and-putt golf course. Camp Curry had a dance hall plus a "Kiddie Kamp" recreational area for children. There were swimming pools at Camp Curry and at Yosemite Lodge. A skating rink and a toboggan run at Camp Curry were available for wintertime activities.

When I was young I once rode the railroad line that carried passengers from Merced to El Portal, just outside Yosemite Valley, until the 1940s. The train was the best way to get into the Valley until the "all year" Highway 140 was opened for automobile traffic in the 1920s.

I had a hobby of collecting beer bottle caps. I scrounged the campgrounds for them, and with my artist mother's help, fashioned them into ashtrays, using the caps for the sides and a jar lid for the tray itself. I then sold them to the other residents of The Row. This was my first business venture.

The Valley society was divided between the children of Company employees and children of Park Service employees. There were friendly rivalries and a different mission between the two caretakers. There were baseball games and social events, but no real animosity between the two groups. There were a few in the small community who were not employees of either The Company or the Park Service. They included the doctor, the dentist, the Ansel Adams family and the postmaster.

We built forts in the meadow and made trails that wound through the flowers and grasses, creating conditions that might have troubled contemporary environmental purists. The meadow survived. Each spring it would come back with all evidence of our previous play completely wiped out by the verdant new growth.

During the summer months, Half Dome served as my alarm clock for bedtime. My mother told me to come home when the glow of the setting sun left the top of Half Dome.

Even though our community was somewhat isolated from the culture and events of the outside world, we were living in one of the world's most popular tourist destinations. Visitors frequently included notable celebrities. I remember watching President Franklin D. Roosevelt as he rode in an open convertible around the Ahwahnee meadow. Walt Disney came for a visit, and several of us gave his daughter Diane Marie a personal guided tour of our school.

The Ahwahnee has always been a luxury hotel. Years ago one of the hotel's transportation agents, Jack Curran, almost turned away a scruffy-looking visitor. As Jack looked over the register, however, he noted the signature was that of Herbert Hoover, who had just returned from a fishing trip.

Foreign dignitaries visited. Haile Selassie came from Ethiopia. The king of Belgium came. When he left, the king of Belgium thanked everyone profusely and then offered special thanks to Herman Hoss. Everyone wondered what Herman had done to earn the praise of the king. Herman revealed that he had gone into the men's restroom and heard a faint tapping on one of the stalls, revealing that the king had locked himself in. Herman rescued him. On the same trip the king was introduced to a wrangler named Billy Nelson, who greeted the king with the famous quote "Just call me Billy, and I'll call you King."

Yosemite's resident children were occasionally granted access to the

YOSEMITE SOCIAL LIFE 1930S AND 1940S

Above, left: Ahwahnee Great Lounge, scene of Yosemite Winter Club Cocktail Party and Dinner. Above, right: left to right, Hil Oehlmann, Luggi Foeger, Bill Janss (a director of Y.P. & C. Co.), Ann Janss (Bill's wife, who later was tragically taken by avalanche while skiing at Sun Valley), Ahwahnee Hostess Irma Cunha, and Mary C. Tresidder, Company president. Courtesy of Nancy and Bob Eckart.

Right: After-ski parties.
Left: Hil Oehlmann.
Rght: Herman Hoss.

DISTINGUISHED VISITORS TO YOSEMITE

Nelson Rockefeller, Hil Oehlmann, circa 1958. Courtesy of Bob and Nancy Eckart.

Hil Oehlmann, Supt. John Preston, Emperor of Ethiopia Haile Selassi with Secret Service and an interpreter. Courtesy of Bob and Nancy Eckart.

Ahwahnee Hotel. Sundays were dress-up days, during which we were invited to attend elegant dinners. I did not look forward to leaving my play clothes behind. Before dinner, my mother made me bathe and clothed me in one of my dress outfits. I was uncomfortable sitting there with a white cloth napkin on my lap.

Christmas in Yosemite Valley was a magical time. Many years snow would fall, granting us a white Christmas. The Ahwahnee Hotel provided a temporary home to a gigantic and resplendent Christmas tree. Santa Claus rode up to the hotel in a sleigh with a bag full of Christmas presents to deliver to the families of hotel guests.

Don Tresidder, The Company top executive, had no children of his own. He loved playing the role of Santa Claus for the local kids gathered for the event in the Curry Pavilion. He was a convincing Santa who helped me remain a true Santa believer for quite a few years. Locals knew him as "Uncle Don."

Uncle Don had a treasured Palomino horse that was the envy of all horse lovers. I never cared much for horses or horseback riding. Uncle Don liked to give local children rides on his beautiful Palomino, but I always demurred, until one day my parents insisted that I accommodate the wishes of the man who was, after all, their boss. So I reluctantly rode the horse around a meadow for a little while, got off, and thanked Uncle Don for the ride. When I got out of range, I said, "Well, thank goodness that's over!"

Our close-knit group of park employee children swelled in the summer to include new playmates, children of guests who spent the entire summer at Yosemite Lodge.

While on vacations ourselves, we were occasionally able to take advantage of the hospitality of hotel operators in other areas. Hotel owners had a custom of providing complimentary accommodations to each other, so we would often be upgraded to the most expensive rooms, which were the most seldom rented. I recall staying in the most expensive suites in the old Del Monte Hotel in Monterey and the Mark Hopkins Hotel in San Francisco, playing with the children of the rich and famous who were staying there at the time.

While I was growing up, Yosemite Valley had no "wrong side of the tracks." There was no social group with whom we were not to associate. I was afraid of no one. I can't remember any playground bullies. I have only a vague memory of a skinny kid, inappropriately named Kit Carson, who used to complain that Indian kids picked on him on his way to school.

Winter sports in Yosemite

Left: Camp Curry skating rink. Right: Dog sledding in Yosemite Valley. Courtesy of Yosemite Research Library.

It was a privilege growing up in such a community. I was unaware of any racial prejudice, social distinctions or evil people. We didn't lock our doors. We didn't know if we were rich or poor. The egalitarian character of the Yosemite Valley culture shaped the values that have endured throughout my life. We lived in a natural paradise that, to some extent, became reflected in the good society that I was part of as I grew up.

School Days in Yosemite

When I approached school age, my mother and Ansel Adams' wife, Virginia, started a kindergarten class in the Yosemite Lodge cafeteria. Nancy Loncaric, the wife of a Company executive, was the teacher. She formed a rhythm band. We joined together in making what sounded to us like great music on a variety of sticks, boards, plates and bells.

When I finished kindergarten, I discovered that my birthday was ten days shy of the cutoff point for going to first grade in the two-room grammar school that we referred to as the "big school." As a result, I had to endure the humiliation of going to kindergarten for a second year.

The experience of being held back was devastating. I believed I was prevented from entering the "big school" by mindless adherence to a bureaucratic rule that I felt made no sense.

I experienced vindication when I finally was able to enter first grade, because it took only three weeks before my teacher realized that I was doing second-grade level work. I was restored to my rightful place with my buddies, who had left me behind when they had begun first grade. The promotion in that two-room school meant that I moved up a single row to sit with the other six members of the second grade. We had the same teacher.

This experience probably contributed to a lifelong aversion to the bureaucratic mindset that regards an arbitrary rule as an inviolate law. I came to believe that it should be incumbent upon all public servants to avoid the making of any decision that would reinforce Honoré De Balzac's observation: "Bureaucracy is a giant mechanism operated by pygmies."

My connection with Yosemite sparked my interest in other parts of our burgeoning National Park System. I studied atlases and learned the name and location of every national park in the system. I developed a lifelong passion for geography. At the age of seven I could recite the population of every state and every major city in the United States, as well as details about countries and cities around the world.

We had only sporadic contact with the outside world. These were years before television. Radio reception was unreliable in Yosemite Valley. My father tried to listen to football games and was frustrated by the poor reception. The news of the bombing of Pearl Harbor and subsequent war details arrived in fragmented fashion.

We responded to the war like other Americans. We grew victory gardens and bought war bonds. I wrote to a pen pal in Russia, our ally at the time.

EJECTED FROM EDEN

During the early years of World War II, Don Tresidder, top management executive of The Company, developed a severe case of pessimism concerning the future of The Company. One dark day he summoned the members of the Company management team, which included my father, into his office and summarily fired many of them. "Uncle Don" then resigned his position to become president of Stanford University, where he achieved some fame, or possibly notoriety, for abolishing campus sororities.

Don Tresidder left Hilmer Oehlmann, Sr., in charge of what he imagined would be the process of shutting off the lights. Hil was my father's best friend and long-time colleague. In addition, by a strange twist of fate, Hil was destined to one day become my stepfather.

While my father was resigned to the earth-shaking changes that were taking place in our lives, my mother resented Don Tresidder's seemingly hasty decision.

Sailors took over the Great Lounge, which the Navy called Ward A. (SS Collection.)

Naval Convalescent Hospital in Ahwahnee Great Lounge during WWII. Courtesy of Yosemite Research Library.

Her negative feelings did not carry over to his wife, Mary Curry Tresidder, who remained a close friend.

As my father looked for a job at age 48, possessing a law degree but little practical experience, he spoke words that have remained with me all my life: "Your worst troubles start when you blame someone else for them."

Ultimately, Don Tresidder's pessimism was unjustified. Instead of shutting down The Company, Hil went on to fashion The Company into a thriving and prosperous business which flourished for many years, serving a steadily growing influx of Park visitors that reached more than a million a year before his eventual retirement. It wasn't long before The Company found it necessary to install a new management team to replace the one that had been dismantled.

Don Tresidder did not live long enough to realize the mistake he had made in not having sufficient faith in the ability of The Company to thrive in spite of challenges. He died suddenly on January 28, 1948, after only five years as president of Stanford University. He was only 53 years old.

My upbringing in the relaxed and friendly culture of Yosemite Valley during those days inspired a veneration of Yosemite that has endured. Yosemite is my home. My roots are planted in the meadows, along the banks of the lazy Merced River, and beneath those towering cliffs.

I feel a sense of belonging when I return to Yosemite that is unlike any other I feel anywhere on earth. In contrast, large cities, whether in America or in foreign countries, have never held lasting appeal to me, no matter how exotic. The excitement soon wears off. I become claustrophobic if I am stuck in any big city for more than a few days. Flatlands bore me. Mountains call me.

CHAPTER 3

MY YOUTH IN YOSEMITE (1942–1950)

Although my father might have been able to resume his prewar position on The Company management team, he found a new life in San Francisco working for the Schwabacher–Frey Company, which was owned by one of the city's leading families. We had become comfortably settled in the pleasant town of Palo Alto, which, at the time, was still a semi-rural environment and home of Stanford University. The separation from Yosemite was not complete, however, because for the first seven years we lived in Palo Alto we rented our house from Frank Kittredge, who was superintendent of Yosemite National Park.

After my family left, my enthusiasm for the Valley remained as strong as ever. The family began returning in a series of visits that have continued unbroken to this day. In the years immediately following our departure from Yosemite my family and I often visited our numerous friends who remained in Yosemite. I maintained contact with some of my schoolmates who remained in the Valley.

HOMECOMINGS

Our frequent visits were a return to our roots. Trips to Yosemite always felt like homecomings, and we left after each visit with a sense of loss.

Every year my talented mother drew the pictures for our Christmas cards. One year after we had left Yosemite, her holiday card was a picture of Half Dome with tears streaming down its granite face.

During the summers of 1945 and 1946, in the midst of the war, I spent some time at a summer camp on the Orme Ranch, not far from Prescott, Arizona. We took side trips to the Grand Canyon and the Indian Country. My childhood friend Dick Otter joined me.

A series of trips to national parks impressed me with the amazing diversity of these dedicated reserves. None of the places I visited was at all like the others. All of them differed from Yosemite. Each park in the National Park system is special in its own way. However, I continued to regard Yosemite with a fondness deeper than I could hold for any other place. Yosemite is my roots.

FIRST MAJOR HIGH COUNTRY TREK

My early experiences with Yosemite while growing up had been mostly confined to the Valley. I had only glimpsed the High Country splendors that stretched away from me on all sides. I finally was able to visit this world during the summer following ninth grade when I joined a group of other thirteen and fourteen year olds for a three-week adventure into the very heart of the High Country. Two adults led us on our trek into the High Country. I will be eternally grateful to them.

Accompanying us were a couple of pack mules that carried most of our equipment and all of our supplies. None of us had any mountain man skills. We learned by experience how to pack the mules efficiently. At times the mules turned out to possess the stubborn attitudes for which their breed is famous. They held opinions of their own that occasionally differed from ours, notably when to begin walking and when to stop.

Our route through the mountains followed the circuit of the Yosemite High Sierra Camps (see Chapters 7, 16). We climbed mountains that lay along our course, including 13,000-foot Mount Lyell, the highest point in Yosemite National Park. Our descent from Mt. Lyell was accomplished by simply sliding down the prominent Lyell Glacier on the mountain's northern slopes, a technique known as glissading.

The trip was strenuous. Mt. Lyell lies more than ten miles from the nearest trailhead. None of those miles was like walking in a city park. A pleasant respite from the hiking occurred during a two-day layover at Tuolumne Meadows. We stayed adjacent to Parsons Lodge by the Sierra Club campground. Parsons Lodge is an impressive stone structure built in the 1930s. Inside the building was an archive of registers in which those who ascended peaks recorded their impressions. I was nearly as motivated by the accounts those climbers left behind as I was by my own personal experience of making some of the climbs myself.

The shared exertion of all those miles of walking served to draw the members of our small group close to one another. We became a band of brothers. Making that hike successfully was rewarding. We returned to civilization with smiles on our faces and pride in our hearts at having overcome the challenges of the new territory that we had discovered.

The following summer I went back to Yosemite High Country for a two-

Hiking from Tuolumne Meadows to Glen Aulin.

day trip with a friend. On the first day, we found a pleasant campsite beside the river that cascaded through a series of mini waterfalls. We had planned to hike farther up into the backcountry the next day, but discovered the irresistible pleasure of carving twigs into little boats and then racing them, like Pooh sticks, against each other down the river. We spent the entire day staging our miniature regattas.

Tent at Housekeeping Camp. Courtesy of Yosemite Research Library.

CHAPTER 4

HIGH SCHOOL SUMMER IN YOSEMITE (1950–1951)

In the summer of 1950, when I was sixteen and had just finished my junior year in high school, the great influx of post World War II Yosemite visitors had begun. I landed the first of what would become a series of full-time summer jobs as a Yosemite Park & Curry Company employee. Company policy would not permit a young person, except for local residents, to obtain summer employment before age eighteen. Those who were in charge agreed that I satisfied the "local resident" requirement. Showing up for my first day on that job was like coming home.

My first assignment was as a houseman at the Housekeeping Camp, which offered tents with hardwood floors for accommodations, plus beds, linens, stoves and utensils. Housemen rented equipment to people seeking a more basic camping experience.

Some of the tents in the Housekeeping Camp were in prime locations right along the river. Others were crowded into less desirable spaces, especially in one location that we called the Dustbowl.

For the most part, we were serving groups of happy people of modest means. In many cases, the Housekeeping Camp provided visitors with their initial and sometimes sole contact with nature. They often fell in love with the experience. Some would return year after year.

My duties as a houseman included maintaining the camp as required. We drove around in trucks picking up dirty linen where the maids had piled it after making up the tents. We loaded camping equipment on people's cars, stacked firewood for sale, and policed the grounds. The lowest job that a houseman was called upon to do was to walk around the camp picking up papers with a wooden pole with a spike on the end, which we called an idiot stick. One employee stoically manned an idiot stick for an entire summer at Camp Curry and was dubbed by a sardonic desk clerk as "The Bengal Lancer."

The task of cleaning restrooms was another lowly job. My father said that an old janitor, John Powell, once said to him, "They said Job was a patient man, but Job never had to clean johns." I learned what he meant by that.

The head housekeeper assigned the tasks to us and managed our work.

She regarded all of us with maternal affection and thought of us as her extended family.

Most of us who worked at those summertime Yosemite jobs were college or local high school students on vacation. The college students came from all over the country.

MEMORABLE SUMMERTIME CHARACTERS

I still remember many of my fellow employees. I remember one who had just returned from military duty in Europe, bringing with him the first VW Bug that any of us had ever seen. It was a curiosity.

A few fellow workers were older transients who moved from menial jobs in one resort to another and lived a nomadic existence. Some of them would work summers in Yosemite and winters in places like Palm Springs. Some of them left indelible impressions on my young mind. I remember our pot washer, though I can't recall his name. He possessed a colorful, if vulgar, vocabulary that was occasionally shocking, but always entertaining. He owned a hot rod that he called the "Dragg'n Wagon." It attracted as much attention as some of the natural scenery.

We nicknamed one of the maids "Dirty Jan" because of the vulgarities she often used in her speech. When Dirty Jan got near the pot washer we were regularly amused by their colorful repartee, each making comments about the habits of the other as well as features of the other's anatomy that "nice" people might not have expressed.

We nicknamed another fellow employee "Big Jim" because he stood six-foot-nine. Jim had a serious case of wanderlust and would spend his days off trying to see how far he could hitchhike from Yosemite Valley and get back in a single day. Because people were curious about his height, Big Jim had no trouble hitching rides.

In the middle of the summer, Big Jim decided that his day trips weren't really scratching his itch for travel, so he hatched an elaborate scheme whereby he would hitchhike across the USA while giving his parents, who probably would not have approved of the project, the impression that he was still at work as a Yosemite employee. He involved us in his ruse, which consisted of leaving behind a stack of postcards he had pre-written to his parents, describing his invented life in Yosemite. After Jim was gone, we would post one of the cards every week so his parents would see the Yosemite postmark and not be suspicious.

While on his trip, Big Jim himself would faithfully send us postcards informing us of the progress of his journey. We would keep track of his sojourn by sticking pins into a U.S. map that hung in our pot-washing room. While sleeping on a bench in a Florida park, Big Jim was nearly arrested for vagrancy, but he talked his way out of it. He spent his longest stretch, from Winnemucca, Nevada, to Cleveland, Ohio, in the company of some unsavory characters with whom he would not, under other circumstances, have willingly spent ten minutes.

Big Jim finally grew tired of his nomadic experiences, and in mid-August he suddenly showed up at the door of the employment office, got his old job back, and finished the season as though nothing unusual had happened. Big Jim ended up graduating from Cal Tech, teaching at MIT, and raising a family. I wonder if he ever told his folks about his unauthorized cross-country adventure.

I caught the hitchhiking bug from Big Jim's adventure. Following my second summer in Yosemite, I hitchhiked to Oregon to visit a girlfriend, encountering some interesting characters along the road. Once I got a ride from a candidate for Oregon Attorney General, and helped him post campaign signs. On the same trip a Greyhound bus actually stopped and picked me up. It turned out that the driver was deadheading back to his headquarters. The man drove the bus recklessly. As he careened around the curves on a mountain highway, he complained about the fact that he was about to be fired for reckless driving. After the trip was done, I gave up hitchhiking.

That first summer job in Yosemite provided a heady environment for a high school student away from home and on his own for the first time. I stretched my wings, experimented with life, made some mistakes and learned some valuable lessons.

One mistake I made was representing myself as a Stanford student to a maid I wanted to impress. She was a college student. I reasoned that I wasn't actually telling a full-blown lie, since I was, in fact, planning to attend Stanford. My ruse lasted a couple months, but it was destined to fail because too many people knew who I was. When my lady friend learned the truth, she was angry at the deception, and I was ashamed at having misled her. The relationship ended badly. I learned a helpful lesson about honesty and truthfulness. We acquire good judgment through experience, which we acquire through bad judgment.

Things were different the second summer that I worked in Yosemite. I was still a high school student, but by then I had been admitted to Stanford. I had learned my lesson and now knew better than to falsely represent my status.

At the end of the summer of 1951, three of us, including Big Jim, departed on a cross-country tour of national parks in my old 1938 Buick. We attempted to convert the car into a camper by knocking out the partition between the back seat and the trunk. We would take turns sleeping and driving. In that way, we managed to make an odyssey of the trip, traveling 4,500 miles in a ten-day whirlwind and making flying visits to the Tetons, Yellowstone, Glacier, Mt. Rainier, Crater Lake and the redwoods in Northern California.

FREEDOM OF WHEELS

The biggest change that took place my second year was that I now owned a car purchased with earnings from that first summer. Mobility assumed a prominent role in my life. During my first summer, my ability to move about freely was severely limited. If I wanted to venture outside the Valley, I had to find someone who owned a car and was willing to give me a ride. Ownership of my own vehicle set me free to come and go from Yosemite Valley as I wished on my days off.

When I drove into Yosemite that second summer, proudly sitting at the wheel of my 1938 Buick, the car was no stranger. Nancy Loncaric, who had been the leader of the rhythm band of my kindergarten class, had previously owned it. Nancy had maintained the car in an immaculate condition, but I soon changed that. Before long the car gave every appearance of being owned by a teenager. On one occasion, Nancy saw the terrible thing that had happened to her beautiful vehicle and broke down in tears.

I took full advantage of the freedom which car ownership gave to me. On days off a carful of my buddies and I would explore the back roads that surrounded Yosemite, including the Mother Lode country as well as the land to the east of the Tioga Pass as far as Reno and Lake Tahoe.

During the halcyon days of that summer I was completely enjoying bumming around with friends, checking out new places, and reveling in the new reality that on my days off I could go anywhere that lay within a day's drive.

GETTING THE "GLAD TIDINGS"

"Climb the mountains and get their glad tidings and Nature's peace will flow into you and cares fall off like autumn leaves." ~ John Muir

I first quoted this in the dedication. At this point in my young life my friends and I began to absorb its meaning. Understanding the "glad tidings" is an evolutionary maturing process that many have experienced. Even though the summer employees loved to party and have a good time, we also became increasingly conscious of the grandeur that surrounded us. The beauty of Yosemite Valley created within many of us a growing appreciation of nature. This was prior to the movement for environmental protection. We became pragmatic environmentalists, striving to preserve the beauty around us, not because of some philosophy, dogma or romantic fantasy, but simply because we sensed in our hearts that this beautiful place deserved to be preserved and protected.

Many of the young people I worked with during those three summers had been born and raised in an urban environment. They had not imagined the existence of the splendors that surrounded them. We began venturing into the High Country. As they began to experience Yosemite, many developed an infatuation with the Park and a desire to protect its beauty from being despoiled by clueless, thoughtless people. This experience provided living proof of a viewpoint John Muir often expressed, that people who are exposed to Yosemite will naturally want to protect it and will be offended by anyone degrading it.

Of course, not everybody is willing to take sufficient time to develop the appreciation for Yosemite that Muir described. We heard tourists ask inane questions like, "Is there anything to see around here except rocks and trees?" "What is there to do?" "Are there any shopping areas?" "Do they turn off the waterfalls at night?" "Where is the other half of Half Dome?" I developed a stock answer to the latter question: "It is in the shop getting a new coat of glacial polish."

We felt contempt for visitors who would simply congregate in one of the Valley's public areas while buying hamburgers, post cards and souvenirs, and then drive back out without making any attempt to understand or appreciate the beauty that they were so blithely passing by. We referred to such visitors as "peasants."

Some of these visitors are simply clueless, and some of them are truly incorrigible. For the latter, the ideal is Las Vegas or Disneyland. They will never be content to visit a place that doesn't have anything comparable to a slot machine or a thrill ride. To turn a blind eye to the "glad tidings" is a choice. Although available to everyone, Yosemite is simply not appropriate for everyone.

We became upset when we found tourists strewing litter about, and not just because we would have to clean it up. We felt in our bones that littering was tantamount to an act of desecration.

CHAPTER 5

COLLEGE DAYS AND YOSEMITE (1951–1957)

Following high school graduation, I was accepted as a freshman at Stanford University. When I returned for the third year of summer employment, I was transferred from the Housekeeping Camp to Camp Curry and promoted to the prestigious position of porter. My job was to show visitors to their tents and to attend to their minor needs. Porters formed the aristocracy in the summer employment hierarchy, because we were the big earners, earning tips, making as much as $1,500 in a single summer. That was good money back in those days.

I continued as a porter for three summers, from 1952 through 1954. Every year I would eagerly anticipate the coming of summer and look forward to my return to Yosemite. We worked eight hours a day, six days a week. There was plenty of time for recreation. There was a recreation hall that had a number of games such as Ping-Pong, plus a piano, but in Yosemite Valley we had little need for it. During fine weather our social activities centered around beach parties located on isolated beaches along the Merced's twisting course. We would often build a bonfire, drink beer and sing, with couples sitting around the fire snuggling together and "doing what comes naturally," as Doris Day sang at the time. We would occasionally entice single females who were staying at Yosemite to join us at our beach parties.

Impromptu street dancing was another social activity. We would drive our cars to a parking lot on one of the roads leading out of the Valley, turn on the car radios and dance.

Some of the more adventurous among us would visit a watering hole located at Indian Flat, which was about 15 miles from the Valley in Merced Canyon. The establishment was named "Sammy's," after the portly Indian who ran the place. Sammy's was a place where patrons could drink, play songs on a jukebox and misbehave if they wanted to. No one was supposed to drink unless they were 21, but Sammy didn't check too many IDs. Company management was not enthusiastic about Sammy's, because the road back to the Valley was winding and dangerous after drinking, but Sammy was impervious, being outside the Park.

Life was not all parties. Many summertime employees would congregate at a beach near the base of El Capitan. We could fish. We could also play Ahwahnee's nine-hole pitch and putt course, or the nine-hole golf course at Wawona.

A choir of employees under the direction of Glenn Willard (aka Keith Bee) known as the Valley Singers rehearsed and performed show tunes from popular musicals.

Yosemite's majestic and looming rock faces lured some of us into climbing. The sport as a serious pastime, with elaborate equipment and standardized techniques, was just beginning to come into its own. However, the inclination of boys to climb over rocks has been around for as long as there have been boys and rocks.

In addition, Yosemite's extensive system of trails beckoned us to hike. As we ventured out on the trails, we began to develop a desire to see more of the seldom-visited areas of the Park. My interest in exploring the Yosemite High Country increased throughout the summers of my employment in Yosemite. My job as a porter required me to walk ten to fifteen miles in a normal workday, walking from one end of Camp Curry to the other and back in endless cycles, so I was in splendid shape.

Despite a regulation that forbade rafting down the Merced River, one night three of us violated the rule and took a spectacular ride through the Valley beneath a brilliant full moon. The experience was memorable.

Today park visitors in droves legally float down the river on rented rafts, but I suspect that relatively few people have had the unique experience of drifting down the Merced beneath towering cliffs illuminated by a full moon.

VISITING THE ANSEL ADAMS HOME

Ansel Adams married Virginia Best in 1928. She was the daughter of Harry Best, who was an early Yosemite entrepreneur, an artist who started a studio in Yosemite Valley. Ansel initially came to Yosemite Valley as a young piano prodigy from San Francisco, contemplating a career as a classical pianist. He became entranced by Yosemite's beauty and began taking photographs and hiking the High Country in search of the glad tidings that John Muir had announced. The Adams family lived above Best's studio, which Virginia managed. Mike and Anne, Ansel and Virginia's children, were my childhood playmates.

When I began hanging around the Adams home, Ansel was a very busy person, traveling everywhere, taking photographs of natural scenes and pursuing the environmental causes that were playing an increasingly important role in his

Ansel Adams playing the piano at his home. Courtesy of Adams Family Collection.

life. Ansel would show up following one of his sorties, tell us some jokes, play the piano for us and just shoot the breeze.

During the 1930s and 1940s, Ansel was regarded as an eccentric, likable mountain man. By the time I worked in Yosemite in the 1950s, he was evolving into the American icon that he eventually became.

Even when home, however, Ansel Adams remained a very busy person, conducting photography classes for groups of eager learners and evolving his photographic art form in the darkroom that Harry Best had built behind his studio. Ansel completely rebuilt it in 1968.

I continued to hang around the edges of the Adams family life. Virginia, who, like me, was a native of Yosemite Valley, entertained a continual flow of interesting visitors.

Virginia had a reputation for her generous hospitality and warm heart. Her personality, together with the food and drink she offered, created an irresistible combination. Her daughter, Anne, told me that her mom would routinely prepare enough food for six extra diners just in case people would happen to drop by, which they frequently did.

I continued visiting the Adams home during all of the time that I worked in the Park. The Adams house was my home away from home. Virginia's hospitality was as genuine as it was warm, and she always made me feel that I was a welcomed guest. More than a mere hostess, Virginia had a strong maternal instinct and was glad to serve as my surrogate mom during those summers when I was away from my parents for the first time.

Virginia's life was almost as busy as Ansel's. In addition to her activities as a sought-after hostess, she managed the studio while running her home with grace and efficiency. She had somehow mastered the no-doubt difficult art of being married to a certified genius.

I was equally welcome in the home of Hil Oehlmann, my father's best friend, and enjoyed his hospitality also, but he was the boss of all the employees. I thought that hanging out at his house too much might appear presumptuous to my fellow workers.

CHAPTER 6

THE GRADUATE COMES HOME (1955–1956)

For the final two years of college, I transferred across the country to Cornell University in Ithaca, New York, mainly to get away from Palo Alto, my hometown, and to see another part of the country. I graduated with a degree in philosophy and no particular direction.

Following graduation from Cornell, I planned to drive the old Studebaker that I had acquired by then across the continent back to our California home. The old engine had seen a lot of miles, so to prepare the car for the trip my friends and I rebuilt the engine, carefully putting tags on all the parts as we disassembled it, so we could make sure to get it back together properly.

My parents flew to Ithaca, New York, to attend my graduation and then joined me for the trip back to California. We made it only as far as Virginia when we discovered that an oil seal had been improperly installed and could be replaced only by pulling the engine, which took a couple of days. The breakdown occurred in Shenandoah National Park. A friend of my father was CEO of the concessioner, so he housed us in the park's most luxurious accommodations, typically reserved for visiting dignitaries. I spent a couple of days exploring the Park but wasn't able to make friends with the Park employees, who regarded me as a visiting dignitary rather than as one of the boys.

Because of the time spent repairing the engine, my parents were unable to finish the trip with me. They flew back to California, leaving me to proceed on my own from Little Rock, Arkansas. I stopped briefly at Mesa Verde National Park in Colorado and met a friend, Roger Hall, whose parents owned the concession there. I had another national park to explore.

I visited another friend in Helper, Utah. His father was a Coors beer distributor. I spent a couple of days helping him make beer deliveries and received two cases of Coors for the road. That turned out to be an indispensable gift, because, in the middle of the night, while driving across Highways 6 and 50 (which had the reputation of being "the loneliest road in the nation"), my radiator overheated. Lacking any water, I filled the radiator up with Coors. I drove into a service station in Ely, Nevada, at 5 a.m. When the attendant opened the radiator cap, a foaming head flowed out and over the engine, filling the station with the smell of beer. If it could have been captured on a video, the reaction on that attendant's face would have made a hit on YouTube®.

I made it as far as the east approach to Yosemite at Lee Vining, adjacent to Tioga Pass. There I had a flat tire, and spent my last three dollars buying a new tire. This forced me to approach the Park entrance with empty pockets, hoping that the ranger would permit a person who had been born in Yosemite to enter without paying the $3 fee. He wouldn't do that, but did allow me to enter with the promise that I would get money from my friends and pay on the way out.

WHAT NEXT?

I had graduated from college, but my next step was uncertain. I was drawn to academic life. I might have become a teacher at the college level, but had no desire to immerse myself in any particular subject.

I considered applying for a managerial position with the Yosemite Park & Curry Company, which at the time was considered to be a good launching ground for people wishing to become managers and executives in the hotel business. I lacked any management experience. There was the growing certainty that I would eventually have to face up to my military obligation, long deferred.

Even though I had been accepted by Stanford Law School, I decided to volunteer for the Army, get my military obligation out of the way and, while doing so, figure out what I really wanted to do with my life. When I finally returned home, I visited the draft office and obtained the appropriate form to volunteer for the draft, but decided on an impulse not to submit it until the next day. This decision turned out to be life changing: That night a friend, Guy Shoup, who was about to report for duty as an officer with the U.S. Navy, told me I was crazy. "The army has no use for philosophers," he said. "They will make an infantryman out of you." He went on to tell me that the Army did have a use for lawyers. If I showed up with my law degree in hand, they would commission me as an officer. The plan seemed instantly attractive to me, because I was painfully aware I lacked the required skills, attitudes, aptitude and certainly enthusiasm to become a soldier. My acceptance for admission to Stanford Law was still viable, so I decided to continue with school.

Since the summer months had suddenly arrived, I jumped into my car, drove to Yosemite and told the people in the personnel office that I would take whatever job was available. They needed a desk clerk at the Housekeeping Camp.

That was fine with me. I was home!

It is strange how my life turned on such a simple thing as my having held my application for a day and my friend just happening to learn of my plans.

Four students who had made the trip to Yosemite by crossing the country from the University of Mississippi (Ole Miss) showed up one summer. The four arrived before Memorial Day, which was before most California schools let out, so the jobs were there for the taking. The four spent what seemed a pleasant summer away from the summertime steam-bath humidity of the Deep South.

At the end of the summer, the four went back to school and told their friends of their summer in Yosemite. As a result, for the next few summers we had 40 or more Ole Miss students, more than from any other college, showing up, ready to work at Yosemite. Southern drawls reverberated through the Valley.

At that time all male seasonal employees lived in a small-tented community called "Boys Town," which was located at the end of the Camp Curry parking lot. Female employees lived in an elevated area called "The Terrace," located above the main units of Camp Curry.

Girls were supposed to be in their tents by midnight. Any infraction was punishable by being fired. All of us guys regarded The Terrace as a potential garden of earthly delights. It was strictly off-limits, so we confined any adventures in that direction to our imaginations. If a boy ever did venture onto The Terrace's sacred ground, a cry would go up: "Man on The Terrace! Man on The Terrace!" The trespasser would be forced to beat a hasty and shamefaced retreat.

When I was working summers in Yosemite, the twisting course of Highway 120 crossed the Tuolumne River at one point above a waterfall that dropped about 30 feet into a large pool, forming a world-class swimming hole, surrounded by large rocks, from which one could dive into the invigorating waters.

In those days the veranda of the Cliff House Restaurant hung over the pool, affording a perch from which anyone with enough daring could make the long leap into the waters below. Across the road from the Cliff House was an old mine tunnel. A bar had been built inside the tunnel, offering a retreat that remained cool on the hottest day. During our free time, we would visit this wonderful place and spend unforgettable times swimming, partying and hanging out together. Today a high bridge crosses the river, the mine has been filled in, and decades ago the Cliff House vanished in a fire, leaving behind a few concrete blocks on the edge of the pool. The place is now the site of Rainbow Pool County Park.

The summer of 1955 ended with three weeks working as a camp helper at Tuolumne Meadows Lodge, which led to a fondness that would have great later significance. I entered law school two days after finishing at Tuolumne Meadows.

THE GREAT FLOOD OF 1955

I returned to Yosemite during the midwinter break and secured a temporary job at the Ahwahnee for the holidays. My job this time was as doorman, elevator operator, and, occasionally, as a replacement bellman.

People are accustomed to opening their own car doors these days, parking their own automobiles and handling their own baggage. The position of doorman and even bellman was much more important in former times than it is now. Traditions change slowly at the Ahwahnee, however, and they still employ doormen and bellmen, but no longer an elevator operator for a six-floor ride.

There had been a lot of early snow that fall and winter. The snow pack was very deep. Just after Christmas an unseasonably warm rainstorm melted the snow, creating torrents of water that came rushing into the Valley, flooding parking lots and roads, stranding everyone who was in the Park for several days.

The Valley is relatively small compared to the immense watershed of the surrounding mountains. The effect was similar to holding a teacup under a rushing rainspout. Everywhere we looked we could see waterfalls cascading down the Valley cliffs. Water was running everywhere, but it was brown with the soil that accompanied it.

The Ahwahnee is on high ground above the reach of any flood. However, the general store at the Old Village was flooding. We waded into the store and began throwing cans up into the rafters. Some of the canned goods became water-soaked and lost their labels. The store subsequently held a sale on the unlabeled cans. People could purchase the unmarked cans for a low price, but they wouldn't know what they had bought until they opened them.

After doing what we could to salvage goods in the store, at the height of the flood we drove back across the Valley to the Ahwahnee through water that was so deep we worried that the engine compartment would flood, leaving us stranded in the midst of the floodwaters. The often sleepy Merced River had become so swollen that we were uncertain of the actual path of the roadway we were trying to navigate. Fortunately, the old Studebaker had sufficient clearance, and we made it across the Valley.

Cabin Living and Interesting Characters

In the winter of 1955 two other temporary employees from the Ahwahnee and I rented a cabin outside Yosemite in El Portal. Our rent was $15 per month. We converted the cabin to a party headquarters with blankets on the walls, a stereo, a stack of records, plus a notebook in which visitors could record their philosophical observations. We made ourselves at home in our cabin and created a Bohemian pad. It was the age of the beat generation in San Francisco, which inspired us. We spent hours engaged in discussions that we considered to be filled with profound insights. When the party spilled out the front door, as it sometimes did, there was a decrepit trailer for the overflow. The ambience of the cabin provided a welcome respite from law school.

We continued to rent the cabin throughout my last two years in law school. I dutifully paid my five dollars each month, hoping I was getting my money's worth. We eventually discovered that our landlady was a squatter and did not own the property. Nevertheless, we paid her. We used to play music on a record player. One night we played a recording by Eugene Ormandy and the Philadelphia Symphony Orchestra. The next day our landlady came by and said, "You sure had a nice band there last night."

Detour to the Tetons

After my first year in law school I decided I wanted the experience of working in another national park. I took a job as a desk clerk at Jackson Lake Lodge in Grand Teton National Park, remembering my first view of the Tetons after crawling out of the reconverted 1938 Buick in 1951. The Tetons were spectacular. The hiking was marvelous. I had many adventures and made good friends with employees who were college students from many different locations. However, it was not the same. I did not develop relationships that lasted a lifetime, as I had in Yosemite. I was not a model employee and did not elect to return, which did not trouble management. This also helped me determine that I was not cut out for a career in hotel management.

High Sierra Camp at Merced Lake.

CHAPTER 7

AN EVENTFUL FINAL SUMMER (1957)

THE PLAN

In 1957, following the end of my second year at Stanford Law School, I returned to Yosemite for the final summer before beginning a law career.

At that time Syd Ledson, a friend from childhood, managed the Yosemite Maintenance Department. Syd was a benevolent bear of a man with a hearty laugh. One of his favorite assignments was managing the crew that set up the High Sierra Camps in early spring and took them down in late summer. The jobs of setup and takedown each required about three weeks.

For a long time I had been telling Syd that I wanted to work on one of those crews, and the spring of 1957 finally afforded me the ideal opportunity of fulfilling that long-standing desire. I reasoned that if I worked the three weeks for setup and the three weeks for takedown, I could earn enough to survive during the rest of the summer. That would leave me two full months to spend a last Yosemite summer at my cabin retreat and do nothing but hang out in glorious indolence, taking hikes and partying with my friends.

SETTING UP THE HIGH SIERRA CAMPS

The Yosemite High Sierra Camps are a series of tented accommodations located seven to fourteen miles apart, to which visitors can hike and stay in relative comfort or arrive on horseback trips. They are very popular. The maintenance employees were unionized, so I had to become a member of James Hoffa's powerful Teamsters Union. At first, the experience went according to plan. We spent a week setting up the Tuolumne Meadows High Sierra Camp, the only camp that was accessible by road. Some items were trucked up from Yosemite Valley. Others were stored in a permanent stone building, which, when emptied, was transformed to its summertime function as camp kitchen. We set up the tents that comprised he Tuolumne Meadows Lodge.

It was amazing to me how carefully the camp fixtures and utensils could be stored in that stone building. The old hands on the crew knew where every single item was stored. Everything had been so carefully and tightly packed into the stone building that it seemed that every square inch of available space was occupied. When we had removed the items needed in the camp, we swept up the left-behind poison pellets that rodents hadn't consumed. Syd sat in a camp chair at a folding table, keeping careful notes on a pad of paper, tracking and orchestrating the progress of the unpacking.

After spending a year of law school engaged in sedentary educational tasks, the hard labor required to set up the camp felt good. In the evenings we ate meals that were especially tasty. After dinner we would have a few drinks, tell stories, play cards and just enjoy each other. The older hands, in particular, seemed to enjoy the brief respite from the demands of wives and family responsibilities.

When the Tuolumne Meadows Lodge was fully set up, we moved to Merced Lake Camp, about 14 miles from our Yosemite Valley staging area. We rode horses and led pack mules that carried in everything required that hadn't been stored at the camp itself. Merced Lake was a smaller site, but the routine was similar to the one we had just carried out at Tuolumne Meadows Lodge.

A close friend from my Yosemite years, Roland Summit, was getting married in Los Angeles the weekend after we set up Merced Lodge High Sierra Camp. I rode horseback down to the Valley, drove by car to the Fresno Airport and then took a plane to LAX. The transition from the untrammeled Yosemite High Country to crowded Los Angeles in such a short length of time was a culture shock.

After the weekend, back in the clear air of Yosemite High Country, we repeated the setup at Glen Aulin, May Lake and Vogelsang High Sierra Camps. After finishing with Vogelsang, I elected not to return by horseback to Tuolumne Meadows with the rest of the crew, but rather to climb Vogelsang Peak and then hike back.

THE PLAN ALTERED AND ABANDONED

By July 4, I had completed the first segment of my summer employment and looked forward to settling in for the rest of the summer and not working again until fall arrived, at which point I would assist in dismantling the High Sierra Camps. But as Robert Burns reminds: "The best laid schemes o' mice an' men / Gang aft agley." My plans to kick back for the summer did "gang agley" with a vengeance, because Guy Shoup, the same friend who had convinced me to go to law school rather than into the U.S. Army, precipitated another life-changing

Booth Lake High Sierra Camp. Now replaced by Vogelsang, one mile away. Courtesy of Yosemite Research Library.

experience by suggesting that the two of us spend three weeks touring the Pacific Northwest and British Columbia.

We conducted a very low-budget trip, staying in campgrounds and cooking our meals, but unplanned expenses depleted my meager savings to the point at which I realized I had to look for another job when I returned to Yosemite.

As it turned out, a fellow Yosemite native and a close friend, Bart Hooley, was also looking for work. Bart had just returned from six weeks of active duty with the National Guard. We took off together to Yosemite in search of work, and showed up at the Yosemite employment office looking rather seedy. We tried to make up with enthusiasm what we lacked in style, telling the woman at the employment desk that we really needed jobs and that we would gladly do any she had available. The woman responded coldly, telling us that there were no jobs available in the park, and that, furthermore, we need not come back, because none would be available in the near future.

We asked her if she wouldn't check more carefully, adding that we were natives of Yosemite and deserved whatever special treatment she could provide.

We weren't getting anywhere, but just then the Park's personnel director, a pleasant woman whom we only knew as Miss Pat, emerged from her office. She greeted us warmly and invited us in. She told us apologetically that she had only two openings available, both of them as dishwashers at the Ahwahnee. We told her that we would gladly take the jobs.

After we had washed dishes for only four days, Miss Pat called us with the news that two other jobs had opened up. One was my previous job as desk clerk at the Housekeeping Camp, and the other was as a camp helper at Tuolumne Meadows Lodge. Miss Pat left it up to Bart and me to decide who would take which job.

Bart and I would both have preferred the Tuolumne Meadows job. After working there for three weeks at the end of the summer in 1955 I vastly preferred working there rather than in the Valley. However, Bart was much more of a mountain man than I would ever be and would have been in his element at Tuolumne Meadows. In a gesture of magnanimity for which I shall forever be indebted, and one that ended up changing my life forever, Bart agreed to take the desk job without even challenging me with some rock-paper-scissors or coin-toss competition that would have given him a chance.

Bart not only graciously offered to take the Housekeeping Camp job, but he also provided me with a face-saving reason for his choice. He said that his knee had been injured in a ski-jumping accident, and it still bothered him occasionally. At Tuolumne Meadows Lodge he knew that he wouldn't have been able to resist the opportunity of climbing mountains, cliffs and rock faces at every opportunity, perhaps re-injuring his knee. I knew that Bart didn't really mean what he said. Bart didn't know the meaning of such caution. He was simply giving me a reason for his gracious choice so that I wouldn't have to feel so grateful to him. It didn't work. I couldn't have been more grateful for his choice.

DESTINY AT TUOLUMNE MEADOWS LODGE

I left the dirty dishes at the Ahwahnee for someone else to clean and set off to my new job with a bounce in my step, a smile on my face and joy in my heart, unknowingly making my way toward the person destined to become my wife.

Patti Kozicki was a coed from Sacramento State. She was working her first summer at Tuolumne Meadows Lodge, but had previous experience working in the Valley the summer before. Even though she had worked in the gift shop at Camp Curry across from where I was working as a porter, our paths had not crossed.

Patti had fallen in love with the Valley and had first regarded her assignment to a High Sierra Camp as banishment, but was developing a passion for hiking. That led her to fall in love with Tuolumne Meadows.

One day Bart and I were going to drive over Tioga Pass and north up Highway 395 to visit his parents in Reno, which was a two-hour drive from Tuolumne Meadows Lodge. I asked Patti if she wanted us to bring her back anything. I thought she might ask for something easy like socks or mosquito repellent, but she said that she had gone the entire summer without a chocolate milkshake and now had a real craving for one.

In Reno I purchased the milkshake and stowed it in an insulated container I had brought along. When we returned to camp at 3:30 in the morning, I woke her up to deliver her chocolate milkshake. She seemed impressed with the rather extravagant effort I had made to satisfy her craving.

I learned that Patti and I had the same day off, together with Harkjoon Paik, a native of Korea, who worked at the Tuolumne Meadows Store, which was two miles down the road from Tuolumne Meadows Lodge. Like the lodge itself, the store was located in a tent that was erected in the spring and taken down in fall.

Two Korean students were working at the store that particular summer. The two had received their education in the United States and were debating with each other about whether they were now under a moral obligation to return to Korea and contribute from what they had learned in America to improve their country, or whether they were free to pursue American citizenship and then to seek their own version of the American Dream. They held widely divergent viewpoints on the matter.

Harkjoon Paik and his girlfriend, Beverly, who worked in the Valley, joined Patti and me for a visit to my El Portal cabin. There we spent the day and eventually the entire night hanging out. The ambiance of the cabin worked its special magic on us. We filled the time with talking, listening to music, and swimming in the Merced River. We shared our life stories.

Nothing of a romantic nature transpired. The four of us simply had an extraordinary time of fellowship together. By the time we drove back to Tuolumne, with dawn breaking the new day, the four of us had become fast friends and comrades. More than that, the event started Patti and me on a road that would lead to a relationship that would endure 42 years of marriage. As noted in Chapter 23, my path would cross Harkjoon's later in life.

WORKING, PLAYING AND FORGING A RELATIONSHIP

That month at Tuolumne Meadows was memorable. We had a wonderful time making our own fun, hiking the trails and exploring the area. I spent the whole time running on adrenaline and thriving on only four hours of sleep a night.

I had a number of memorable experiences. One night several of us drove over Tioga Pass to a casino in Hawthorne, Nevada. Luck was a lady that night, and I made enough at blackjack to allow me to put all my earnings at Tuolumne into a savings account.

On another night we had a different sort of fun by getting out of bed at 4 a.m., removing part of the dining room tent, carrying the manager's Volkswagen Beetle into the middle of the dining area, and then reinstalling the side of the tent. The next morning the manager showed his good nature by being more surprised and amused than angered by our elaborate practical joke.

I worked hard at my job and tried to do the best I could. I had one bad adventure when the manager assigned to me the task of defrosting the camp's refrigerators. We weren't able to use hot water, so the manager told me to do the job with a Coleman lantern. I objected to the assignment, telling him that it was not a safe thing to do, but he ordered me to do it, so I put the lantern inside the refrigerator. The danger of the plan lay in the possibility of the door to the refrigerator accidentally closing, which is just what happened. The ensuing fire melted the plastic brackets supporting the refrigerator trays and created a terrible mess. That manager took full blame for the problem and let me off the hook.

A hundred Coleman lanterns, all of which had to be refueled on a regular basis, illuminated the High Country tents. When it was my turn, my thumb felt like it was going to drop off from pumping for so long before I got to the end of the row of lanterns.

A wood-burning unit that had to be kept stoked by hand fired the boiler for the showers. The task required some diligence, because the boiler wasn't large. When it ran out of hot water, simultaneous screams would come from the showers as freezing mountain water hit the bathers.

Tents at Tuolumne Meadows Lodge.

All too soon the magic month was over, and it was time to rejoin the maintenance crew in dismantling the High Sierra Camps. We took down the tents and packed furniture and gear into the storage units from which we had unpacked them three months earlier, loading perishable items onto mules and hauling them down to the Valley.

When the maintenance job was finished, I drove to Sacramento to visit Patti and to meet her mother and father. I wasn't completely surprised by the growing romance, because I had often thought that I was destined to meet my wife in Yosemite. The timing was right, because that was the last year of my summer Yosemite employment.

The sense of destiny was underscored by a number of coincidences: our both having been assigned to work at the same place; having the same day off; my tour of the Northwest forcing me into the extra work; and Bart allowing me to take the job at Tuolumne Meadows Lodge. These circumstances, if altered in the smallest way, would have sent my life down a different path.

BACK TO LAW SCHOOL

When the eventful summer ended, I returned to Stanford for my final year of Stanford Law School. Several of my classmates were talking about the stimulating summers they had spent working in some law office or another. I just smiled. I

Michael and Ansel Adams on Tenaya Lake, circa 1950. Courtesy of Adams Family Collection.

could not bring them to the place where I had been. I had an entire lifetime to work in a law office. The actual practice of law seemed far off. Indeed, it would be a long time before I finally started practicing law.

My life would continue to be involved with Yosemite, but the idyllic days of living and working in Yosemite were over.

Life in Yosemite for summer workers in those days was more laid back and enjoyable than it is now. Unions now control most of the jobs, which are filled by year-round employees and by older transient hospitality industry employees. In addition, the Park Service has grown less tolerant of the kinds of adventures in which we used to indulge. One is more likely to find foreign temporary workers than college students working in guest services of one kind or another. The life we summer employees lived has largely vanished. Yosemite culture is diminished by this passing. Something precious has been lost.

CHAPTER 8

AWOL FROM YOSEMITE (1958–1960)

My attitude in 1958 when I finally graduated from Stanford Law School was that of relief rather than triumph. Although my parents were proud of my accomplishment, I was simply glad after 19 years of classroom instruction to finally get out in the world and do something else. The "something else" at that point meant to pass the bar exam and await the inevitable draft.

I spent some time in my parents' home in Palo Alto, a few days in my Yosemite cabin, and most of my time in San Francisco taking refresher courses. Those few weeks in San Francisco were the only time in my life that I have lived in a big city.

Patti had taken a job teaching school in Sacramento. As the only child in her family who was still single, she was caring for her father following the death of her mother. I never proposed to her in any formal way. Our relationship simply grew to the point where we began to talk about getting married as a shared understanding.

The bar exam turned out to be more physically taxing than intellectually challenging, because it required three days of furiously analyzing hypothetical legal issues. I returned home the day after my bar exam was finished to find my induction notice from Uncle Sam ordering me to report for duty in three weeks. I had been anticipating the letter. My deferments had run out.

I spent a final few poignant days in the cabin. September turned into October. Most tourists had gone home. My friends had all returned to school. Autumn leaves flamed on the mountainsides.

IN THE ARMY NOW

I reported for basic training at Monterey County's Fort Ord. I was a soldier by neither attitude nor aptitude. Basic training was like imprisonment. Watching cars driving down Highway 1 from the rifle range reminded me of Johnny Cash singing "Folsom Prison Blues." My situation exactly suited the line, "I know I can't be free; but those people keep a-movin' and that's what tortures me." Basic training was followed by eight weeks of intensive instruction, during which I obediently learned the duties and acquired the skills of a military clerk typist. I impatiently awaited the results of the bar exam that would qualify me to apply to become a legal officer. I was able to get to Yosemite a couple of times during that period.

I was assigned for duty in Vicenza, Italy, in the Judge Advocate office as a legal clerk. I was serving in a peacetime army. The Gulf of Tonkin Resolution lay six years in the future. Most Americans had never heard of Vietnam, and almost none of them could have pointed it out on a map. The Korean War had ended.

Patti and I had discussed the idea of marriage in general, but had not firmed up details, because I was not sure where the Army would send me. Then, suddenly, I found myself in Italy. I developed a set of cold feet, and suggested that perhaps we should wait until after my tour of duty ended and I returned to the U.S. Patti would hear none of it, and sealed her fate for the next forty-two years by responding "I am coming—you promised." And so it came to be. At the time, Patti owned a classic MG TC. Three weeks before her announced departure, the car was severely damaged in a collision, and we were never able to repair it. I would later joke that the bargain was an 18-month European vacation in exchange for co-ownership in a classic MG TC, and I was the one who kept my part of the bargain.

When the results of the bar exam came and I learned that I had passed, I was offered a JAG commission. It would have required me to extend my tour of duty by another year, and to be transferred for advanced training from Italy to Fort Benning, Georgia.

I said "No, thanks" to becoming a legal officer. I was in Italy, married, and living off post. No war was going on. We had 30 days' leave in Europe. It was like a paid vacation. I could not improve on this situation.

BACK TO YOSEMITE

It was October 1960 before I saw Yosemite again. Half Dome and El Capitan hadn't changed, but my life had changed in significant ways. Notably, I returned to Yosemite accompanied by my wife and a three-month-old son. A shattering change was the discovery that my old cabin retreat had been bulldozed to make room for a mobile home park for employees. Forty years would pass before I finally would learn the story of how my beloved cabin had come to be destroyed.

Otherwise, it was a joyful homecoming. While in Europe I had visited the Alps, but still preferred the mountains, valleys and waterfalls of my first home. We drove past Mono Lake, over Tioga Pass and into Yosemite Valley, then back home to Palo Alto, where I began my first serious job in the legal profession working with a federal appellate judge in Fresno, only a two-hour drive from Yosemite.

My return to Yosemite was destined to mark the beginning of a whole new era in my relationship with the Park. We spent very few weekends in Fresno that first year because we were back in the Park every chance we got, spending most weekends in a very pleasant fashion as guests at the Wawona Hotel where my friend, the late Ned English, was experimenting with opening the hotel in winter.

The winter of 1961 remained snow-free until mid-January. We could still drive the road to Glacier Point because it was clear of snow, and because the caretaker of the Glacier Point Hotel, an acquaintance of ours, loaned us the key to the gate.

One memorable day that winter we staged our own unofficial fire fall (see "The Fire Fall" in Chapter 12, Yosemite Traditions). Ned English, the manager of Wawona, went with us up to Glacier Point. The hotel on the top had been condemned and was living out its final days. We sat around a huge fireplace that evening, feeling like feudal barons. Then one of us said, "We should have a fire fall!"

We called the desk at the Ahwahnee Hotel to say that we were going to produce a winter fire fall. We conducted our impromptu celebration at 9:00 p.m., the same time it was performed during the summer months. We escaped both detection and punishment for this indiscretion.

Martino and Vince on top.

CHAPTER 9

INTRODUCING THE FAMILY

Our two sons were exposed to Yosemite from their infancy. Each summer we took them camping at Tuolumne Meadows. As soon as they were old enough to put on a pair of skis, we took them skiing at Badger Pass in the winter.

I took our first son, Martino, for his inaugural camping trip to the High Country when he was three years old. We also took a teenage neighbor and his girlfriend. We camped at Porcupine Flat, a remote campground, and hung our food in the trees in the prescribed fashion in order to protect it from bears. However, the mother bear had trained her cubs to crawl along the slender branches and dislodge the pack holding the food.

The next morning my three-year-old son and I had a conversation that was confusing for Martino, but amusing for me. "Martino," I said, "we have to drive to Tuolumne Meadows for breakfast."

"Why?" he asked.

"Because the bears got our food," I answered.

"Where was the food?"

"In a tree."

"Dad, why did you hang the food in a tree?"

"So the bears wouldn't get it."

Martino couldn't think what to ask next.

Later that same day we came upon a mountain stream that had a sign posted that requested that people not contaminate the water since it was part of a water supply. A group of people was sitting in front of the sign, dangling their feet in the stream. Martino marched right up to them, looked them in the eye, and said, "You are contaminating the supply of water."

Without saying a word, the group pulled their feet from the water, put their shoes on, and slunk away, rebuked by a three-year-old.

My younger son, Vince, soon followed his brother into the mountains. The family visited Yosemite on camping, hiking and ski trips at least once a year until both Martino and Vince started working in the High Country after graduating from high school. Martino worked at Tuolumne Meadows Lodge for five summers while attending college. Vince worked at Sunrise High Sierra Camp for three summers while attending college.

HALF DOME CLIMB WITH VINCE
AND THE BOY SCOUTS

I took Vince and four other Boy Scouts on a Half Dome climb when they were about 12 years old.

We camped overnight in Little Yosemite Valley, above the top of Nevada Fall. Yosemite Valley is the home of many bears, which are known for foraging food from campers. In those days the prescribed method of protecting food from bears was still to hang food above the ground. A large cable had been strung between two trees in Little Yosemite. The prescribed procedure was to hang backpacks full of food from the cable. It took a cooperative effort of the campers to lift the packs up and bring them down.

A resident ranger stationed in Little Yosemite Valley gave a nightly ranger talk in the early evening that included an explanation of how to protect food from bears. The talk took place after most campers had eaten dinner, but before they had stowed food in packs for the nightly ritual of hanging food in packs from the cable. While most of the campers were at the ranger talk the bears came and cleaned out the camp. We returned to the camp to find our breakfast strewn about. Bears are messy eaters. They do not take everything, however, so we were able to salvage something for breakfast.

We proceeded to complete the planned ascent of Half Dome up the cable. Our arrival at the top was greeted with exclamations from the boys in terms such as "wow," "boss," "cool," and similar expressions of the day. One of the scouts, a more scholarly type, said, "I feel a great sense of satisfaction." When we arrived at Camp Curry, we decided to spend the night in one of the tent cabins rather than drive home at night. This added to the adventure.

One of the scouts was the son of the then-mayor of Salinas. I ran into him forty or so years later. He remembered both the trip and me and said it was one of the highlights of his life.

CHAPTER 10

LEGAL SERVICES FOR
THE CONCESSIONERS (1964–1972)

Beginning in 1964 I entered into a more mature relationship with Yosemite.

During the 1960s, my father asked me to replace him, together with attorney Dale Doty, as co-counsel for the National Park Concessioners Association. Securing Dale Doty's services had been a great coup for the concessioners' organization because he had served a previous administration as Under Secretary of the Interior. After retiring from government, Doty switched allegiances and began working for concessioners.

A young attorney starting out in law practice, I jumped at the opportunity my father had offered. I served for several years as co-counsel for the association. We attended annual meetings in Washington, D.C. We advised various concessioners, most of whom were pioneer family businesses in national parks.

Those activities brought me into contact with representatives from another organization that also contracted with the government. This organization represented river runners in various national parks and monuments, including the Grand Canyon.

During the 1960s, an unanticipated development changed forever the nature and management of national park concessions throughout the entire national park system in general, and in Yosemite in particular.

Most of the concessions, for business and tax purposes, had incorporated, making them potential targets of conglomerates owned by entities outside the parks. By acquiring stock in a corporation that already had a contract with the government, the conglomerate could acquire control of the concession without having to negotiate a contract with the government. The concessions appeared to be profitable, because many of them had a virtual monopoly on visitor services provided in a national park. Visitation to national parks was expanding rapidly.

Big business began operating visitor services, rather than pioneer family businesses. Original owners either sold out or were acquired by hostile takeovers.

The conglomerates had their own way of doing business and their own lobbyists to represent them, so, before long, Dale Doty and I were replaced. I was sad to lose the business; the conference had been an impressive client for a young lawyer.

In 1972 the National Park Service staged a celebration in Washington, D.C. in honor of the 100th anniversary of its initial creation, recalling the three people who sat around a Yellowstone campfire and first promoted the idea of the federal government, centrally administering a series of national parks.

The Park Service celebrated the centennial by gathering together a group of people dressed in tuxedos, political functionaries and socialites, many of whom had never had anything to do with any national park. I was there in the company of Ansel Adams. The person sitting next to me, however, was a military man who knew nothing about national parks, just there to enjoy a nice meal.

I was struck by the irony of the whole celebration. Washington staff people know how to put on a good cocktail party and formal dinner, but they chose an incongruous way to honor the memory of the people who had worked so tirelessly to bring the National Park Service into existence.

PAVING THE WAY FOR THE SHUTTLES

Toward the end of the 1960s, my friend Stuart Cross, then-CEO of the Yosemite Park & Curry Company, asked me to help negotiate a contract for the operation of the shuttle bus system that they were planning to initiate as a way of alleviating auto traffic on the Valley floor.

The Park Service lacked the funds to make this idea work, so they contracted with a third-party transportation company to provide the buses and to operate them. The company loaned the money. The Park Service offered the shuttles as a free public service. The original draft contract was a nearly unintelligible document drawn up by a government attorney who was totally unfamiliar with what the Park Service and The Company were trying to accomplish. We were walking a fine line, because if we made too many changes, the contract would be sent back to Washington, D.C, where it was liable to fall into a bureaucratic black hole from which it was likely never to emerge into the light of day.

We successfully managed to rework the contract to the point that The Company could live with it. This saved us from having government lawyers rewrite a contract they didn't understand.

The shuttle system was successfully put into place and is still in operation. It covers about a third of the Valley floor, which is now closed to private vehicles, though still open to pedestrian traffic and to bicycles. The system has been praised as a great step toward the reduction of automobile traffic in Yosemite Valley. I am pleased with the role that I played in contributing to the success of this effort. I am reminded of it when I stroll through the upper third of the Valley and enjoy the tranquility of the area out of sight and sound of automobiles.

A HOSTILE TAKEOVER

During the late 1960s conglomerates had focused their attention on acquiring Yosemite Park & Curry Company stock. The winds of change were blowing. A hostile takeover was unfolding. Loyalties were divided. Mary Curry Tresidder, commonly considered the matriarch of the Yosemite Park & Curry Company, died in 1970. Hil Oehlmann succeeded Mary Curry Tresidder as chairman of the board. He was eventually named honorary chairman of the board. Those titles allowed him to maintain a residence in Yosemite Valley.

An out-of-the-area conglomerate commonly referred to by the initials "USNR" began trying to acquire the Yosemite Park & Curry Company concession in a hostile takeover. They could do this only by buying stock in the corporation, not by acquiring the contract with the government directly. Stanford University had a large amount of non-voting stock that was held in trust. Employees and former employees who were not top management also held stock. USNR made tender offers at high prices. Loyalties were divided. Eventually USNR acquired a controlling voting interest in the stock. This allowed USNR to operate under the contract between Yosemite Park & Curry Company and the government. Another conglomerate, which we knew as Shasta, then succeeded to the controlling interest that had been acquired by USNR.

The CEO of Shasta was Don Hummel, a former mayor of Tucson, Arizona, who had operated concessions in other national parks and who had been a president of the National Park Concessioners Association while I was co-counsel. I knew him but had little contact with him during his short tenure in Yosemite. Because of the circumstances surrounding his arrival in Yosemite, his presence in Yosemite was not received in the friendliest manner by the old-timers, who were my friends and also Don Hummel's friends.

I am glad that my father, who died in 1971, did not live to witness the above events. It was the beginning of the unraveling of his most stellar legal achievements.

A NEW LIFE FOR DELLA

Shortly after the annual Conference of National Park Concessioners Association in Washington, D.C., in 1971, Hil Oehlmann's Else also died. The two couples had been the closest of friends for years. In 1972 my mother married Hil. The marriage ceremony took place in Washington, D.C., before our final association meeting. Patti and I were the sole witnesses at the event.

Hil and Della moved back to Yosemite and lived there a short time during the twilight of Hil's career, with The Company under new management. Stuart Cross, the handpicked successor of both Hil and Mary Curry Tresidder, moved on to run the Hotel Utah operations for the Mormon Church out of Salt Lake City. By this time he and Lenore, Hil's daughter, were divorced. Stuart had remarried. Ansel and Virginia Adams moved out of Yosemite Valley to Carmel Highlands in 1962. Doctor Avery Sturm and his wife, Pat, who were beloved by everyone in Yosemite, retired and moved to Mariposa, where they built a replica of their Yosemite home behind the hospital.

My mother was not happy living in Yosemite in these times. There were too many changes and too many old friends gone away. When Hil's tenure in management was finally phased out, Hil and Della moved back to Palo Alto, where Della was more comfortable, but Hil less so. Hil adjusted somewhat and started writing his memoirs, but the change was hard on him after so many years in Yosemite.

This period of time afforded me the opportunity to become better acquainted with Hil and to know more of this remarkable man who had been such a close friend of my father for so many years. Hil and I held long philosophical discussions as he sat in the same chair my father had occupied for so many years.

During all this turmoil in Yosemite, and in the life of Hil and my mother, I was wrapped up in my law practice in Salinas, California, and raising a family. I was not personally involved in Yosemite affairs. I did, however, manage backpacking trips into the Yosemite High Country and skiing in the winter at Badger Pass each year.

I thought that an unbroken reign of my personal acquaintance with top management executives in Yosemite Concessions was finally coming to an end, but that was soon to change dramatically and unexpectedly. First I learned that yet another corporation controlled from outside of Yosemite National Park had acquired The Yosemite Park & Curry Company stock owned by Shasta. The new operator was Music Corporation of America (MCA), which was headquartered in Los Angeles and owned mostly recording studios. One day at my mother's home in Palo Alto I learned that MCA had selected Ed Hardy as its top management executive. Ed was one of the first kids I had met in Palo Alto when we moved out of Yosemite. Ed and I had gone to school together from the fourth grade through high school. Ed and I ran in different circles in high school. I was an academic. He was an athlete, a swimmer and water polo player. I lost track of Ed for about twenty years, but we remembered each other. I was off to a new and different relationship with Yosemite.

Now for the first time the chief operating officer (as Ed was called) of the Yosemite Park & Curry Company was of my generation, as well as someone I knew personally.

Peter Hoss, Martino Hoss, Matthew Adams, and Jeanne Adams, late 1960s. Tenaya Lake. Courtesy of Adams Family Collection.

CHAPTER 11

BECOMING A PRIVILEGED VISITOR (1972–PRESENT)

With the advent of the MCA era, my involvement with legal matters affecting Yosemite ended, and my association with Yosemite was changed to that of privileged visitor. During subsequent decades I created additional friendships and associations with organizations that support Yosemite.

On my first visit to Yosemite following his new assignment, Ed greeted me with a warm, "Welcome home," and bought me what was to become the first of many rounds of drinks at the Ahwahnee bar.

Ed completely captured my loyal affection the subsequent Christmas by inviting me to play the role of Visiting Squire at the Ahwahnee's annual world-famous Bracebridge Dinner (see Chapter 12). I was able to boast of the upward mobility that elevated me from the job of parking cars and being in the event as a lackey to playing the role of visiting squire.

Ed routinely kept me informed on what was happening in Yosemite.

At the end of each season, Ed would sponsor a gathering of his friends, which he called The Hardy Party, at one of the High Sierra camps after the season had closed. I attended one of these at Merced Lake. Ed really did know how to party hearty. We spent three bibulous days in high spirits and having good fun.

In 1990 I and three other former employees organized a reunion of Yosemite employees who had worked at Camp Curry during the 1940s and 1950s. I didn't know the other three well, but they asked me to help organize the event because they knew of my friendship with Ed Hardy. Ed was glad to help us in any way he could, graciously opening the Curry Pavilion and playing the role of host.

I discovered that a couple of the other organizers were making plans to use the reunion as a forum for criticizing MCA's current management policies. This situation afforded me a way of repaying Ed for some of many favors that he had done for me. I told the other organizers that their intention of blasting the person who was hosting the event was in poor taste. Ed agreed to drop by and welcome the group if I would introduce him. I used the introduction as an opportunity to recognize a considerable list of good accomplishments that Ed and MCA had done for Yosemite.

I also was able to introduce another visitor, Stuart Cross, a former Yosemite Park & Curry Company CEO who had followed Hil Oehlmann. Stuart had previously been a Company employee and had worked alongside many of the people at the reunion long before his promotion. Ed and Stuart made presentations that melted any spirit of criticism. I feel pleased to have been instrumental in creating something positive out of an event that had threatened to become a vehicle for criticism and censure. The occasion became one of great joy mixed with nostalgia, a time for renewing old friendships with people who had gone in a number of directions and were pursuing a variety of careers.

A number of the people at the reunion had, like myself, attended the Yosemite Grammar School. We formed the idea of creating another reunion of people who had attended the school at some point throughout the school's lifetime. The reunion took place. We had a joyous and nostalgic homecoming together. There may have been other reunions of the Yosemite Grammar School, but I am not aware of them.

When the Delaware North Company (DNC) replaced MCA in 1992, it was the end of five decades of my nearly unbroken association with top management executives of the concessioner in Yosemite. There had been a lot of prestige and personal advantage involved in being a friend of Yosemite's top management executive. I had been able to use my influence to do such things as get tickets to the Bracebridge Dinner and acquire preferential room reservations for my friends. It was a blow to have the connection at the top cut off. The situation gradually improved as I met the management of DNC, and I was able to continue my personal relationship with top management.

During my 42 years of marriage with Patti, we continued returning frequently to Yosemite, where we enjoyed a succession of renewals, including Patti's sixty-fifth birthday celebration. That proved to be her last birthday, as well as her final visit to the Park. It was a visit that I especially cherish in my memory. Patti died in 2001.

BOARD MEMBER

In November 1999, after retiring from law practice, I found myself in yet another new association with Yosemite. It began when our friends Don and Kay Pitts (see Chapters 14, 22 and 23), who were going on a trip, invited Patti and me to housesit for them at their Yosemite Peregrine Bed and Breakfast, in

Yosemite West, a development just outside the Park, near the junction of the road to Badger Pass and Glacier Point. Don was a former magistrate. The reader will learn more about Don in Chapter 14.

Patti and I spent three weeks at Don and Kay's home, the longest time I had spent in Yosemite since my final summer of college work. During those three weeks, I made connections that propelled me toward becoming part of three separate park-related organizations. I became acquainted with what was then the Yosemite Fund and is now the Yosemite Conservancy. I joined the John Muir Heritage Society, which is a select group of people who have agreed to donate $1,000 or more annually to the Fund. The Fund uses the money for projects that the chronically underfunded Park Service cannot afford. I spent quality time with Mike and Jeanne Adams. I was able to give them legal advice about litigation in which the Ansel Adams Gallery was involved. This led to an invitation to join the Board of Directors of the Ansel Adams Gallery, one of the last family-owned businesses in the national park system.

Mike Adams acquainted me with a group called A Christian Ministry in the National Parks (ACMNP). Mike had been involved for a number of years as a member of the Advisory Board. Mike told me that when he first encountered ACMNP representatives, he was totally upfront with them. "I don't go to church," he said, "but I know a lot about national parks." That kind of honesty, as well as his knowledge about national parks, appealed to them. Mike and his wife Jeanne still enjoy participating in the organization. I joined the ACMNP Advisory Board in 2000 and became a trustee of the organization in 2010. More on ACMNP in Chapter 16.

The writing of this book represents the final evolution of my role as park champion. In all the tumult and controversy about Yosemite, the voice of the visitor is not heard as loudly as it should be. Visitors are largely a silent majority, but Yosemite, after all, belongs to the visitor.

Climbers on El Capitan. Courtesy of Tom Frost.

PART 2

Yosemite's Passions and Politics

Visitors should not do this.

An early photo of bears and automobiles in the Park.

CHAPTER 12

YOSEMITE TRADITIONS

Yosemite is more than a place. Yosemite's rich history has created a number of entrenched traditions that have brought people together and created long-term associations. Some of them are known throughout the world. Others are familiar only to residents and repeat visitors. These traditions as well as other experiences have become part of Yosemite lore.

The following pages describe some of these traditions.

BEARS IN THE PARK

Bears surely antedated the white man in Yosemite, and quite possibly the Indian. They have never totally surrendered the territory. Grizzly bears are long gone in California. The bears in Yosemite are black bears (*Ursus Americanus*). They come in colors of brown, cinnamon, or blonde, but they are still of this species. California bears are often referred to as "golden bears," but, technically, a golden bear is a grizzly bear, no longer found in California. The black bears that now inhabit Yosemite are smaller and more benign, but they are powerful and capable of inflicting damage to visitors and visitors' vehicles that contain food. Although injuries from attacks by bears in Yosemite are rare, visitors need to exercise caution. One should never venture between a mother bear and cubs. Above all, the visitor needs to remember that bears are wild animals, not pets. Instances of clueless tourists trying to place children on bears' backs to take pictures are not unknown. Visitors must not attempt to play Goldilocks.

Bears have developed a sort of symbiotic relationship with humans, who are attracted to seeing them. The bear is the mascot of both major branches of the University of California, Berkeley and UCLA.

Bears in Yosemite were a spectacle in the days before I was born. At night bleachers were erected near a lighted garbage dump so visitors could view them foraging for food. This may have been a relic of Buffalo Bill's Wild West shows and the bull and bear fights that entertained the early California miners. The tasteless spectacle of bear feeding was discontinued before my birth.

I must confess to continuing the bear-feeding tradition in a modified fashion when I worked at Tuolumne Meadows. Part of the duties of camp helpers at Tuolumne Meadows Lodge was to haul garbage to a dump frequented by bears. We observed the bears and even named them. I remember one we named Polychrome. We noted that the larger bears staked out territory in the center of the dump and drove smaller bears toward the fringes. We resolved to disturb the social order by separating some of the more choice morsels of garbage and placing them on the fringes for the smaller bears as an egalitarian gesture. The larger bears continued to occupy the center.

On a couple of occasions guests inquired where they might see bears. I accommodated them by driving them to the garbage dump and explaining our social experiments. Management would surely not have condoned this personalized service. Fortunately, it was not discovered and did not appear in my personnel records.

I have had numerous other encounters with bears in Yosemite Valley and in the High Country. Bears are often sought after, but seldom spotted, in Yosemite Valley. Once while working at Camp Curry I was showing guests to a tent. Upon inquiry, I stated truthfully that I had not seen a bear all summer. At that precise moment a bear emerged from one of the tents. To the credit of the guests, they stayed on and did not cancel their reservations.

Various devices have been developed to discourage or prevent bears from stealing food from backpackers. Hanging food in trees was once the prescribed method. However, mother bears trained cubs to crawl out on slender branches and knock down the bags of food. I have observed this more than once.

The Yosemite Fund, now the Yosemite Conservancy, has developed state-of-the-art bear-feeding canisters. Some food lockers have been placed at backcountry campsites, and smaller canisters that can be carried by backpackers are available. Visitors are routinely advised to refrain from leaving food in tents or vehicles, and surely to avoid tucking a midnight snack into a sleeping bag. This has helped, but some visitors remain heedless.

Efforts are currently being made by the Park Service to wean bears away from being dependent upon foraging food from tourists, and to reintroduce bears to their traditional feeding habits. This is easier said than done, because bears pass on their knowledge of food gathering to the next generation. A ranger naturalist is currently assigned to this program, which is a worthwhile effort at preservation. Rangers also have identified problem bears and have attempted to tranquilize them and haul them away. There have been instances in which the bear has made it back before the truck that hauled it away. Bears have a keen homing instinct and are able to cover many miles of roadless territory very quickly.

Bears will forever remain a part of Yosemite. Viewing them will continue to be an attraction to visitors, as the rest of the man and bear story unfolds. Education should continue to play a major role in this endeavor.

THE FIRE FALL

The Yosemite fire fall was among the most famous of all the traditions. Visitors and residents alike assembled to view the nightly summertime spectacle.

The fire fall started around the turn of the century. A man named James McCauley, who was manager of the Glacier Point Hotel, originally conceived the first fire falls. The spectacular sight impressed David A. Curry, who transformed it into a nightly spectacle during the summertime season. Curry discovered that flaming embers from a special red fir bark would create particularly spectacular sparks. The bark was from dead or downed trees. It burned hot and fast to produce coals, but not so hot and fast that it turned to ash.

David A. Curry had a flair for the dramatic. Each day a great bonfire would be laid out on the top of Glacier Point, 3,000 feet directly above Camp Curry. The fire would be ignited to a roaring pitch. At precisely 9:00 p.m., a caller from Camp Curry would shout, "Hello Glacier!" A caller atop Glacier Point would respond, "Hello, Curry!"

Pushing the fire fall from Glacier Point. Courtesy of Yosemite Research Library.

The Camp Curry caller would then give the command for which everyone had been waiting: "Let the fire fall!" The original call, "Let 'er go, Gallagher!" was replaced by the more straightforward "Let the fire fall!"

The Glacier Point caller would respond, "The fire will fall!" Yosemite employees on Glacier Point would then push the flaming bonfire over the edge with rakes. The flaming embers fell vertically for about 1,000 feet, landing on a rocky ledge, where they would burn harmlessly into ashes. There never was any danger of the falling fire starting a conflagration, because no trees or bushes were anywhere near the ledge where the flames landed. While the flames were falling, a singer would entertain the watching crowds by singing "Indian Love Call."

All activity in Yosemite Valley would cease while the fire was falling. People stopped their vehicles to watch the spectacle. Cars would turn off their lights. Everyone would stand in the darkness breathlessly watching the orange embers cascading down the cliff side.

Tom Bopp Comments on the Fire Fall

Tom Bopp, the Yosemite musical historian whose comments are included in Chapter 22, describes the spectacle and its demise in more lyrical fashion:

"It is 8:58 on a summer evening in Yosemite Valley, and something is up. The campgrounds are suddenly, strangely still. Cars have pulled off the roads; hushed, excited groups are forming in the meadows. Electric lights have dimmed, and the silent masses gaze at a pinpoint of fire three thousand feet above at Glacier Point. You're wondering if some kind of religious ritual may be about to begin.

"A sudden, singing bellow erupts from the nearby encampment: 'HELLLLOOO … GLAAAAACIER!!' As the echo fades, down through the silence comes the thin reply from the cliff-top, 'Helllooo … Camp … Curry!' Then the nearby voice howls, 'IS …THE FIRE … READY?!' and the faint reply wafts down, '… the fire is ready.'

"It appears that you're watching some kind of communal event in which all turn toward a sacred point—the bonfire on the cliff—listening to the ritual, responsorial calls … (the voice booms once more), 'LET… THE FIRE… FALLLLLLLL!!!' … (pause)… 'the fire is fallllinggggg.' What's this!… the coals of the bonfire gently urged over the cliff form a wafting, glowing emulation of Yosemite Falls while a voice is singing '… when I'm calling yooooooooo…' You think, 'Interesting choice of liturgical music—but what religion is this?'

"The *Fire Fall*, accompanied by the singing of *Indian Love Call*, is remembered by thousands as a cherished part of their Yosemite visit. The combination of song and spectacle provided a deep-rooted, powerful symbol of all that has been brought to Yosemite since the glaciers melted and allowed life to move in. Fire codependent with plant-life, songs inseparable from birds, human behavior—all of these elements share equal status as natural imports to Yosemite. The *Fire Fall* also symbolizes, ironically, how life impacts itself even while celebrating itself.

"This gentle, beautiful symbol of the forces of fire and song that connect humans to their environment was altering Yosemite meadows, as increasing numbers of spectators nightly trampled the delicate grasses. Its embers left an additional streak on the cliff face. Red-fir bark stripped from fallen trees and used to fuel the *Fire Fall* became scarce, requiring its collectors to cover many miles per summer. These fallen trees being hotels for massive amounts of insect species, it is even possible to quantify the impact on the insect and bird populations, not to mention the yearly labor and equipment costs to the Yosemite Park & Curry Company.

"Increased managerial, environmental and fiscal impacts of the *Fire Fall* spelled its demise, but other kinds of 'artificial entertainment' joyfully persists wherever it does not impair our efforts to protect Yosemite. The last *Fire Fall* took place on January 25, 1968—a victim of its own popularity.

"For many, the *Fire Fall* may have satisfied some unconscious need for a communal ritual when visiting Yosemite; it has often been described as a deeply moving, spiritual experience, a sort of religious service. It was a chance for many at the same time to pause in the mundane doings of camping, eating and preparing for sleep, and stand in awe at a cultural icon unique to Yosemite, listening to the ritual *Fire Fall Calls* and music. Watching the sunrise from Glacier Point may satisfy this need for some, but many crave the kind of man-made, cultural event as in a church service, to express a deeper, spiritual communion with Yosemite's natural beauty. That is why the *Fire Fall* died so hard and why some are still angry about it. To dismiss it as 'kitsch,' or as artificial, is for many to scoff at the power and beauty of symbolism that takes place in a religious ritual.

"Still, the histories of the *Fire Fall*, bear-feedings and tunnel-trees teach good lessons for how we may monitor and manage our cultural interaction with the Park. Even *Fire Fall* diehards will often accept the reasons for its elimination if the explanation is respectful." – Tom Bopp

* * *

One of the distinctions during my summer employment was that for three years during the 1950s I was one of the elite corps of fire fall callers. It was part of a summer job as a porter at Camp Curry.

To some it was the highlight of a visit to Yosemite. Not everyone was enchanted; some thought it corny. Environmental purists considered it inappropriate since it was not a natural phenomenon, even though it was comprised of natural elements.

In 1969 the Park Service put an end to the famous spectacle for a number of reasons, none of which seem compelling to me. I believe they succumbed to the opinion of environmental purists who

CAMP CURRY'S FIRE FALL.

Courtesy of Yosemite Research Library.

condemned outright any show that Mother Nature herself hadn't staged. There were complaints about traffic congestion, but during the fire fall itself, there was none. Everyone was stopped and watching. Another reason given was the supposed shortage of the special bark used in the fire, which I have been unable to verify.

Park Service personnel cited one reason that had some validity—the impact that the gathered swarms of people placed upon the Yosemite environment. Cars reportedly drove into the meadows, where they parked to get a better view of the event. Crowds reportedly gathered in masses and trampled the meadows.

The Park Service supplied an explanation for suspending the fire fall in a 1999 issue of the Yosemite Guide: "It was halted amid a growing trend to eliminate artificial, manmade attractions, and to end massive nightly traffic jams, crowding, and exodus that drew visitors from throughout the Valley to the best viewing sites in the east end."

The fire fall remains a nostalgic memory for thousands of visitors who witnessed it during the many years of its existence. My viewpoint is that this is not a preservation vs. enjoyment issue, because the fire fall did minimal damage to the environment while providing a maximum of enjoyment to many who revered it. Visitors were free to ignore it.

THE BRACEBRIDGE DINNER

The Bracebridge Dinner is another Yosemite tradition, tracing its origins back to 1927, the first year of operation of the Ahwahnee Hotel. The dinner was initiated to attract visitors during the Christmas season. It remains a cherished annual observance today.

The Bracebridge Dinner is held in the Ahwahnee's grand dining room. It features a formal seven-course dinner conducted in a style intended to characterize a banquet served by an 18th century English squire. The first dinner cost $22 per couple, which was a hefty price in those long ago years. After more than eight decades, the cost has risen to about $325 per couple.

The Great Hall at the Ahwahnee seats 375 guests who are served in true regal style at the Bracebridge Dinner. All guests are simultaneously served each course by a small army of 60 table servers. The traditional courses include The Relish, The Soup, The Fish, The Peacock Pie, Baron of Beef and Boar's Head, The Salad, and Pudding and Wassail.

In the earlier days the Bracebridge Dinner was a one-time affair on Christmas Eve. Tickets were in great demand. Because the same people would monopolize them year after year, a lottery was conducted for the tickets. Almost 2,000 people would vie for the 300-plus tickets. The production is now staged on several days in December; thus there is no need for a lottery.

The performers are all dressed in period costumes. The clothes worn by the squire and his lady are elegant. While a young lad, I began my own association with the Bracebridge Dinner as a lackey, accompanying the courses as they were brought in to the hall with great fanfare. As indicated previously, I rose from this lowly position to be the Visiting Squire, a one-time honor.

The dinner officially begins with the entrance of the couple playing Squire Bracebridge and his lady, accompanied by the Visiting Squire and his lady. Each course is accompanied by old English Christmas carols and a jester, the Lord of Misrule.

The dinner was inspired by Squire Bracebridge's Yule celebration, which was part of a series by Washington Irving called The Sketch Book of Geoffrey Crayon.

Irving told the complete story of the event surrounding the Bracebridge dinner in five episodes in his Sketch Book, including "Christmas," in which he reflects upon the meaning of Christmas; "The Stage-Coach," in which he rode with children to the country manor of Squire Bracebridge; "Christmas Eve," which recounts the holiday celebration at Bracebridge Hall; and two final episodes, "Christmas Day" and "Christmas Dinner," both of which describe in detail all the parts of the Christmas celebration at Bracebridge Hall.

Don Tresidder originally conceived of the event as a means of encouraging wintertime patrons to patronize the newly completed Ahwahnee Hotel. Ansel Adams produced the annual spectacle. Ansel characterized the event as "A Christmas Tradition that never really happened but that lives in everyone's heart." He hired Ted Spencer, a prominent architect, and his wife, interior decorator Jeanette Dyer Spencer, to create the set. Spencer played a key role in the restoring and refurbishing of the Ahwahnee after the Navy trashed it in World War II.

In 1931, Ansel Adams became Major Domo, the Head of the Household, and Virginia Best Adams became the Housekeeper, leading villagers who entered the hall from outside.

The Squires Bracebridge Dinner head table at the Ahwahnee. Top: left to right, Herman Hoss, Della Hoss, Don Tresidder, Mary Tresidder. Herman Hoss as Parson. All of The Squires' guests, 1927. Courtesy of Adams Family Collection.

Every year until his death in 1948, Don and Mary Curry Tresidder played the Squire and his lady. Ansel Adams played the role of the colorful Lord of Misrule, a jester dressed appropriately. My father played the Parson, who blessed each course, one of the key roles. Singers were recruited from the prestigious Bohemian Club from San Francisco.

Ansel Adams managed the production until 1973, after which Eugene Fulton and his family began to manage the production. Eugene died in 1978 of a heart attack just following a dress rehearsal. His daughter Andrea carried on the production that night, and has only recently retired. She directed the dinner for over 60 years and continued to add events and touches to the celebration, writing original songs and adding a female choir, as well as an impressive candlelight procession to open the performance.

After participating in the event as a lackey and as Visiting Squire, I began to attend as a guest. The performance is a little different each year. Far more than a meal, The Bracebridge Dinner is a unique pageant that must be seen to be experienced.

The Bracebridge Dinner has nothing to do with Yosemite Park's history, nor is it a natural phenomenon. Predictably, it has been criticized by an environmental purist.

In 1997 I had an exchange of correspondence with Allan Shields, Professor of Philosophy Emeritus, from San Diego State University. He was a former seasonal Ranger/Naturalist at Tuolumne Meadows who characterized himself as a "publisher of Yosemite and regional books."

As part of a letter to Stan Albright, who at that time was the Yosemite superintendent, Dr. Shields stated:

"The devotees of the Bracebridge Dinners have had their fun now, since 1927, give or take a war or two. Based on Washington Irving's *Bracebridge Hall, or the Humorists* (1822, not 1819 as the Ahwahnee tradition has it), it is a fictional celebration of British traditions of a farcical character and, as such, is altogether appropriate for some California Renaissance Fairs, and is not appropriate in a National Park. Does anyone else dare to point this out? It is elitist *in extremis*."

I responded to Dr. Shields in the following words:

"Your comments about The Bracebridge Dinner interest me, because they raise a broad philosophical question to which I am going to devote some attention. That question is 'How does anyone determine what is appropriate or not appropriate in a place such as Yosemite, considering varying public tastes, and the dual mission of the National Park Service for leaving it unimpaired for future generations and to be enjoyed by present generations?' Is there any rational way of doing this? Is it political in the sense that it should be responsive to what a majority of the public want? Is it utilitarian, in the sense that it should respond to some criteria of the greatest good for the greatest number? Are there any principles that can be developed?

"Viewing this question vis-à-vis The Bracebridge Dinner, you are absolutely right that a traditional English Christmas has nothing to do with Yosemite. However, it is a 70-year tradition that is greatly enjoyed by many people. You have to really stretch to say that this even poses any threat to the environment. So what is wrong with continuing it? What do you gain by ending the tradition? What is the countervailing value?"

Dr. Shields did not respond to these questions.

Although Ansel Adams opposed the fire fall, he could hardly oppose The Bracebridge Dinner, having been a founder and integral part of it for years. These positions have been deemed to be inconsistent by some environmental purists.

The best response to this criticism is the famous dictum of Ralph Waldo Emerson (who was an enthusiastic visitor to Yosemite): *A foolish consistency is the hobgoblin of little minds.*

Top, left: Upski sled at Badger Pass before lifts; right: skiers at Badger Pass. Courtesy of Yosemite Research Library
Bottom, left: Upskiers at Badger Pass; center: Badger Pass Ski Lodge during heavy snow; right: Mary Curry Tresidder, 1935 skier.

THE STORY OF BADGER PASS

In 1935 Badger Pass became the first ski area in California, when Don Tresidder and the Yosemite Winter Club opened the Badger Pass Ski Area, a 45-minute drive from Yosemite Valley, under ideal conditions. Instructors were imported from Austria to teach Americans what was then a fledgling sport, relatively new to the USA.

Development of the ski area met with initial opposition from the California State Chamber of Commerce, which was dominated at the time by representatives from Southern California who thought that the mention of snow and skiing would detract from their image of California as the land of sunshine and beaches.

Don Tresidder made a valiant effort to bring international attention to Yosemite winter sports by working with the Olympic Steering Committee, to make Badger Ski Area the venue for the 1928 Winter Olympic Games. He lost the bid when Lake Placid, New York, was selected instead. In spite of the failure to bring the Winter Olympics to Yosemite, Don Tresidder pushed forward to create what was then a premium class winter sports facility. The first lift was built in 1933. The slopes were used for the first slalom race held in the state. In the beginning, Badger Pass could be reached only by a winding and difficult road. That problem was solved in 1933 by the completion of the Wawona Tunnel. Two years later the Glacier Point Road to Badger Pass opened as well. That same year, Yosemite's first ski lodge was built.

Ski equipment, featuring lace-up boots and bear trap bindings, was primitive by today's standards. In the early days, to reach the top of Badger Pass' longest hill, skiers removed their skis and rode to the top of the hill on an Upski, which was a large sled that carried six skiers at a time to the top of the hill. Winter sports at Yosemite began to boom, and in 1935 more than 25,000 skiers had made the trip to Badger Pass.

A great number of people hold fond memories of learning to ski at Badger Pass, and it continues to provide a wonderful wintertime getaway for families and beginners. It now features groomed trails for people who enjoy cross-country skiing and snowshoeing.

Imagine how a proposal to build a downhill ski resort in a National Park would be received today. Badger Pass has only been able to survive because it has been grandfathered in by the Park Service with support of thousands who hold cherished memories of Badger Pass.

One of Yosemite's more colorful traditions, held on the Badger Pass closing day, consists of employees from various parts of the lodge designing dummies that they then let loose to careen down the hill. On the same day, contestants ski across a water hazard at the bottom of the hill.

The Wawona Tree. Peter's maternal grandmother, Ellen Stobbs Taylor, with her brother William, and Ollie Stobbs. Courtesy of Mary FitzGerald Beach.

THE WAWONA TREE

One of Yosemite's most popular traditional tourist attractions used to be located in the Mariposa Grove of Big Trees. A giant Sequoia was cut so as to allow an automobile to pass through it, so gawking tourists could snap pictures. The tree was hardy enough to survive this indignity for a number of years, before it toppled over prematurely.

I stand behind the environmental purists on this one. To create a spectacle of this kind from a living tree is on a par with feeding bears garbage under lights. In my opinion, there can be no justification for defacing a living tree in a National Park. To me there is a difference in kind between doing this and creating what some regard as a non-natural spectacle in the fire fall, which harmed no living thing and did no perceptible damage to Mother Nature.

The Conversation Club

The Conversation Club began in the year of my birth, 1934, fifteen days after my birthday, and continued as a Yosemite institution through which overqualified Company executives and Park Service personnel educated themselves on topics of public interest. The founder was the then-Superintendent Colonel Charles Goff Thomson, who had belonged to a similar organization in New England. Colonel Thomson had authored some novels. Both my father, Herman Hoss, and stepfather, Hil Oehlmann, were charter members. As Hil observed on the 20th anniversary of the Conversation Club, "The Colonel was quick to observe the great field of fertile intellect lying fallow in this masterwork of nature and concluded that it could be made to yield a priceless harvest of wisdom." Regarding the character of Colonel Thomson, Hil noted: "In an early meeting Mr. Ackles (Secretary Treasurer) addressed the Chair with some remarks of warm appreciation of the spirit of comradeship which the club had engendered in the hearts of its members. He then proposed that we dispense with formality in addressing one another. The Chair, without inviting comment from the floor, made it clear that there was distinction between liberty and license. To my knowledge, neither Mr. Ackles nor any other member thereafter addressed Colonel Thomson as "Charlie."

The Conversation Club adopted bylaws, and even a bill of rights, which were not consistently followed. The bylaws prohibited discussions of sectarian religion and partisan politics and prohibited the service of alcoholic beverages before meetings. Hil noted in his 20th-year reminiscence that "there existed among the membership a deplorable lack of acquaintance with the Constitution and Bylaws of the Organization."

Meetings were held at homes of members. The procedure of the club was that each member, on a rotating basis, would present a typewritten paper in bound form which would be distributed and read, with discussion following. Among topics presented, as noted in Hil's reminiscence, were Mussolini's invasion of Ethiopia, American Youth Problems, Trial of Facts at Law, Our Labor Problem, Honesty, Semantics, Mnemonics, State Medicine, Venereal Disease, Outdoor Advertising and the Armament Industry.

I have found some of these papers among my father's possessions, and they are impressive. The Conversation Club is an example of what made Yosemite special as a haven for the inquisitive and overqualified.

YOSEMITE CEMETERY

Many visitors may be unaware that there is a cemetery in Yosemite. The cemetery is located across the road from the Visitor Center, adjacent to the Park Service housing. It has not been well tended over the years. Instead of manicured grass, one shuffles through leaves to look for the markers.

Some prominent Yosemite pioneers are buried in the Yosemite cemetery. Perhaps most notable among them is Galen Clark, a contemporary of John Muir, known as the caretaker of Yosemite. Also buried in the Yosemite cemetery are: J.B. Hutchings, one of the first publicists in Yosemite and an early innkeeper who employed John Muir in his sawmill (see page 110); his daughter, the first Caucasion child born in Yosemite; George Anderson, who made the first ascent of Half Dome; and Gabriel Souvelesk, a cavalry officer instrumental in building many trails in Yosemite. According to my friend, Charlie Castro, a Yosemite native (see page 259), the last person to be buried in the Yosemite cemetery was his grandmother, Louisa Tom, in 1955.

I was reminded of this information and a Yosemite tradition connected with the cemetery not through personal experience or from the Park Service, the concessioner or the Yosemite Conservancy. Rather, it was through a report from visitors to Yosemite, Dr. Joe and Linda Hancock, who are old friends from Salinas who happened to be in Yosemite on Halloween and heard of an event unknown to the present superintendent and Mike Adams. They heard about it from a desk clerk at Yosemite Lodge. This event is an annual Halloween cemetery tour in which participants are given a marker to find in the dark, with the aid of a flashlight. They are then given information about those buried under the marker, an interesting educational experience, which my friends thoroughly enjoyed.

This is an example of a bright idea that illustrates the creation of new Yosemite traditions. It is this type of ingenuity inherent in the people attracted to Yosemite which makes Yosemite such a special place. A visitor never knows what he or she may stumble upon, even if familiar with Yosemite and its traditions. This one was new to me.

CHAPTER 13

YOSEMITE SUBCULTURES

THE CLIMBERS

The first recorded ascent of a prominent Yosemite peak occurred on September 7, 1869, when John Muir, working as a Tuolumne Meadows shepherd, ascended Cathedral Peak, climbing barehanded up a crack that most climbers today would not ascend without a rope.

On October 12, 1875, five years after Josiah Whitney declared Half Dome unable to be climbed, George Anderson became the first person to make the ascent, inserting handmade eye bolts into holes that he drilled a few feet apart. Each bolt provided Anderson with a foothold upon which to stand while he drilled the next hole.

Today visitors stand in line to climb Half Dome after a long hike. They make the ascent by holding on to a cable and walking up a series of wooden steps. In 2010 the Park Service determined that the number of climbers was creating a safety hazard, particularly when changing weather conditions created a "get down fast" motivation, although there were no serious injuries.

The Park Service began to require permits to climb Half Dome on weekends in 2010. As of 2011, permits were required every day. The Park Service reported 40,656 ascents of Half Dome in 2010, averaging between 300 and 872 per day. The cables are not up in late fall, winter or early spring.

During the 1940s the challenge was to climb Lost Arrow, a pinnacle near the top of Yosemite Falls. The ascent was first accomplished by a traverse, with a rope thrown over the pinnacle. Later the famed climbers Nelson and Salathe made a direct ascent, straight up The Lost Arrow.

In the 1950s climbers began flocking to Yosemite because it had become a rock-climbing mecca. In particular, they had come to ascend El Capitan, which they referred to as "El Cap." El Capitan is a single gigantic boulder, the largest in the world. Before the 1950s, it had been widely believed that nobody would ever be able to scale El Capitan's towering 3,000-foot granite face. However, the "impossible" was accomplished in 1958 when three men—Warren Harding, Wayne Merry and George Whitmore—successfully completed the first ascent of El Capitan, scaling the surface that climbers call "The Nose."

Tom Frost, at home on any wall. 1960.

El Capitan profile.

Cool aid. Royal Robbins climbs the third pitch of the Salathé Wall.

The two greatest climbers of their generation, Chuck Pratt and Royal Robbins atop El Cap Spire, the Salathé Wall, El Capitan.

The powers that be. From left: Tom Frost, Royal Robbins, Chuck Pratt, and Yvon Chouinard. El Capitan summit, October 30, 1964, after their ten-day ascent of the North American Wall.

Tom Frost's name conjures for us that spirit of the Golden Age of Yosemite rock climbing when adventure was in the air and the style of the ascent was what counted. In the early 1960s, Frost made ascents of the Nose, the Salathé Wall, and the North American Wall of El Cap with pioneers Royal Robbins, Chuck Pratt and Yvon Chouinard.

Robbins was the prima facie leader of Yosemite's Golden Age. He showed us a style for climbing El Capitan. Chuck Pratt, a beloved Camp 4 personality, displayed uncanny virtuosity on the rock. As Chouinard once asked, "Did anyone ever see Chuck's foot slip?" We don't think so. Chouinard was unoffical philosopher for the Camp 4 community. He and Frost also worked together to design and produce much of the climbing hardware that is still in use today. In his younger years Tom Frost raced sailboats at Newport Harbor, then went on to study mechanical engineering and rock climbing at Stanford University. It was he who, on every one of their El Cap climbs, carried his Leica screw-mount camera, with 50mm collapsible Elmar lens, and up to 30 rolls of black and white film. These photos are but a sampling of the images he captured on those climbs.

Text and photos courtesy of Tom Frost and Matt Dealy.

Harlan atop the fou.

The initial climb required 18 months of preparation, using a method that involved assembling and putting into place a system of clamps linked together by manila ropes, pitons and expansion bolts. The actual climb took 45 days and 30 nights, during which the climbers climbed back and forth to staging locations.

Three years later, four men—Royal Robbins, Joe Fitschen, Chuck Pratt and Tom Frost—used other climbing methods to make the ascent in only seven days. The time is now down to hours rather than days, as records continue to be broken.

The late 1950s ushered in what came to be known as the Golden Age of Climbing in Yosemite Valley. Three of its icons were Royal Robbins, Tom Frost and Yvon Chouinard. Chouinard went on to found the highly successful Patagonia line of clothing and equipment. In September 1960, Robbins planned a second ascent of the route taken by Harding, Merry and Whitmore, which was a continuous ascent using no fixed rope. He was accompanied by Frost, Chouinard and another climber, Chuck Pratt. They completed what had been planned as a ten-day climb in seven days. Frost is quoted in the January-March edition of the *Yosemite Gazette* as saying at the end of the climb, "I thought when I stepped off onto the summit from the last move I was stepping right into Heaven. It was that big of an experience for me."

Frost credits Robbins for having been the impetus for the Golden Age of Climbing in Yosemite. He said of Robbins in the same *Yosemite Gazette* issue, "Climbing as we know it would not exist without Royal Robbins. The way we move, behave and even think is, 30 years after the end of his Yosemite reign, shaped by Robbins." Robbins pioneered many firsts and new routes, innovative climbing techniques, as well as the "leave no trace" philosophy that required the second man following each climber to remove pitons hammered into the rock so that the next climbing party would find the route in the same condition.

Many notable climbers, too numerous to mention, followed the Golden Age of Climbing and are still following it. One among them deserves mention. The late Galen Rowell climbed in the far corners of the earth and produced many coffee table books of magnificent color photography. To me, Galen Rowell is the Ansel Adams of color photography. His studio, Mountain Light, located in Bishop, California, houses some of the greatest mountain photographs taken.

During the Golden Age of Climbing, and through the present day, breakthroughs in climbing equipment and technique were invented, tested and developed in Yosemite. One of the techniques is free climbing, utilizing few or no ropes. Climbers have continued to find new routes up El Capitan as well as other Yosemite cliffs. There are now more than 70 established routes up El Capitan. Time for climbing El Capitan has been reduced from months to days to hours. It is pointless to mention a record because it will be broken before this is read. However, most climbers do not climb to establish speed records. Many climbers report cherishing the time they spend on the granite face and the challenge of finding new handholds and footholds as being the essence of the experience, the journey rather than the destination being the prize.

The sight of climbers making their way up the face of El Capitan has become a major tourist attraction. In the minds of many visitors, the climbers have become as much a fixture of Yosemite as the rocks themselves.

Another result of the Golden Age of Climbing was the establishment of a subculture. Climbers tend to be independent and to want to hang out with other climbers. Many of them are willing to live in a state of near poverty because they prefer climbing to work. At first, climbers were reluctant to accept women into their subculture, but soon females established their proficiency as climbers and came to be accepted, as in so many other fields.

Climbers came to congregate in a Campground known as Camp 4, across the road from Yosemite Lodge, near the site of the now vanished Indian Village. Climbers from all over the world came to Camp 4 to climb in Yosemite. For some years the relationship between the climbing subculture and the Park Service and The Company was somewhat less than harmonious. Some of the climbers had a scruffy, unkempt appearance, and some of the more impecunious of them were known to venture into the Lodge cafeteria and pick up leftovers or even beg food, although this was by no means widespread. There was pot smoking in Camp 4. At one time, both the Park Service and the Concessioner discouraged interaction between visitors and climbers.

All this came to a head during the tenure of the late Stan Albright as superintendent, when the Park Service renamed Camp 4 "Sunnyside" in an attempt to encourage more non-climbers to camp there. The climbers protested and asked that the name "Camp 4" be restored and placed on the National Register of Historic Sites. The climbers hired legal counsel, and threatened litigation. There was a settlement in which the climbers prevailed. A maintenance crew even found the original sign, which was reinstalled and later disappeared. To climbers, Camp 4 has always been a shrine.

The Park Service assigned rangers interested in climbing to interact with the climbers. Climbers assisted rangers in rescue efforts. Relations have moved into peaceful coexistence, described by the present superintendent as positive. Another noted climber, Ron Kauk, participates in educational programs conducted by the Yosemite Conservancy. The current concessioner operates the Yosemite Mountaineering School and Guide service, which teaches climbing techniques to visitors and novices.

Climbing has become and is destined to remain an established, appropriate and exhilarating activity in Yosemite.

EXTREME SPORTS IN YOSEMITE

When climbing El Capitan had become a regular experience, a number of courageous, perhaps foolhardy, people pushed forward to something more challenging by making unauthorized "base jumping" parachute leaps off the top of El Capitan. This is a risky adventure because of the unpredictable winds that often swirl around that granite face. Two men made the initial jump on July 24, 1966. They both survived, although with broken bones.

The Park Service experimented briefly with base-jumping permits in 1980, but soon discontinued the practice. Park rangers have a policy of confiscating base jumpers' equipment when they catch the jumpers, who have been at odds with the rangers. The relationship between jumpers and park authorities reached its lowest point when a successful jumper fled from Park Rangers after his jump, leaped into the Merced River—and drowned. Jumpers continue to complain about the ban on base jumping.

On October 23, 1999, a 60-year-old woman named Jan Davis became eligible for the Darwin Awards (commemorating those who assist natural selection by removing themselves from the gene pool) when she leaped off the top of El Capitan to protest the ban and died when her borrowed chute failed to open. Davis reportedly borrowed some cheap equipment, not realizing that the ripcord on her borrowed equipment was in a different place than on the more expensive chute that she left behind.

Hang gliding off Glacier Point has also been pursued. The granite walls are certain to beckon those who pursue extreme sports.

CHAPTER 14

A DIFFERENT KIND OF LAW

MY FATHER AS COMMISSIONER

Because Yosemite is under exclusive federal jurisdiction, a federally appointed magistrate presides over a court in Yosemite Valley. My father served part-time in this capacity, while serving as a full-time employee of the Yosemite Park & Curry Company.

A commissioner's duties consisted mostly of dealing with minor criminal infractions that arose in the Park. In the early days, the superintendent could declare a person to be persona non grata and banish that person from Yosemite. This practice has been discontinued, creating a de facto civil right to be a troublemaker in Yosemite.

One day a guest approached my father at the Camp Curry desk and asked him whether the magistrate judge might be amenable to fixing the traffic ticket that the man had been issued. With a completely straight face, my father replied "I don't think that is a good idea with this particular judge. Just be straight with him, and he will be fair with you." When the visitor later approached my father while he was in his role as magistrate judge, the man was mortified to discover the identity of the judge. My father gave no clue that he had ever seen the man before in his life.

Another episode in my father's judicial career illustrates the atmosphere in the Yosemite community in which we lived. Wendell Otter, a management employee of The Company and father of my close childhood pal, Dick Otter, and a friend, also an employee, were cited by a ranger for illegally rafting on the Merced River. When they appeared before the Magistrate, my father dutifully fined them and they all went out for a cup of coffee. I don't know who paid.

LIFE ON THE BENCH
WITH DON PITTS

Don Pitts is a close friend and colorful character by any definition. Don, an appointed magistrate, provided me with some highlights of his judicial career.

Kay and Don Pitts.

One day Don was walking the short distance from his home in Yosemite Valley to the courthouse. A man drove by, accompanied by a lady, and asked for directions to the courthouse. Don provided directions and continued his walk. The driver continued on to the courthouse and appeared before Don to answer a charge of driving without a license.

On another occasion a couple appeared before Don to answer a charge of camping in an area not designated as a campground. They explained that they had arrived late at night and were unable to locate and check into the proper campground, so they pulled into the Ahwahnee parking lot and threw their sleeping bags down nearby until they could get their bearings in the morning. The ranger who apprehended them had a somewhat different story. While patrolling on horseback above Mirror Lake, over two miles from any road head, he encountered dogs and investigated, only to find the couple encamped in an idyllic location up against a cliff with their own small private cascade. The location was so well hidden that the couple never would have been discovered had it not been for the dogs. Don invited his wife Kay to visit the place and they were impressed with its isolated solitude. This story should disprove any notion that it is not possible to commune with nature in a very private way in Yosemite Valley.

Don't Trifle with the Magistrate
or "How to Turn a $25 Fine into Four Days in Jail"

Mr. B and friends decided to raft the Tuolumne River in October, but they did not get a permit. The permit notifies the rafter when water is released from the upstream dam, enabling rafters to "catch the current." The group of five launched Mr. B's raft at the put in. Two of the three women soon became afraid of the swift water and decided not to continue. They had a rough hike getting back to the car. They had forgotten to get the keys from Mr. B. The remaining rafters planned to return by late afternoon, but did not return by nightfall. The two women, who lived in Boston, were not used to being alone in a remote area. They spent a miserable night huddled by the car. The next day they began a long hike to the nearest highway and were fortunate to encounter a car approaching. Two fishermen drove them to a phone, and they reported the rafters missing.

A search was launched with an airplane and a helicopter, and the rafters were finally spotted just as they reached the take-out at the end of the day. The raft had been trapped in low water. The three spent an uncomfortable night.

They were each given a citation for rafting without a permit.

The fine for this offense was $25. They chose not to pay the fines. Letters were sent from the court and returned unopened with "wrong address" scrawled on the envelopes. Don used an old strategy, which was to send the same letter to the same address in a plain, unmarked envelope. Sure enough, the official envelope was again returned but the plain envelope was not, which meant that the addresses were correct.

Magistrate Pitts issued a notice to appear in court, and this certainly got the girlfriend's attention. She showed up several hours early. She related how Mr. B had intimidated her and his friend, instructing them to ignore the letters and court summons. He had also threatened the two women from Boston. Don became curious and called the women in Boston, who confirmed that they had been told to not give out any information. Meanwhile, another rafter did show up in court, and he and the lady were each given a fine, which they both readily paid.

Instead of showing up for court, Mr. B began calling everyone believed to have power, such as his congressman, the chief judge of the District Court, and the Federal Public Defender, complaining that he was being persecuted. Magistrate Pitts, getting tired of wasted court time, increased the fine to $500, the maximum allowed. When Mr. B still ignored the court summons, Don called the U.S. Marshalls and asked them to phone the scofflaw and explain how serious a matter this was becoming. Mr. B laughed at the marshalls, saying, "There's nothing you can do to me!" Not a very bright statement to make to a federal marshall.

On a Friday afternoon Mr. B was arrested at work in Menlo Park and taken to jail in San Francisco. The magistrate in San Francisco had left for the day, so Mr. B remained in jail over the weekend. When Mr. B came before the magistrate the following Monday, she read the note from Magistrate Pitts, which was attached to the file, which explained the circumstances of the arrest. She took the case under advisement and sent Mr. B back to jail for the night. The next day he was instructed to appear in Yosemite, or else!

Mr. B then hired a lawyer who tried to recuse Don as magistrate. There is a right to recuse a state judge but not a federal judge. Had the lawyer done his homework, he would have known this. The court hearing lasted most of the day. The recusal was disallowed. Mr. B was fined $500. An appeal was filed and later dropped. Don figured that the lawyer's fees were probably around $2,000, so the total cost to Mr. B was $2500 + four nights in jail, all for not getting a permit, which was free.

Moreover, the case illustrates the importance of obtaining a permit, so that officials responsible for the safety of visitors can be alerted if they do not return when expected, as the ladies from Boston experienced.

TEACHERS

A middle-aged couple, both school teachers, stopped at the Visitor Center in Tuolumne Meadows on a weekend. There they saw drawings by John Muir showing how Yosemite Valley was formed by glaciation, which was contrary to the thinking of the day. They wanted to get copies for their classes but were informed they would have to contact someone during the week. They continued driving west and reached the Crane Flat area, where they saw a ranger.

The ranger was in the process of arresting someone. Ignoring the obvious signs of confrontation, a ranger's car with flashing lights, the couple crossed the street, walking between the suspect's car and the ranger's car. They confronted the ranger, asking him for copies of the John Muir drawings. In Yosemite there are enforcement rangers ("fuzz") and interpretive rangers ("fuzzies"). Not having a clue as to who the teachers might be and hoping they weren't friends of the suspect, the ranger asked the couple to return to their car until he was finished with the arrest. The wife went back, but the husband insisted on his rights as an American citizen. Insisting once too often, he was arrested and put in the car with the other suspect and taken to jail.

Don met the couple in a settlement conference and hinted broadly that pleading to a charge of interfering with an officer would carry a small fine and relieve the man of having to return to court. The husband said, "No. I am an American citizen and have a right to trial."

On the day of the trial the husband waived his right to a federal defender and chose to act as his own lawyer. The arresting ranger testified that there was a space of about 30 feet between the suspect's car and the ranger's car. The husband stated that he believed that there was at least 60 feet, which would mean that anyone might have wandered through the space. Perry Mason then called his wife. "Oh no, Dear," she corrected. "I'm sure the cars were only 20 feet or less apart." Unfazed, the husband testified, "The ranger said I swore at him. But I did not." The wife testified, "Dear, I'm sure you did. I definitely heard a God damn, you son-of-a-bitch."

Holding on to his seat and trying not to laugh, Magistrate Don found the defendant guilty and fined him $100, the same amount he would have paid for pleading guilty. Don often wondered what happened to the marriage. The wife was last, seen in the foyer crying, being consoled by Don's secretary. "But I swore to tell the truth!"

ENCOUNTERS WITH A 90-DAY WONDER

Don and Kay were backpacking in the Yosemite High Country in early July over 20 miles from a road head when Don slipped on a rocky slope and severely injured his ankle. After a long, sleepless night they made their way to the backcountry ranger station on the Merced River, 16 miles above Yosemite Valley. The ranger could not telephone for help as the line had been removed to the Merced High Sierra Camp. To get help the ranger had to either hike to the camp or climb to the ridge to get radio contact. With the help of two passing hikers who were able to climb part way up the ridge, messages could be conveyed by shouting up or down the hill.

The ranger requested a helicopter to transport Don out. He was told that since Don was not a Park Service employee, Don would have to pay for the rescue. Don's reply, shouted by uphill relay was, "I'm going to take some vacation time here and just rest. You can haul the prisoners to Fresno." Realizing what an expense this could be to the Park Service, the next response was, "OK, we'll take the magistrate, but Kay can't come!" Kay shouted that she preferred to walk out anyway. The ranger descended the hill only to find he must go up again for another radio message.

"The helicopter broke down! We're sending Ranger G with a mule to rescue the judge. They can spend the night there and come out the next day."

When Don heard who was to rescue him he could hardly believe his luck, not the good kind. In all the years Don had been in Yosemite, neither he nor his family had ever had difficulty with rangers, with one exception. Ranger G had had confrontations with Don's son Rob, his daughter Ann, and his wife Kay. On his horse Ranger G had chased Rob's car uphill, accusing Robert of speeding because his horse couldn't catch the car. Rob asked Ranger G to think about a horse traveling uphill at 25 miles per hour. He was not ticketed. Ranger G started to cite Don's daughter Anne for failing to stop for pedestrians in a crosswalk. Anne pointed out that the people were not in the crosswalk, but behind a huge yellow pine tree and thus invisible to a driver. Anne was not ticketed. When Kay had to unload some heavy recording equipment to take into court one morning, Ranger G kept insisting that she couldn't park in the loading zone, but must move some distance away to visitor parking. Every other ranger would have offered to help her.

Due to these previous encounters, Don did not feel that his rescue would go well, nor was he willing to spend the night with Ranger G. It was now 1:00 in the afternoon, and Don was determined to walk part way out and meet the ranger so he could get home that night. Kay put some of his essential things in her pack and gave Don her walking stick. Kay started walking while Don organized the rest of his gear for later pickup. After about 11 miles of hiking Kay reached the top of Nevada Fall, where she finally saw Ranger G, who had come four miles. He was having a pleasant chat with a variety of tourists while they admired his horse and the rescue mount. Obviously he was in no hurry. Kay reminded him in a loud voice about his rescue mission.

Ranger G did finally meet Don in Little Yosemite Valley. Don had traveled ten miles on a badly damaged foot. Ranger G made six miles on horseback.

Don and Kay later learned that Ranger G was what is known as a "90-day Wonder," a temporary employee, a notable exception to other rangers. His regular occupation was as a wrestling coach.

I hasten to add that Ranger G is the exception, not the rule.

Following in Footsteps Failed

In the early 1990s I was getting a bit tired of legal business as usual in Salinas and decided that I might like to be a judge. As it turned out, it proved to be the best thing that did not happen to me. However, while musing along these lines, Don Pitts retired as magistrate in Yosemite, and the position became open. Suddenly Yosemite beckoned, and I decided to apply in somewhat of a fit of nostalgia as well as a desire to follow in my father's footsteps, albeit much later in life. The federal district judges in Fresno made the appointment.

I was warned that it was a real long shot, because a retiring California appellate judge with great clout with the district judges was known to be eyeing the position. Eighty-nine eager applicants applied for the position. I made it through the interviews to the top six. However, as predicted, Hollis Best triumphed and assumed the position. It was somewhat enjoyable going through the interview process. I never met Hollis Best while he presided. My interest in my own career returned, and I was glad for the result. My experience in going back to living in a very different Yosemite than I had known as a child and summer employee might well have been similar to that of my mother.

Another Familiar Face Becomes Magistrate

William Wunderlich practiced law in Monterey County in the district attorney's office and became a superior court judge. He was elevated to the U.S. Sixth District Court of Appeals. When the magistrate position in Yosemite next became open, he eyed it with interest as a new adventure in a varied career. He very graciously inquired if I was still interested, not wishing to deprive me of the position I had previously sought. I said that at that point I had no further interest, having retired and not being eager to go back to work, preferring to continue to be a privileged visitor in Yosemite at my choosing. I encouraged him to chase the "glad tidings," and he did so successfully. He greatly enjoyed his experience in Yosemite. I visited him several times, and we swapped yarns.

Like previous magistrates, he acquired a collection of stories. On one occasion he shared them with fellow lawyers in Monterey County. The following is worth passing on:

A house was provided for the magistrate in the area where Park Service personnel live. Nearby lived the chief ranger, who frequently prosecuted cases in front of the magistrate. One day, the neighbor observed an obviously inebriated young man on the porch of Magistrate Wunderlich's house. When he approached him, the young man said, "I live here." The chief ranger said, "I think not." About this time another ranger came by just as the young man was getting sick on the porch of the magistrate, and arrested him for public intoxication.

The next day in court the two rangers appeared before the magistrate, one as a prosecutor, the other as a witness. Magistrate Bill wondered if there might be a conflict of interest, but the issue was not raised. The young man was fined appropriately.

Hetch Hetchy before the dam was built..

CHAPTER 15

HETCH HETCHY
THE CONTROVERSY THAT WON'T GO AWAY

The area of controversy that John Muir considered his greatest failure was his inability to prevent the construction of O'Shaughnessy Dam in the Hetch Hetchy Valley, which is within Yosemite National Park, about 20 miles north of Yosemite Valley.

The dam is a major source of drinking water for millions of California residents in the city of San Francisco and on the San Francisco Peninsula. The dam is an important source of hydroelectric power for San Francisco. Hetch Hetchy Valley is a smaller image of Yosemite Valley with its own set of cliffs, waterfalls and a gently flowing Tuolumne River.

John Muir and the Sierra Club waged a valiant battle against the dam project, but they were on the losing side. The loss served to galvanize environmentalists and became an impetus for the growing preservationist movement.

The movement toward the dam began following the 1906 earthquake and fire that destroyed most of San Francisco. James Phelan, a San Francisco millionaire and politician, purchased land and water rights, including rights to the water flow of the Tuolumne River in Hetch Hetchy Valley, north of Yosemite Valley.

Anyone interested in a blow-by-blow description should read the most definitive book on the subject, *The Battle of Hetch Hetchy,* by an old friend and Yosemite co-worker, Bob Righter. Bob accurately stated that his book is not a polemic, and does not seek to state a position one way or the other on the present controversy over Hetch Hetchy. Rather, the book describes the complex political machinations that led to the dam's being built.

Bob's deliberately neutral position enabled him to describe people on both sides of the battle as being well intentioned. The laudable objectives on either side of the controversy were mutually exclusive. Bob described the conflict as a battle between good guys. His book does an admirable job steering a middle course, recounting the facts though the eyes of an impartial historian. One reviewer wrote about the book, that it was "…something beyond merely the best book anyone has ever written on confluence of canyon, dam and city that so shaped the story of the modern American West. It is both a well-argued history and a beautifully written testimony of hubris and loss, even possible redemption."

By a coincidence often repeated in my life, Bob was a cotenant of the cabin in El Portal described earlier. I was reunited with him after 40 years of being out of touch when he was invited to speak on his book at a forum of the Yosemite Conservancy.

The prevailing controversy of the construction of O'Shaughnessy Dam was not between preservation and development, but between developing the Hetch Hetchy Valley as a tourist destination and developing the site as a source of water and electricity. Ironically, given that posture and those policies, the inundation of Hetch Hetchy Valley behind that dam probably spared Hetch Hetchy from being developed as a tourist mecca, like Yosemite Valley, with hotels and tourist facilities. If the current environmentalists succeed in tearing the dam down, the dam will have been the very thing that saved the wilderness they want to preserve.

Hetch Hetchy reservoir is not an eyesore. In my opinion, it is a beautiful blue mountain body of water, encircled by cliffs. Motorboats are not permitted to destroy the serenity of the reservoir. Waterfalls cascade into it. After walking 100 yards past the corner of the dam, the evidence of human handiwork has largely vanished. The scene is almost indistinguishable from any mountain lake, except that varying water levels leave a "bathtub ring" during low water periods. Beauty really is mostly in the eye of the beholder. Viewers of Hetch Hetchy can be diverted from the reality before them by imagining what they might have been seeing.

A by-product of the dam is the spectacular recreational opportunity provided by the Tuolumne River running through the gorge below the dam, one of the great river runs in the nation. Without the controlled flow from the dam, the river run would be much more difficult and perilous.

There is an energetic movement to remove O'Shaughnessy Dam and eliminate the reservoir. "Restore Hetchy Hetchy" is a 501(c)(3) corporation with an agenda that has attracted a zealous following and significant donations. It is much more than a quixotic band of dreamers. Tearing down the dam and diverting the river flow into a pipeline so as to preserve a water supply for San Francisco is feasible from an engineering standpoint. Some cost estimates have been attempted, but an accurate figure would have to depend on an actual plan and bids by contractors. Both proponents and opponents concede it would be expensive.

Studies have also been undertaken on how long it would take to restore the drained reservoir to its appearance before the construction of the dam. It would be a gradual process, with grass first appearing, then clumps of trees, and finally a forest. Estimates of up to 100 to 200 years have been made before full restoration. What would happen to the Hetch Hetchy Valley during or after restoration is unclear. Environmentalists are excited about the opportunity to preserve an area as wilderness that they see as lost in Yosemite Valley. On the other hand, it could represent just another debate with those who would want to develop more tourist facilities.

As of this writing, the emphasis on restoring Hetch Hetchy is on garnering public support. A vote would be required by voters in San Francisco. Legal theories to force the restoration under the public trust doctrine have been explored.

Mike Marshall, executive director of "Restore Hetch Hetchy," is identified in the organization's promotional material as a veteran political operative who has been hired to sell the project. Marshall has outlined the following plan to obtain support of San Francisco residents:

1. Build a broad coalition in support of a city charter amendment requiring, among other things, the restoration of Hetch Hetchy Valley within a specified time period.
2. Secure six votes of the San Francisco Board of Supervisors for a charter amendment.
3. Build majority support within San Francisco for restoration of Hetch Hetchy Valley.
4. Work with coalition partners to create a separate campaign organization to pass the amendment.
5. Identify legislators at the state and federal level who will sponsor and pass legislation allocating resources for legislation by 2012.

The effort is linked to encouraging more recycling and environmental sustainability.

"Restore Hetch Hetchy" reports a poll of 500 San Francisco residents finding that 42% support restoration, 43% oppose it and 14% are undecided, if restoration would require an increase in utility rates. If the full cost of restoration is paid by the state and federal governments and there is not an increase in utility rates, support jumps to 59%, opposition falls to 31%, and 9% remain undecided. The survey found overwhelming support for investments in water recycling and water efficiency. Not surprisingly, support depends a good deal on who pays for the restoration.

An article in the March 30, 2007, issue of the Sacramento Bee contained the following impassioned summary of the justification for the destruction of the dam:

"The restoration of Hetch Hetchy is about the return of a natural treasure to all of the American people and the addition of a prized piece of the fabric back into the quilt that is our National Park system."

Proponents of the dam removal point out that creating a downstream storage system could mitigate the loss of water by catching the water without the destruction of a natural resource. They note that since 1990 the fresh water storage capacity in California has increased by a volume greater than 17 times the capacity of the existing Hetch Hetchy reservoir.

On the other side of the issue is Diane Feinstein, U.S. senator and former mayor of San Francisco, an outspoken opponent of restoring Hetch Hetchy. She echoed the sentiments of some California residents by offering this quote in the Los Angeles Times, related to the cost. "All this for an expanded campground. It's dumb dumb dumb."

To me, the seminal issue is not the feasibility, but rather the cost benefit ratio, which is unclear at this time. I choose to not take a position.

CHAPTER 16

CHANGING PUBLIC INVOLVEMENT

YOSEMITE VALLEY IS NOT
(AND NEVER HAS BEEN) A WILDERNESS

The notion that Yosemite Valley is "wilderness" is perhaps the greatest of all misconceptions about Yosemite Valley. Any reasoning based on this false premise is basically flawed. This misconception seems to increase with the distance from Yosemite Valley of the person proclaiming it, and with the lack of hands-on experience the proponent has with Yosemite Valley.

The misconception of Yosemite Valley as wilderness has caused rancorous debate by the misinformed, as well as lobbying by agitators who wish to "restore" Yosemite Valley to something it never was. It is too bad that these poor souls cannot enjoy a place of spectacular natural beauty for what it is, rather than what they imagine it could be. It is too bad Yosemite Valley has been "ruined" in their minds.

Yosemite Valley fits neither a dictionary definition nor a legal definition of "wilderness." Wilderness, as defined by *Webster's*, is

a. Any unsettled, uncultivated region left in its natural condition, especially a large, wild tract of land covered with dense vegetation or forests

b. An extensive area that is barren or empty, as a desert or ocean; a wasteland

c. A piece of land set aside by any legislation to grow wild

Yosemite Valley has never been any of the above in recorded history. Miwok Indians settled and cultivated Yosemite Valley for 1,000 years or more before any white man saw it. Yosemite Valley is not covered with dense forests, and it is neither empty nor barren. Yosemite Valley was not set aside by legislation to grow wild. Yosemite Valley had been developed extensively with man-made improvements when legislation designating it as public property was enacted.

Throughout history, wilderness has largely been a negative concept. Wilderness was to be feared, tamed, and converted to the uses of mankind. Wilderness was seen to have no value in its natural state. Wilderness has also been seen as a place to go for spiritual renewal and contemplation. Jesus went into the wilderness for 40 days to resist the temptations of Satan. Poets and writers have romanticized wilderness as land in its natural state, somehow purer than the world in which we live.

In recent times the concept of preserving wilderness for the sake of preserving it, rather than for recreational use or enjoyment, has developed and attracted a following. Some people are comforted by the notion that there remain places that no one can visit, and there has been lobbying for such places to be legally designated as "wilderness."

Yosemite Valley was a developed area devoted to recreation for over 100 years after being designated public property, and 50 years after becoming a National Park, before the idea of preserving areas as wilderness gained public acceptance.

In 1964 preservation of "wilderness" became public policy, representing a total turnaround of the historic view. Legislation was enacted by Congress that excluded from development more than nine million acres of land owned by the federal government. The Wilderness Act also produced a legal definition of "wilderness" drafted by Howard Zahniser of the Wilderness Society, which read more like a poem than a stipulated legal definition:

"A wilderness, in contrast with those areas where man and his own works dominate the landscape, is hereby recognized as an area where the earth and community of life are untrammeled by man, where man himself is a visitor who does not remain."

This definition may appeal to a romanticized vision of "wilderness," but it offends my training and experience as a lawyer. The purpose of a legal definition is not to inspire, arouse or provoke, but to state the point being made in words that cannot readily be misunderstood or misapplied. By this criterion the preceding legal definition fails.

Calling Yosemite Valley "wilderness" is a perfect example of misapplication of a legal definition. Translated into common parlance, the legal definition of "wilderness" means no roads or buildings, no overnight accommodations, with access, if at all, only by hiking trails. It probably means no restrooms, picnic tables or barbecue grills. It means no motorbikes or snowmobiles.

Translated into Yosemite Valley as it exists today, it would mean removal of all visitor accommodations, campgrounds, roads and buildings. It would also mean removal of all rangers and National Park Service personnel, for there would be nothing for them to administer.

For those hardy and adventurous souls willing to see Yosemite Valley as "wilderness," it would mean a day's worth of travel to a trailhead, packing in all gear and provisions, camping as backpackers. If one were to get into trouble, rescuers would be some distance away.

Only a tiny minority advocates this scenario for Yosemite Valley. The minority might be even smaller if its full implications were fully understood. The Park Service has never taken it seriously. Yet there is still a clarion call by vocal proponents. A pragmatic visitor might well protest that the purists and self-appointed saviors have 95% of the Park to enjoy, why must they insist on appropriating the most visited 5% as well?

I recall a conference I attended at the Ahwahnee. A young man, dressed impeccably in garb appropriate for a wilderness advocate (probably purchased at REI or Banana Republic) enjoyed wine and a good meal provided by the concessioner, after having slept in a comfortable bed. He then launched into a tirade, denouncing the Ahwahnee as a pretentious concrete structure, totally inappropriate for a national park.

95% OF YOSEMITE NATIONAL PARK COMES CLOSER TO BEING WILDERNESS

That portion of Yosemite National Park outside of the original grant, and commonly known as the High Country, comprises over 95% of the Park. This area comes much closer to meeting the legal definition of "wilderness," but not quite. There is a road, originally built as a mining road, that bifurcates the park, This road, commonly known as the Tioga Road, crosses the crest of the Sierras at Tioga Pass and connects with Highway 395, running from Reno, Nevada southward toward Los Angeles and San Diego.

Until 1957 a 21-mile stretch of the Tioga Road was one way. Cars had to back up to allow other cars to pass. This stretch of the road was unsuitable to recreational vehicles. The road was improved to two lanes in 1957.

There are campgrounds located adjacent to the Tioga Road. At Crane Flat, where the Tioga Road connects with State Highway 120 toward San Francisco, there are a store, a gas station, and the headquarters of the Yosemite Institute, an educational facility. The drive from Crane Flat to Tuolumne Meadows consists of 39 miles of forest, meadows, breathtaking views of mountains and granite

Mt. Dana and Lembert Dome.

domes, then passage along the shores of the clear blue Tenaya Lake, at the base of Tenaya Peak. The road makes this spectacular drive not "wilderness," but the views from both sides qualify as "wilderness." Only a small percentage of visitors to Yosemite Valley ventures even this far into the High Country.

Tuolumne Meadows, one of my favorite places in the whole world, a treasure trove of family memories, is not wilderness by either the dictionary or legal definition. There are overnight accommodations, a gas station, a campground, a store and grill, a visitor center, stables, a ranger station, a mountaineering store, and cabins and tents where employees live, as well as Parsons Lodge, a stone building near Soda Springs and the current visitor center, which was built by the Civilian Conservation Corps. These facilities are rustic and totally compatible with an encounter with nature.

Tuolumne Meadows is a favored destination of many. It has changed little in my lifetime, except that it grows ever more popular. Few of its many repeat visitors would want to change or upgrade it. This was confirmed at a master planning session I attended in 2007.

There are a few buildings off the road in the High Country. Most notable among them are a string of High Sierra Camps where visitors can get a real taste of the High Country without packing in (see Chapters 3, 7).

I recall a spirited debate with an ardent young environmental purist who was advocating the removal of the High Sierra Camps. He had never visited one. He used the term "enclaves in the wilderness" to describe them. His mental process was to locate an area on a map, designate the area as "wilderness," and draw circles around everything he felt did not belong there. He was concerned that the High Sierra Camps would encourage backpackers to camp near them and overcrowd the area.

As previously indicated, I am very familiar with High Sierra Camps, having put them up, taken them down,and visited them frequently, and having a son who managed one.

Tioga Pass ranger station, circa 1930.

I told the young man that I had never seen any evidence of overcrowding due to proximity to a High Sierra camp. Moreover, all backpackers must obtain wilderness permits allowing them to camp only in designated areas, in order to avoid overcrowding.

Environmental purists, like this young man, are seldom open to altering their extreme views based on new information. He had his mind made up and had moved into a philosophically hardened position that was impervious to any argument. He did not want to be confused with facts.

I have never heard a visitor to a High Sierra camp complain that his experience had been diminished by being in an "enclave in the wilderness."

Part of the problem of coming to a reasonable policy position with respect to Yosemite Park management is that a good deal of the discussion is dominated by opinionated people occupying fringe philosophical positions who loudly clamor to be heard, believing everyone who disagrees with them to be ignorant, uninformed or motivated by some greedy agenda.

I came upon an example of this type of thinking in a letter to the editor of the San Francisco Chronicle by a lady named Carol Paoli from St. Helena, California, who wrote in response to a story about the upgrading of the trail to Yosemite Falls, a major project of the Yosemite Conservancy. The trail had become unsightly in the view of the Conservancy and its contributors. Carol wrote as follows: "Where is it written that the public needs to view Yosemite Falls or the Valley at all? This wondrous happening of nature has been desecrated for years, especially after the National Park Service takeover. Perhaps it's time to express our appreciation to the marvels of nature by pulling out of the Valley completely and letting it return to its original splendor. How arrogant of us to think that the new restrooms, trash cans, and pollution-free vehicles will enhance the beauty of the Valley. For me it is enough to know that it is there. I do not want to contribute to its demise by my attendance."

Where is it written? It is written in Lincoln's 1864 proclamation and the Organic Act of 1916 establishing the National Park Service that the public owns the national parks, whether environmental purists and self-appointed saviors like it or not. Environmental extremists need to be reminded of this. Like the government itself, the American system of national parks should be considered to be "of the people, by the people, for the people."

The Tioga Road closes with the first snowfall in fall and remains closed until May or June in normal years. For those months, the High Country does come close to meeting the dictionary definition of "wilderness." Up to 20 to 30 feet of snow blankets the High Country, up to the rafters of Tuolumne Meadows Lodge and the High Sierra Camps. Access is only by cross-country skis.

Yosemite has been ensnared in a romantic conception of wilderness based on writings by romantic poets. Thoreau's lyrical reflections about nature appeal to us for their poetic imagery. Bryant described the effects of nature upon mind and attitude as follows:

> To him who in the love of Nature holds
> Communion with her visible forms, she speaks
> A various language; for his gayer hours
> She has a voice of gladness, and a smile
> And eloquence of beauty, and she glides
> Into his darker musings, with a mild
> And healing sympathy, that steals away
> Their sharpness, ere he is aware.

Thoreau and Bryant did not base their observations on any experience in wild places, nor did they camp in pure wilderness areas. Every winter Walden's famous pond was the source of a thriving ice business. Bryant's "love of Nature" was more likely focused upon the trees outside his bedroom window than upon the lofty mountains and empty wild lands that, after all, he never gazed upon.

As little as one day in a true wilderness area in bad weather without any amenities might well be enough to cause any reasonable person to distinguish poetry from reality.

AT THE BEGINNING

The Yosemite landscape that I knew as a child was relatively unchanged from its geological appearance when the first white man or first Native American appeared. The big changes were caused by a succession of glaciers over the past 30 million years that ended ten millennia ago. Hundreds of life spans must pass before there is any noticeable naturally-caused effect on the granite walls, domes, spires, waterfalls, and meandering rivers.

THE WHITE MAN "DISCOVERS" YOSEMITE

Native American tribes had been living in Yosemite for a millennium before the initial arrival of Caucasians who "discovered" Yosemite in 1851. A militia unit called the Mariposa Battalion entered Yosemite Valley while in pursuit of Ahwahneechees, who had raided a gold mining camp known as Savage's Trading Post, after its owner, Major Jim Savage, in the Merced River canyon located below Yosemite Valley.

The original inhabitants were eventually driven from Yosemite Valley. Most of the soldiers were intent upon chasing and routing the Indians, but one of them, Dr. Lafayette Bunnell, was awestruck by the scenery. He provided the first recorded description of Yosemite Valley when he wrote:

"Domes, peaks, spires,and cliffs were capped with fresh snow, their walls and slopes dappled with it, marking in strong relief the various sculptured forms. Some were veiled in wisps of cloud, others seemed to rise from a deep blue haze, giving the whole a drifting unreal quality, like a vision... on every side astonished by the size of the cliffs and the number and height of the waterfalls, which constantly challenged our attention and admiration."

Even though the beauties that surrounded him moved Dr. Bunnell to tears, the general view of his comrades was summed up in the obtuse comment that Yosemite Valley was "a gloomy enough place." One member of the party later commented that if he had known Yosemite Valley was destined to become famous, he would have looked at it.

VISITORS BEGIN TO ARRIVE

Descriptions of Yosemite began reaching the outside world when a colorful character named J.M. Hutchings, together with 41 other men, visited Yosemite in 1855, Hutchings emigrated to the U.S. in 1848. He became wealthy as a '49er miner, lost his wealth in a bank failure, then made another fortune from publishing. Hutchings began publishing descriptions of what he saw, using phrases like "luxurious scenic banqueting."

Hutchings and a number of other entrepreneurs immediately saw economic opportunities in Yosemite's extraordinary beauties. Two members of the party built an improved trail connecting Mariposa and Yosemite Valley. They turned it into a toll road and charged the first tourists the then-hefty fee of a dollar for pedestrians and two dollars for riders on horseback. By the time the first stagecoach arrived at Yosemite in 1874, a recorded 2,656 visitors had walked or ridden into the Valley.

Hutchings was able to claim property under the provisions of a piece of legislation called "The Swamplands Act of 1850," which provided the means to transfer federally owned swamplands to the states and thereby to the private sector, for agricultural and commercial development. One of the act's many faults was its failure to define clearly what constituted swampland. Investors capitalized on the imprecision to claim the right to develop Yosemite Valley.

Hutchings was notorious for being so enthusiastic about the scenic wonders of Yosemite Valley that he neglected the proper feeding of his guests, who began to arrive in response to his colorful invitations. It is difficult to enjoy Bridalveil Fall's lacy splendors on a stomach that is growling for food. El Capitan's towering massive wall is hard to appreciate when seen through eyes red and burning from lack of a good night's sleep. As people began to be lured into visiting Yosemite Valley, facilities needed to be created to provide good food and comfortable lodging.

The earliest visitors' need for food and lodging was especially acute after dismounting from a cramped stagecoach ride, during which they bounced around for three days over roadways that were little more than pathways through uncharted territories. Within a year work had begun on the first primitive visitor accommodations, which were opened to the public in 1859. Not even a decade elapsed between the time the first person of European descent saw the area and the time when tourists were able to visit and to stay in visitor accommodations.

Early visitors were a hardy lot, because Yosemite Valley was in a remote area that could be reached exclusively by a long, dusty and uncomfortable horseback or carriage ride. There was an element of danger added to the discomfort: travelers were often accosted by highwaymen who doubtless found unarmed tourists to be easy prey.

A PUBLIC TRUST

Less than a decade following its discovery, Yosemite became the first area in the world to be designated as a public trust to be preserved for the use and enjoyment of the public. President Lincoln somehow found the time to issue the designation on June 29, 1864, while the nation was embroiled in the Civil War. Lincoln granted the land to the State of California, which was only 14 years old at the time. The proclamation referred to the property thus:

"The Cleft or Gorge in the granite peak of the Sierra Nevada mountains, situated in the county of Mariposa… and known as Yo-Semite Valley…. And the Mariposa Big Tree grove."

The proclamation that Lincoln issued was revolutionary, because the proclamation directed the state to…

"…Accept this property upon the express conditions that the premises shall be held for public use, resort and recreation, which shall be inalienable for all time."

It was appropriate that the president who proclaimed the government to be "of the people, by the people, for the people" should have been the same president to reserve scenic property for the sole use of the people, rather than for the enjoyment of the wealthy and powerful.

THE INFLUENCE OF JOHN MUIR (1838–1914)

Yosemite was destined to capture the imagination of the world in 1868 when a Scotsman–turned–mountain man named John Muir came to Yosemite Valley. Muir, who would become Yosemite's most eloquent chronicler, had walked from

San Francisco to Yosemite Valley, passing through the Santa Clara Valley (which a century later would become known as Silicon Valley), and across the Pacheco Pass. This is where he gained his first glimpse of the distant Sierra Nevada. Muir named the mountains "the range of light," which became a frequent description of the Sierra Nevada.

John Muir tended sheep and became the millwright when Hutchings ordered equipment for a sawmill that could manufacture paneling for permanent room dividers in the first inn that Hutchings had built, which was a 20- by 60-foot structure with rooms formerly separated only by muslin sheets.

Few people in the world at the time considered John Muir's occupation of sawing virgin timber into boards to be used for construction as inappropriate. Today no one would defend the propriety of a sawmill in Yosemite Valley.

Muir built a cabin beside Yosemite Falls, where he lived until 1873. He explored Yosemite and the Sierras extensively, becoming the first person to ascend many of the Sierra peaks. All the time he was engaging in exploration, Muir kept copious notes about the flora, fauna and geological features he was observing.

Even though Muir was not trained as a scientist or geologist, he put forth the hypothesis that Yosemite Valley had been formed by glaciers. This contradicted the conventional wisdom of his day. Disputing geologists, he wrote with a very lyrical note:

"In the development of these (scenic features) Nature chose as a tool not the earthquake or lightning to split asunder, not the stormy torrent of eroding rain, but tender snow-flowers noiseless falling through unnumbered centuries."

Muir's theories contradicted the conventional wisdom propounded by the arrogant Josiah Whitney, who dismissed Muir as an amateur. Muir proved to be right. The highest peak in the continental United States should have been named Mt. Muir, not Mt. Whitney.

John Muir went on to write many books describing Yosemite and tirelessly lobbied for its preservation from sheep and timber interests and the would-be caretakers who supported them. Muir referred to sheep as "hoofed locusts" and the caretakers as "money changers in the temple." Muir's efforts were instrumental in raising public awareness concerning the importance of preserving scenic acres for public enjoyment. Muir's appreciation of wilderness was not born from romantic fantasy, but from his experience of exploring the valleys, canyons and mountains about which he wrote.

John Muir never favored preserving wilderness by locking it up. Quite the contrary, he wanted everyone to partake of what he called "glad tidings" and wished for everyone to be inspired as he himself had been. He had an evangelical passion to attract visitors to Yosemite:

"Heaven knows that John the Baptist was not more eager to get all his fellow sinners into the Jordan than I to baptize all of mine in the beauty of God's mountains," Muir wrote.

THE WILD MUIR
Twenty-two of John Muir's
Greatest Adventures

In another place Muir described the spiritual effect of Yosemite's beauties:

"Another glorious Sierra day in which one seems to be dissolved and absorbed and sent pulsing onward we know not where. Life seems neither long nor short, and we take no more heed to save time or make haste than do the trees and stars. This is true freedom, a good practical sort of immortality…."

John Muir was to write enough about what he saw and what he thought that his writings would eventually fill volumes. Of all the observations that he left behind, one paragraph was selected to be inscribed on a plaque in front of the Village Store in Yosemite Valley as a summation of all that he had seen and observed:

"Nowhere before have I seen such a glorious landscape, so boundless an affluence of sublime mountain beauty. The noble walls are sculptured into endless variety of domes and gables, spires and battlements and all a-tremble with thunder tones of falling water."

GALEN CLARK, THE FIRST YOSEMITE GUARDIAN

Another Yosemite pioneer who deserves mention is Galen Clark (1814–1910), known for his tenacity in protecting Yosemite.

I am indebted to the *Yosemite Gazette* for calling attention to some little known facts about this remarkable man. Galen was born in Quebec, Canada, into a family so poor they were reduced to placing their children with other families for room and board. Unschooled but self-educated, he was a prolific reader. He learned carpentry, painting and furniture-making from the families with whom he boarded. He married and fathered five children whom he had to board when his wife died of consumption. Although he failed at farming and several businesses, he joined the gold seekers in the California gold rush. Tiring of the drudgery of gold mining, he became a packer, and in that occupation he discovered Yosemite and became infatuated with its beauty, as John Muir had.

Galen took out an agricultural land grant in what is now Wawona and built a log cabin where he entertained visitors. Noted for hospitality and kindness, he is credited with discovering the Mariposa Grove of Big Trees, which became part of the original grant of Yosemite for public enjoyment made by Abraham Lincoln. He was not as eloquent as Muir or Hutchings. However, reports to some influential visitors whom he entertained and some letters he wrote are credited with reaching those who influenced Lincoln in making the Yosemite grant. Despite his misfortunes, he was an eternal optimist. He settled in Yosemite in poor health and resolved, in his words, to "take my chances on dying or getting better, which I thought were about even." He regained his health and lived to the age of 96.

Galen's role as guardian of Yosemite originated with an appointment to a board of commissioners, which led to a designation as Guardian of Yosemite, a multifaceted role at which he worked tirelessly for 20 years, for little compensation. His property never paid for itself, and he was forced to sell it. John Muir said of him, "He was the best mountaineer I ever met, and one of the kindest and most amiable of all my mountain friends."

PROTECTING THE PUBLIC TRUST: THE FEDERAL GOVERNMENT STEPS IN

Lincoln's proclamation brought the government into conflict with Hutchings and other early innkeepers who had taken over property through the Swampland Act. A lawsuit filed by Hutchings reached the Supreme Court. The public trust concept proclaimed by Lincoln prevailed over Hutchings' private interest. The government bought out Hutchings and other developers. A few other land holdings, which had been acquired under the Homestead Act, referred to as "in holdings," remain privately owned properties within Yosemite National Park today.

In 1872 Yellowstone became the first national park under the control of the federal government, due to the fact that Wyoming, Montana and Idaho were territories, not states. If they had been states, the federal government might not have become involved in preserving areas of scenic beauty for the public, which might have started an irreversible system of state parks.

Yosemite continued to be jointly administered by the State of California and the U.S. Cavalry. California withdrew operations in 1905 when Yosemite was formally ceded to the federal government. The cavalry continued to administer visitor facilities until 1916 when the National Park Service was created and park rangers took over supervision of Yosemite, creating the management system that is in place today.

In 1890, with impetus from John Muir, the Yosemite High Country became a federally administered park, under President Benjamin Harrison, based on the Yellowstone model, and governed in the same manner.

President Theodore Roosevelt was a strong advocate of preserving areas of scenic beauty for public enjoyment. At one point he abandoned staff and admirers who had planned an elaborate reception at the Wawona Hotel, in order to explore Yosemite and sleep under the stars with John Muir. On that and other occasions, Muir inspired President Roosevelt to pursue his vision by establishing the National Park Service.

One area of disagreement between the two men involved identifying what would be appropriate in the proposed park when it came to the issue of hunting wild animals. The question about hunting came into focus because Roosevelt was an avid hunter. Muir may have caused Roosevelt to reflect on the disconnect of killing wild animals inhabiting areas preserved for public enjoyment.

In 1864, when Yosemite Valley and the Mariposa Grove became the first areas to be set aside for public enjoyment, there were no guidelines to decide what was appropriate and what was inappropriate. The earliest activities considered inappropriate were commercial ventures that degraded the environment, such as mining, logging, and pasturing sheep and cattle. The earliest efforts to classify these activities as inappropriate turned into a battle between nascent environmental concerns and the urge to make a profit in undeveloped territory.

Early restrictions against commercial operations went against a strong current in the culture at that time. The prevailing public attitude still held a view of domination and subjection when dealing with wilderness areas. Progress was equated with "taming" wilderness by converting it to commercial use. According to this dogma, the best use for any forest was to chop down the trees to provide materials for building new communities. The best thing that could be done with wetlands was to drain them so that they could be used to grow crops to feed a hungry nation.

Yosemite seemed ripe for development in the eyes of people who tended to value anything from a tree, mountain or meadow in terms of whatever income might be gained from the lumber in the tree or from crops that might be grown in the meadow, or what could be extracted from the mountain in mining. The government took the radical position that Yosemite was valuable for reasons other than its profit potential, asserting that forests should be protected from the loggers, the mountains from the miners, and the Valley from the sheepherders.

When Yosemite was first set aside and protected from commercial enterprises such as mining, logging and ranching, initial park advocates saw no conflict between recreational tourism and preservation. In fact, John Muir and the early Sierra Club members advocated visitation as a method of encouraging preservation. They believed that all visitors who witnessed the splendor of Yosemite would naturally become advocates for protecting its beauty from commercial development.

The National Park Service, established in 1916, assumed the duties of Park administration. Rangers replaced cavalry.

THE NEW DEAL IN YOSEMITE

The diminishing number of visitors during the Great Depression was more than offset by extraordinary development projects that the government undertook as part of Franklin D. Roosevelt's New Deal. FDR was sympathetic to national parks. Moreover, he was facing the challenge of putting people to work. From Roosevelt's perspective, government development projects in Yosemite provided an excellent opportunity for him to work toward both objectives.

The Wawona Road and Tunnel were completed during the Roosevelt administration. The Tioga and Big Oak Flat roads were started, new buildings erected, public restrooms built, and signage, benches, entrance stations and the Mariposa Grove Museum were added.

Besides numerous infrastructure improvements, the Civilian Conservation Corps (CCC), which Congress established in 1933, made numerous improvements. Working under the oversight of National Park Service managers, CCC personnel helped combat beetle infestations by attacking eggs and cocoons. More importantly, they constructed new trails, firebreaks and fire towers, and they laid new telephone lines. They built new fireplaces and picnic tables and created a 300-site campground at Tuolumne Meadows, with restrooms and a Visitors' Center. The design and workmanship was of vastly superior quality. Much of it remains today.

Roosevelt's New Deal was controversial and remains so today. Nevertheless, the improvements have been beneficial to Yosemite. As an added benefit, many of those CCC workers were exposed to the outdoors and to Yosemite's glories for the first time. Their reactions in many cases were no doubt consistent with John Muir's vision of providing a commitment to protect Yosemite.

World War II

World War II profoundly changed Yosemite. The numbers of park tourists dropped precipitously as the effects of gas rationing and tire rationing were felt. The Ahwahnee Hotel was deformed ("transformed" being much too positive a word to describe the change) into a rehabilitation facility for wounded naval personnel.

The wounded veterans who occupied the Ahwahnee during those years differed from every other group of people who visited Yosemite up to that time, because they were there neither for sightseeing nor for work. They were there simply because that is where they were sent. While some of the wounded vets must have been impressed by the majestic views from the spacious Ahwahnee windows, they were not there to marvel at the sights. They were there to recover.

The Ahwahnee had a colorful bar known as the El Dorado Diggins, decorated with mining memorabilia. A heated debate took place between a chaplain who wanted to convert it to a chapel and an officer who wanted to convert it to an officers' club. I don't know who won.

While the nation was preoccupied with the war effort, the American public's focus was not on preserving the nation's natural wonders. Young men and women were off fighting the enemy in distant countries, not hiking Yosemite trails.

POST WORLD WAR II TOURISM BOOM

During the period of the late 1940s and 1950s, following the end of the war, Americans were in a state of euphoria. The war heroes had come home and married, and they were looking for the good life. Many of them believed the good life to be at its best in California, the land of opportunity, with new subdivisions, plentiful job opportunities, temperate climate and wonderful places to visit, such as Yosemite National Park. Many from other parts of the country had been stationed in California during the war. People were moving to California from other parts of the country in droves. Many of the newcomers began to take weekends and day trips to see Yosemite's glorious sights.

After extensive negotiations, the government paid a handsome sum for thoroughly trashing the Ahwahnee. The grand hotel was refurbished and restored to its former splendor.

People who did not live in California also visited Yosemite. Detroit couldn't operate their assembly lines fast enough to create enough automobiles to satisfy consumer demand. Rationing restrictions were lifted. Gas was plentiful and inexpensive. People wanted to drive their new cars with their full gas tanks to any tourist destination they found attractive. Yosemite Valley was one of the most attractive of all choices. Yosemite became flooded with visitors, particularly from Memorial Day to Labor Day. Campgrounds were full, and visitor accommodations often oversold. In 1954, the number of visitors to Yosemite Valley hit the one million mark.

During the 1950s Yosemite Valley had three gas stations; all were operated by Standard Oil of California. One summer, the service station at Camp Curry set the summer record for gallons pumped of any facility in the state of California. Today, one cannot purchase gas in Yosemite Valley. The Standard Oil stations were manned by crews of college students, gaining a sometimes-deserved reputation of being overly aggressive salesmen. They were called SOBs, referring to their being Standard Oil Boys. Some of them would stare at a tire or peer beneath the hood of a car, jump back with apparent shock on their faces, and ask, "How did you ever get here?" They would then sell the confused motorists automotive equipment they did not need.

The decade of the 1950s was one of unabashed striving for maximum utilization of visitor facilities. Visitors were required to make reservations long in advance of their visit. Hopeful people waited in long lines for cancellations.

THE MEDIA BLASTS YOSEMITE MANAGEMENT

The rising tide of visitors to Yosemite Valley, commencing in the 1950s and proceeding into the 1960s and 1970s, led to a proliferation of articles in the media criticizing park management and concessioners with monotonous and persistent regularity. There were two common themes: There was too much traffic and congestion in Yosemite Valley, and the concessioners were greedy profiteers.

Hil Oehlmann predicted this verbal onslaught in 1959 when addressing the annual Conference of the National Park Concessioners Association as follows: "My own far deeper concern lies with the cumulative effect of publicity which I fear is creating an image of our national parks as overcrowded, over-visited areas which are deteriorating rapidly to a state of unattractiveness, if not utter ruin."

Those in the media writing the blasts were listening to purists rather than tourists. The negative press did not stop visitors from coming to Yosemite in record numbers.

An article that appeared in the *Wall Street Journal* on March 27, 1990, by a pundit named Carrie Dolan had some sharp criticism for park management. She charged MCA, the concessioner at the time, with "artificially creating demand for Yosemite by marketing it." She went on to write:

"In the peak summer season, campfires and car fumes create a smog that hangs in the Valley. Hordes of tourists burden the Park with 25 tons of garbage and a million gallons of sewage each day. Some evenings 7,000 people sleep in a four-square-mile area of the main Valley. Holiday traffic creates Manhattan-like congestion."

Much of the criticism of Yosemite is ill advised. Some visitors fly into the Park and back out again in a single day carrying with them only a memory of crowded roads and public places. I read an incredible passage in a book called *The Lost Continent* by an experienced travel writer named Bill Bryson who made just that sort of error. He wrote:

"The great problem at Yosemite today is simply finding your way around. I've never seen a place so badly signposted. It's as if they are trying to hide the Park from you. At Yosemite, the visitors' center is almost impossible to find. I drove around Yosemite Village for twenty-five minutes before I discovered a parking lot, and then it took me a further twenty minutes, and a long walk in the wrong direction, to find the visitors' center. By the time I found it, I knew my way around and didn't need it any more.

"And everything is just hopelessly, depressingly crowded—the cafeterias, the post office, the stores...."

For some reason Bryson, like many other visitors, manage to remain oblivious to the beauties of Yosemite and ignorant of the fact that by walking 100 yards in almost any direction from any paved road, he could have been out of sight and sound of traffic and tourists, and have lost himself amidst the glories of one of earth's most spectacular areas.

DAVID BROWER DEFENDS YOSEMITE MANAGEMENT

The late David Brower was one of the most outspoken and uncompromising preservationists of the 20th century. He had an intimate knowledge of Yosemite, having worked and lived there. He leveled a sharp rebuke to the kind of criticism from afar written by Ms. Dolan. In an article entitled "Give 'Em Bouquets, not Bricks," he wrote in characteristic fashion:

"The periodic assault on Yosemite guardians has gone on long enough. Gnats are being strained at concerning Yosemite management while we in California as a whole swallow camels—the spoiling of waters offshore and on, the reckless destruction of forests and the apparent preference for gridlock over clean air and acid-free rain.

"There were about 37,000 other visitors when I first visited Yosemite in 1918. When I stopped working there twenty years later, the count hit almost half a million. Last year there were more than six times that many, and the Valley looked better and was more enjoyable than it had been a half-century earlier. The impact of visitors on the Valley has been lessened, and the impact of the Valley on visitors has been enhanced.

"Generous credit is deserved by the Yosemite people, government, and company who have been masters of restoration....Yosemite people deserve a toast not a roast....If they annually serve 3 million people so well and protect

Peter Hoss, Patti Hoss, David Brower.

the Park so well that The Company makes a lot of money, don't curse them. Profit is still legal."

I line up solidly behind David Brower and against the tiring rhetoric of Yosemite detractors that I have heard and read most of my life. Dave Brower worked in Yosemite and knows the territory. Anyone who has met him and talked with him, as I have, knows that he speaks with conviction, even if you may not agree with all of his views. David Brower would be the last person to apologize for environmental degradation.

There appears to be a correlation between the intensity of the proclamations about Yosemite Valley being ruined by overdevelopment and overcrowding, and the distance between Yosemite Valley and the place from which such claimants are writing their dire proclamations. I have to wonder where the detractors are getting their information. It clearly is not coming from visitors, who vote with their feet and continue to gravitate to Yosemite in record numbers.

Too much of this discussion is based on personal bias. People who look for beauty in Yosemite will see it. Those who search for ugliness will find it as well. The best suggestion comes from John Muir, who advised us to look up at the waterfalls, treetops and clouds, not down toward dirt and clutter one might see on the ground.

There has been no great change in the physical appearance of Yosemite Valley since David Brower's comments in 1990.

Dave Brower and Virginia Adams at Mariposa Grove.
Courtesy of Adams Family Collection.

CHANGING CHARACTER OF THE PARK SERVICE
RANGERS BECOME POLICEMEN

The growing number of visitors created law-enforcement issues for the Park Service. Beginning in the 1960s, the so-called Counterculture Revolution spilled over into Yosemite. Besides their aversion to the Vietnam War, the "flower children" espoused a back-to-nature philosophy, which led a number of them to move into Yosemite campgrounds, where they set up semi-permanent residences and established a subculture characterized by a carefree attitude, especially towards sex, experimentation with drugs and resistance to authority.

The situation came to a head on July 4, 1970, when holiday celebrations degenerated into a bottle- and rock-throwing melee with park rangers who tried to clear them from Stoneman Meadow. The conflict became ugly, and the rangers called in reinforcements.

The incident marked a turning point. Up to that time, they had conducted themselves mainly as friendly naturalists, but now they were required to become law-enforcement officers, and the hippies thus regarded the park rangers as authority figures. The Park Service began to issue side arms to the rangers, putting them in a position that many of them did not prefer to be in.

Following the Stoneman Meadow battle, charges and countercharges were passed back and forth between the two sides. The rangers were accused of over-reacting. The fact is that the protesters were not nature lovers. They were, in fact, city people who descended upon Yosemite believing that since Yosemite was public property, that gave them permission to do whatever they wished. Their battle cry was "Yosemite belongs to the people; therefore it is our park."

VISITORS BECOME THE ENEMY

As Hil Oehlmann predicted, the media blasts did have an effect, even if not to discourage visitors from flocking to Yosemite. They contributed to a growing feeling among environmental purists, and even some Park Service personnel, that the new enemy in Yosemite was the visitor. In the classic words of Pogo, "We have met the enemy, and he is us." This view has led to more pressure to "save" Yosemite by making visitation more difficult.

The fundamental inconsistency between the concept of the national parks as a public trust owned by the public and available for the enjoyment of the public, and the contrary notion that "preserving" the national parks requires prohibiting the public from using them, cannot be overemphasized. It is a fundamental misnomer to claim that facilities designed for the comfort of the visitor are "commercial." Management decisions must attempt to strike a balance, with the realization there will never be agreement on the proper balance. That is as inherent in Yosemite as the cliffs and waterfalls. Management must also be directed to prevent desecration. Desecration can be either unintended or intended.

I wish that radical environmental purists could follow John Muir's advice to allow the masses of people to enjoy the Valley while leaving the heights for the few who will go there. John Muir remained untroubled by the presence of other visitors who were less appreciative of Yosemite Valley than he was. He wrote:

"We saw another party of tourists today. Somehow most of these travelers seem to care but little for the glorious objects about them, though enough to spend time and money and endure long rides to see the famous Valley. And when they are fairly within the mighty walls of the temple and hear the psalms of the falls, they will forget themselves and become devout. Blessed indeed would be every pilgrim in these holy mountains…. The tide of visitors will float slowly about the bottom of the Valley as a harmless scum, collecting in hotel and saloon eddies, leaving the rocks and falls eloquent as ever and instruct with imperishable beauty and greatness…. The Valley is full of people, but they do not annoy me. I revolve in the pathless places and in higher rocks than the world and his ribbony wife can reach."

Yosemite icons like John Muir and Ansel Adams managed to create an impression of Yosemite in the hearts and minds of those who have never visited Yosemite—or at least who have visited it only in brief, sporadic or transient fashion. The impression and state of mind has created a vision of Yosemite greater than the place itself.

The concessioner is in business to serve the guests. The credo of the hotel business is that the guest is always right. The Park Service is there to regulate the business and, to some extent, to determine what in Yosemite is appropriate. In their opinion, park guests are not always right.

Some Park Service managers and rangers have difficulty understanding the businessperson, who can remain in business only by taking care of the bottom line. Sometimes the Park Service would propose to regulate activities in a far more rigorous fashion than anyone would who had any accountability to the people they were regulating.

Yosemite's ultimate destiny should remain in the hands of the silent majority comprised of people who want to come to Yosemite and enjoy it. No one should prescribe for American citizens the proper way in which they should utilize this American resource, beyond the requirement to keep it from being desecrated.

Most visitors uncritically accept management decisions of the Park Service even when they can't understand the rationale for the decisions. Access to some parts of the Valley has been cordoned off in order to allow areas to be left in or restored to their natural states. Visitors to the High Country are urged to abide by standards of pack-in/pack-out applied to all non-biodegradable materials. All Yosemite visitors are urged to conform to the credo, "Leave no trace."

There must be a certain amount of amenities for the visitor. It is left to park service officials and concessioners to define a middle ground between maintaining primitive conditions and erecting casinos and strip malls.

Former Secretary of Interior Bruce Babbitt, citing the contrast between children romping in the meadows and rock climbers scaling the face of El Capitan, described Yosemite Valley as: "One of nature's most awesome creations…the personal blend of the pastoral and the sublime."

Babbitt made his comment in 2004, at a time when the number of visitors to the Valley had swollen to an estimated 4,000,000 per year and many of the self-appointed saviors had begun lamenting the fact that Yosemite had been ruined by its success. In their opinion, the sheer numbers of tourists, rather than shepherds and loggers, had become the problem.

Bruce Babbitt, like John Muir, refused to allow the presence of visitors, even in great numbers, to impair his vision for Yosemite. And neither should anyone else.

EMERGING ROLE OF THE NONPROFITS

Expenses of building and maintaining capital improvements in Yosemite and providing enhancement of the visitor experience have always out stripped resources the government can make available.

The presence of nonprofits in Yosemite Valley goes back to the 1920s. Stephen Mather, the first director of the National Park Service, called for a museum in every national park. In 1922 a small museum was opened in Yosemite Valley and received 33,000 visitors. In 1923 the Yosemite Museum Association was formed to raise private funds for a larger museum. In 1924 this organization expanded its purpose, and the Yosemite Natural History Association was formed. A new two-story museum opened in 1926 in a building that still houses the Visitor Center. In the same year the publication "Yosemite Nature Notes" was started, and the Glacier Point Lookout was built with part of the funds raised for the museum.

In 1937 the Junior Ranger Program was created by the association. In 1940 the association functioned as an auxiliary of the National Park Service. The chief naturalist served as the director of the association. In the 1950s the association commenced publishing books about the natural and cultural history of Yosemite. In 1974 the association took over operating and maintaining the Ostrander ski hut, located eight miles from a road. This facility provides an overnight accommodation for cross-country skiers wishing to enjoy the majesty of Yosemite in winter. In 1976 the association held its first annual membership meeting.

In 1985 the association changed its name to "The Yosemite Association" and established its office in a railroad building in El Portal, outside Yosemite Valley. The association began providing volunteers to assist with restoration projects. Volunteers helped establish the Parsons Lodge Summer Series in the Parsons Lodge at Tuolomne Meadows.

In 1979, at the request of Yosemite Superintendent Bob Binnewies, the Yosemite Association spun off a private fundraising effort called the Yosemite Fund, in order to raise funds to make capital improvements in Yosemite. Executive Director Henry Berrey worked with others and the Park Service to create wish lists. In 1984 the association began a fundraising effort that they called "The Return of Light Campaign." At the beginning there were ten couples, including my childhood pal Dick Otter and his wife Ann.

Dick was the fourth chairman of the Yosemite Fund. He hired Bob Hansen to be fund director. The fund had been raising a couple hundred thousand dollars a year, but took off under the leadership of Dick Otter, Bob Hansen, Byron and Ellie Nishkian, and Bill Lane, Jr., (son of the founder of *Sunset Magazine* and ambassador to Australia), and raised as much as $8 million. The fund entered into a contract with the Park Service to become the primary fundraising organization for Yosemite, establishing a true public-private partnership, which has become a model for nonprofit fundraising. The fund secured permission to issue license plates featuring a picture of Yosemite Valley, which alone bring in over a million dollars a year.

Among the first projects of the Yosemite Fund were: removing an unused sewage plant near Bridalveil Fall; improving trails in the Bridalveil Fall area; placing museum displays in the old Fish Hatchery at Happy Isles; and restoring Galen Clark's cottage in the Mariposa Grove of Big Trees. A leach field for the bathroom at Glacier Point replaced the practice of dumping the sewage from the bathroom over the cliff.

In 1992 the Yosemite Fund became a separate 501(c)(3) corporation and moved its headquarters to San Francisco. The Yosemite Fund works as a partner with the National Park Service to raise money for trails, habitat, wildlife, visitor center exhibits and cultural preservation projects. During the first two decades of its existence, the organization raised more than $45 million dollars through the generosity of some 100,000 donors, contributing to more than 200 park improvement projects.

Projects too numerous to mention include: improving overlooks at the Tunnel View on the Wawona Road, Olmsted Point on the Tioga Road, and at Half Dome overlook on Highway 120; as well as the remodeling of amphitheaters in Yosemite Valley campgrounds; remodeling the studios of the famous painter Thomas Hill at Wawona; and establishing the Pioneer History Museum in Wawona. There is an active program of trail restoration. Bear-proof canisters have been developed for backcountry visitors. Research on big horn sheep, as well as restoration to their former habitat in the Yosemite backcountry, has been undertaken.

The Yosemite Fund works in close cooperation with the Park Service, who originates projects. It has been a true public-private partnership.

The services that the fund brings to Yosemite have become increasingly important because of the great number of visitors that are now pouring into Yosemite. Park rangers are burdened with the duties of policing and managing the visitors rather than providing the naturalist services that are more characteristic of their traditional role.

In 2009 a merger was announced that restored the previous association of the Yosemite Association and the Yosemite Fund. This will help them to be more effective in augmenting the activities of the Park Service in serving park visitors.

The merger will be under the leadership of Mike Tollefson, who resigned in 2008 as park superintendent in order to assume this position.

Under the leadership of Mike Tollefson the newly formed Yosemite Conservancy in 2010 launched a one million dollar fundraising campaign directed toward youth in Yosemite.

The focus will be on outdoor learning opportunities that will encourage environmental stewardship and foster a lifelong connection with nature.

The youth in Yosemite program brings together several projects in Yosemite that offer opportunities for youth of all ages to participate in the Yosemite experience and to help encourage future stewards of Yosemite. These projects encompass both experimental learning with young people working alongside National Park Service employees to build knowledge, leadership skills and a love for the outdoors along with Junior Ranger programs and exhibits that will reach an even broader audience of children visiting Yosemite.

The California Conservation Crews will repair frontcountry trails in Yosemite Valley, near Wawona and in the Merced River watershed, and over 60 miles of backcountry trails. The Youth Conservation Corps summer program will bring young people into Yosemite to work on a variety of restoration projects. A Student Conservation Association program will allow college students to work in the backcountry and on visitor service projects in Yosemite Valley.

Junior Ranger programs and exhibits at Happy Isles Nature Center will be expanded to engage more children in nature and the environment in Yosemite Valley.

Young people growing up in urban areas are losing contact with nature. Many of them look for amusement with video games, computers and other technological pursuits. It is anticipated that this program will change lives by bringing young people in contact with "glad tidings."

A CHRISTIAN MINISTRY IN THE NATIONAL PARKS (ACMNP)

Yosemite has always held a connection with matters spiritual. The Indians associated Yosemite Valley features with deities, and they named and created legends about them.

The white man carried on the association. The writings of John Muir are laced with biblical references. His dour, rigorous father required John to memorize the Bible at an early age.

The oldest building in Yosemite is the Chapel, which was built in 1879, long before there was a National Park Service. Almost every other National Park has a history of religious observance. Few, however, can support full-time pastors.

In 1950 Yellowstone experimented with student ministers employed in the Park. They conducted Sunday morning services, held vacation Bible schools, and offered music programs, special programs for children and other activities designed to meet the needs of those who lived in and visited Yellowstone. In its second season, similar programs were started in Yosemite and other national parks that the National Council of Churches considered a national movement. The National Park Service indicated general approval of an interdenominational ministry, emphasizing that its relationship had to be one of cooperation, not sponsorship or funding.

It took a visionary to coordinate these efforts and translate them into an organization that has grown, prospered and lasted 60 years. That visionary was the late Warren Ost, one of the original student ministers, who worked as a bellman at the Old Faithful Inn in Yellowstone in 1951.The organization was called "A Christian Ministry in National Parks" (ACMNP). Warren Ost deserves to be recognized as the founder of ACMNP, as well as the catalyst in perpetuating the vision. Warren Ost was a dynamic, highly motivated and tireless individual. He was able to attract donors to support the organization, including wealthy families. I never met him, but stories about him are legion.

ACMNP provides an opportunity for worship in national parks that might not otherwise exist. It provides seminary students an opportunity to test their career aspirations in the real world. It may also provide an opportunity for student ministers from urban environments to experience places of great natural beauty in a spiritual context. By and large it provides employers with dependable employees. It is most often a win-win situation. Furthermore it is an example of a proper balance of church and state. It protects the First Amendment right of free exercise of religion, while at the same time observing the proscription against the government's establishing a religion.

The Board of ACMNP is an interesting conglomeration of Park Service and concessioners personnel, pastors and religious educators, plus some members who are simply interested in the program. The Board meets once a year in a different national park, always an enervating experience.

ACMNP has operated under three different executive directors. The current executive director is Rev. Spencer Lundgaard. AMNCP operates out of Denver, Colorado, with a small staff of full-time employees largely engaged in recruiting and training employees and identifying prospective employers. In addition there are many volunteers.

The organization is in the process of revising its mission statement and strategic plan to adapt to changing times. There is less emphasis on the conducting of traditional worship services and more emphasis on discipleship, counseling and helping coworkers and visitors rid themselves of destructive lifestyles. There are a number of lost souls who work in national parks and who visit them, people who would never think of seeking guidance in a traditional church setting.

The current tagline adopted by ACMNP is "Encountering God in the Wonders of Creation." This leads to an environmental connection presently being explored, which is for ACMNP representatives to become stewards of the natural beauty of the national parks in order to protect the wonders of God's creation. This goal would tie directly into the mission of the National Park Service and support that goal by adding a spiritual element to it.

ACMNP is ecumenical and open to all branches of the Christian faith. There is no reason why practitioners of other faiths, Jewish, Muslim, Buddhist, Hindu or even secular humanist atheists cannot create a similar program reflective of their own faith communities and beliefs. National parks in general, and Yosemite in particular, have always evoked some level of spiritual awakening or renewal.

GETTING SMART ABOUT ENTRANCE FEES

For many years the Park Service collected entrance fees at all national parks. These fees became part of the general fund. The practice prompted cynics to claim that their entrance fees were being used to pay for bombs and guided missiles. There was no incentive for park officials to be diligent in collecting fees, since there was no connection between how much they collected and the maintenance and welfare of Yosemite and/or other national parks.

Finally, Congress passed legislation that allowed a portion of entrance fees collected to be allocated for use within each national park. The resulting increase in revenues was a great advantage for park management, providing much-needed funds without requiring the Park Service to compete with other demands for government appropriations.

GETTING DUMB ABOUT FIREARMS

Until very recently firearms were prohibited in Yosemite National Park and other national parks. They had to be checked at the entrance station. During the final days of the G.W. Bush Administration, Park regulations were modified, rescinding a previous order that forbade visitors from bringing firearms into Yosemite.

In my opinion, granting people permission to bring firearms onto Park property deserves to be ranked high on the list of dumb policy decisions. Hunters are the only civilians who should be permitted to carry firearms into areas that are administered by the Forest Service. Since hunting is forbidden in Yosemite, there remains no clear reason for carrying a gun.

Any argument about the necessity of carrying a gun into Yosemite for the purpose of self-protection is not persuasive, because the knowledge that people can have guns in the Park serves to make Yosemite a much more dangerous place than it would be if all the visitors were disarmed.

It may be simply a matter of time before some redneck with too many beers takes a potshot at a deer, or someone will engage in road rage. I can imagine that someone with a firearm stowed among his/her camping gear might be tempted to fire a bullet into the tent of the camper who is playing heavy metal music at 2 a.m.

Yosemite should have remained one of the places where Americans could leave behind our obsession with guns.

CURRENT PARK SERVICE RESPONSIBILITIES

A superintendent in Yosemite may appear to have the power to make things happen in Yosemite. This is realistic only to a limited extent. A Yosemite superintendent is subject to considerable outside pressures that may limit his or her capacity to accomplish personal goals, or the goals that the Park Service directs. The Park Service is a bureaucracy within the federal government, subject to political pressures from above and outside. The tendency of some employees of a bureaucracy, public or private, is to avoid making decisions that are either controversial or innovative and to adhere slavishly to the rules. Also, in a bureaucratic setting, there is often not a penalty for delaying a decision, which may drive a concessioner dealing with priorities crazy. Most Park Service personnel are not trained in business principles. In this setting it is not uncommon for there to be long delays in the renewal of concession contracts, which continue in force under the old terms, like a lease. Many Park Service personnel are creative and innovative, but they may be prisoners of a bureaucratic system. Most Park Service personnel are dedicated to their jobs. It is not just another government job.

Considering these factors, it is really quite remarkable that joint control of Yosemite by the Park Service and concessioners allows the Park to function as well as it does, albeit with some grumbling. In my experience one overriding factor is that both Park Service and concessioner top management share a profound love of Yosemite and a desire to carry out the enjoyment and preservation mission inherent in public ownership as best they can.

The third and neutral full-fledged member of the partnership is the nonprofit Yosemite Conservancy. It provides both capital improvements and naturalist programs which the Park Service cannot provide. The Yosemite Conservancy is more insulated from political pressures than the Park Service, and does not have to make a profit, like the concessioner. This makes the Yosemite Conservancy an ideal buffer.

This type of three-pronged partnership in public ownership is not unique. It exists in other national parks, but it is more fully developed in Yosemite. I believe that encouraging people to come to Yosemite to enjoy nature, rather than to enjoy entertainment that one can enjoy elsewhere, is an educational process—not a directive to be forced on visitors.

The Park Service must pay attention to assuring the safety of visitors. This sometimes means rescuing the clueless from dangers into which they have placed themselves, and also rescuing those who have an unfortunate accident. The recent popular book about how visitors have met their death in Yosemite reinforces my view that there are more of the former than the latter. In my observation, this is what the Park Service does best.

The Park Service must also deal with enforcement of traffic rules and rules against conduct which is offensive to other visitors. In this role rangers must become policemen. There have been instances in which some rangers have become overzealous in this role, just as some policemen have. The *Los Angeles Times* recently reported an incident in which an Australian couple was thrown in jail after being stopped for driving after having had a couple of glasses of wine at the Ahwahnee. I personally have experienced being stopped by a ranger for driving a little over the centerline on a one-way road and being subjected to being tested for excess alcoholic consumption in a thoroughly offensive fashion. I was let go when the Breathalyzer failed to function. The resident magistrate is there to protect against overzealous conduct and should not operate as a rubber stamp for whatever a ranger does. Due process does not end when one enters a national park. The overzealous conduct described is by no means typical and should be dealt with just as overzealous police conduct is dealt with elsewhere.

The Park Service must also deal with maintaining roads, sewers and other infrastructure in need of repair. This creates a good deal of distraction from broader goals.

The more visitors there are, the greater the regulatory responsibility of the Park Service. This can sometimes lead to the mindset that the public is the enemy. Whatever the Park Service does is almost certain to displease someone. Park Service personnel are underpaid for what they are expected to accomplish and the challenges which they face daily.

Some of my comments in this book may appear critical of the Park Service personnel. Indeed, some of them make mistakes, being human. So, however, do concessioners, visitors and self-appointed saviors. My overall observation is that Park Service personnel are largely a dedicated class of people who actually do a commendable job of caring for Yosemite, considering all the pressures they must contend with, coming at them from all sides.

CHAPTER 17

EVOLUTION OF THE CONCESSIONERS

Concurrent with the evolution of Yosemite Park as a government-run institution is the story of the growing role of the concessioners that manage and operate the inns, stores and other facilities that serve Park visitors.

THE INNKEEPERS AND EARLY AUTOMOBILES

The first automobile entered Yosemite in 1900. During subsequent years several of the curious "horseless carriages" would show up every year. Antipathy was shown toward automobiles even when there were only a dozen of them. In 1907 automobiles were officially banned from entering the park.

When the ban was lifted in 1913, green motor stages belonging to the newly organized Yosemite Transportation System began transporting passengers, and continued to do so for many decades following. Even after the reintroduction of automobiles, some people continued to enter Yosemite on horseback and with horse-drawn vehicles. As recently as 1920 automobile tags issued by Yosemite contained the note that "Horse-Drawn Vehicles Have the Right of Way."

The tide of technology had turned, however, and people increasingly were driving into Yosemite in private automobiles. The introduction of the Model T Ford served to make automobile travel affordable for middle-income

Parking lot on the Valley floor, circa 1930.

*Left: Chief Ranger Townsley welcomes early
visitor. Courtesy of Yosemite Research Library.
Right: Buick convertible entering Yosemite.
Courtesy of Adams Family Collection.*

families. America was on the road and the road often headed toward Yosemite.
Automobiles in Yosemite remain a leading source of controversy to this day.

During the ensuing decades, nine lodging facilities were built to meet the
needs of the ever-growing throngs of visitors: Leidig's Hotel, Paregoy's Mountain
View House, James McCauley's Mountain House on Glacier Point, Wawona
Hotel, the Sentinel Hotel, and the La Casa Nevada Inn. Except for Wawona,
they have long vanished. Their existence is preserved only by records, memoirs
and fading photographs.

IMPACT OF DAVID A. CURRY AND THE
CURRY FAMILY ON YOSEMITE

The impact of the Curry family on Yosemite has been profound, running from
1899, when David A. Curry and Jennie Curry established what became Camp
Curry, until 1970, when Mary Curry Tresidder died, just as the original Yosemite
Park & Curry Company was unraveling.

David A. Curry (1860–1917) was known as "the Stentor" (which educated
people of his day would have recognized as "a person having a loud and powerful
voice"). His devoted wife Jennie described him: "Big in body, mind and soul,
interested in life and people, simple in ways and habits, absolutely without any
affectation, his friendly spirit and genial whole-souledness appealed to people
and made him the perfect host."

I never had the privilege of meeting the famed Stentor, who died many years
before I was born, and by that time legend about him was becoming separated
from reality. However, I did know Jennie Curry, who carried on as president
of the Curry Camping Company after David's death, during some tumultuous
years, regarding both the business and the family. She lived 87 years, long enough

Above: Mother Jennie Curry.

Right: David Curry as the Stentor.

Below: Camp Curry visitors.

to see the 50th anniversary of Camp Curry. She was known to all local residents as "Mother Curry" and was held in great reverence by guests and locals alike. She lived in a bungalow in Camp Curry most of her days after David's death. In contrast to the sometimes aggressive, strong-willed and confrontational behavior of her husband, she was devout, kindly and gentle but just as iron-willed as David. She occasionally succeeded in accomplishing by charm what he failed to achieve by bombast. David died during an often-pitched battle with the Park Service and unfriendly competitors. "Mother Curry" persevered and played a major role in the Curry family legacy of being the most well-known innkeepers of Yosemite, and a household name to thousands of visitors.

For a description of events in the history of the concession before my birth, I rely heavily on the books of the late Shirley Sargent, whom I regard as the leading and most credible chronicler of the people who have hosted visitors to Yosemite. Shirley's research is exhaustive. Her leading book, *Yosemite and Its Innkeepers,* is filled with names of people I know or knew; reading it is nostalgic. I am even featured in one of her books, called *Children in Paradise,* about kids, like me, who grew up in Yosemite. If Shirley reports an event, I believe it (more about Shirley in Chapter 23). I will therefore recount a few facts about the Curry family, citing *Yosemite and Its Innkeepers* as the source.

David and Jennie Curry grew up in Indiana and Kansas. They were heavily influenced by David Starr Jordan, the first president of Stanford University, who lured them to California. David became principal of Sequoia High School in Redwood City, California. Another influential person early in their lives was Rufus Green, a famed professor on the first faculty at Stanford, who was involved in setting up Camp Sequoia, which eventually became Camp Curry, at an abandoned campsite.

Rufus Green was on the Board of Directors of the Curry Camping Company and a trusted advisor for many years. When he met Don Tresidder, a young prospective medical student from Indiana, he was the first to suggest that Tresidder visit Yosemite. Tresidder boarded with Green at Stanford. Green is the grandfather of Stuart Cross, who later became CEO of the Yosemite Park & Curry Company. Thus, connections with Yosemite and Stanford begin at the inception of Stanford, long before Tresidder left Yosemite to become president of Stanford in 1942.

Camp Curry offered a different experience in Yosemite Valley from the other early accommodation, the historic Sentinel Hotel, which was pricier at $4 per night. In its first year of operation in 1899, Camp Curry hosted 290 of the 4500 visitors to Yosemite. By 1902 the house count rose to 800, and by 1902 and 1903 it was at 1300. David and Jennie Curry were devoutly religious and insisted that the entertainment they introduced be wholesome and family oriented. David objected vocally when a competing concession was allowed to sell alcoholic beverages. Thus, the unique ambience of Camp Curry developed.

David and Jennie brought three young children with them—son Foster and daughters Mary and Marjorie. They grew up in Yosemite and helped to run the operation.

Foster shared some of his father's attributes and ran Camp Curry for a few years following his father's death. However, he did not share his father's sobriety or nonviolent nature. He had numerous run-ins with the Park Service over drinking and fighting episodes, which continued after he promised to repent. Finally, in 1921 he was banished from Yosemite by the superintendent, in the days when that was an option. He was forced to sell his interest in the family business, leading to great bitterness that lasted throughout his lifetime. Foster started an operation similar to Camp Curry at Camp Baldy in Southern California. He died in 1932, never returning to the Yosemite he loved, but directed that his ashes be spread over Yosemite from an airplane.

Foster's sons were invited to return to Yosemite and did so, even with the possibility of working their way into top management because they had the magic Curry name. Son David opted out of Yosemite for a career with Stanford Research after working several seasons. His younger brother, the late John Curry, did work his way into top management but left to work for Disney and eventually for Sea Pines in South Carolina about the time the Yosemite Park & Curry Company was unraveling. I know David and knew John. David offered early encouragement for writing this book.

Mary graduated Phi Beta Kappa from Yale and returned to Yosemite. She later married Don Tresidder, who had been hired by her father in 1916 as a porter along with Hil Oehlmann. Both would become CEOs of the Yosemite Park & Curry Company. Mary authored a book entitled *Trees of Yosemite*, which my mother illustrated with woodblock prints. They were close friends.

Mary was an adventurous, avid hiker and skier who loved Yosemite passionately. After the passing of Mother Curry in 1949, Mary assumed the role of the nominal head of the Yosemite Park & Curry Company and the matriarch. In her later years she maintained a suite on the sixth and top floor of the Ahwahnee Hotel. Mary's contributions to Yosemite are lasting and enduring. Don and Mary had no children.

Mary's sister Marjonie married Bob Williams, who was from Illinois. He remained as a director and shared top management with Don Tresidder until he had a falling out with the board over a stock redemption issue that led to a lawsuit during the depths of the great depression of the 1930s. The Williams family lost the lawsuit, and Bob Williams left for Hawaii and eventually returned to the family business in Illinois. Marjorie remained on friendly terms with Mother Curry and Mary and returned frequently to Yosemite. However, both Mary and Marjorie remained so estranged from Foster that he refused blood from them when dying of leukemia. I knew who Marjorie was, but I did not know her well.

Even though I have little personal recollection of many of the above events, because they occurred when I was an infant, they deserve mention as an explanation of why the Curry name has prevailed, while the names of other concession operators have fallen by the wayside.

CONSOLIDATION OF COMPETING CONCESSIONERS

After the formation of the National Park Service in 1916, while Camp Curry was developing as an institution in Yosemite, competition was also developing. Again, my source of information is *Yosemite and Its Innkeepers* by the always-accurate Shirley Sargent.

Joe Desmond, described by Shirley Sargent as "impulsive, arbitrary, energetic and purposeful," found backers and came to Yosemite with ambitious plans. Desmond had previously been in the restaurant business in San Francisco, had built construction camps for the aqueduct from Mono Lake to Los Angeles and had run a string of concessions at the Pan Pacific Exposition in which he introduced hot dogs to the West Coast.

Desmond's company remodeled the old cavalry headquarters into the old Yosemite Lodge, which has remained at its location near the base of Yosemite Falls on the sunny side of Yosemite Valley. In the late 1950s Yosemite Lodge was entirely rebuilt. Desmond had plans for a grander hotel, but his ambition did not match his financial resources, and his major creditors, mostly hotel suppliers, had to step in and become part owners.

They formed a new company called the Yosemite Park Company and absorbed some of the smaller businesses in Yosemite Valley. David A. Curry adamantly refused to be absorbed, and there was continual conflict between the competitors as to who would operate concessions in Yosemite Valley. There were continual efforts by both entities to secure contracts with the Park Service.

Finally in 1924 the Park Service tired of the conflicts and the politics and decided that the visitor would be better served by a regulated monopoly. The Park Service forced a consolidation with Don Tresidder and Bob Williams of the Curry interests in charge of management, with the creditors who largely owned the Yosemite Park Company becoming stockholders and directors of the new company. Desmond was out. By the time I was born, the consolidation was a totally done deal, and it was as if there had never been competing companies running visitor accommodations in Yosemite Valley.

The Curry Company operated every business in the Park except for Standard Oil, and two other exceptions that operated under a separate government contract. One was Degnan's. Degnan's originated with the wife of a construction worker who sold donuts. The business evolved into a bakery, restaurant and gift shop across the street from The Old Village Store. After the passing of the founder, her resourceful and tenacious descendants managed to parlay the informal business into a concession contract with the Park Service.

When the buildings were removed from the Old Village, the Degnan heirs had an opportunity to realize their long-standing dream of building a larger facility. They lobbied the government heavily for the right to build a new delicatessen adjacent to the post office in the government center. Ironically, with its larger overhead, Degnan's was able to operate the new facility only for a couple of years before going broke. The facilities were assimilated into the operations of the Yosemite Park & Curry Company. The delicatessen is still referred to colloquially as Degnan's in recognition of its original owners.

Best's Studio was the other business that successfully remained independent of the Yosemite Park & Curry Company. Harry Best originally owned the studio. His only daughter, Virginia, married Ansel Adams in 1928. The studio name was later changed to The Ansel Adams Gallery. The gallery is still in operation and is managed by descendants of Ansel and Virginia Adams. This enterprise possibly has the distinction of being one of the last family-owned businesses operating in any national park.

Stephen Mather, the first director of the National Park Service, believed that there should be a place in national parks for luxury hotels in order to attract affluent visitors whose support he counted on for the development of national parks. The luxurious Ahwahnee Hotel was built in 1927.

Don Tresidder, the first president of the Yosemite Park & Curry Company, was a visionary who realized the potential power of winter sports to attract off-season visitors to Yosemite and in 1927 created an organization called the Yosemite Winter Club. An initial attraction was a four-track toboggan slide and ice-skating rink developed near Camp Curry. The following year the Winter Club opened the first California ski school with a staff of experts in winter sports headed by a Swiss ski instructor named Jules Fritsch. The team led ski treks into the High Country.

By 1927 Yosemite visitors were able to choose from a number of recreational options including campfire entertainment, a free nature guide service, a livery with saddle horses, the nightly fire fall, bait and tackle service for fishermen, swimming holes, a Kiddie Kamp for children, a cafeteria, a post office, a bath house, tents, bungalows, a main dining room that could accommodate 750 people, a barber shop, beauty parlor, garage and filling station, a store, a laundry, a dance hall, medical services, church services and a museum.

The tremendous influx of park visitors in the 1950s saw a corresponding increase in services designed to meet the visitors' needs and wishes. There were swimming pools at Camp Curry and Yosemite Lodge, and continuous entertainment at Camp Curry. The placid Merced River offered a number of swimming beaches where young people swam during the day and held beach parties at night.

For adults in the upper income brackets, the Ahwahnee offered more sedate entertainment options where the rich and famous would gather, the women in gowns and the men in coats and ties, to feast on sumptuous evening meals. They also enjoyed golf on the local pitch-and-putt golf course and tennis on the courts surrounding the hotel.

The number of services has been steadily declining over the decades. Standard Oil of California formerly operated service stations with the largest volume of gasoline sales in the state of California. Today visitors and residents are unable to buy gasoline any place on the Valley floor, though fuel is available at a couple of the remote areas in the park.

While I was growing up Yosemite afforded many recreational opportunities that have since been removed. Critics who complain about a trend in Yosemite toward commercialization are not aware of the fact that 60 years ago the Park was far more commercialized than it is now. There are actually fewer overnight accommodations. The full-service hospital in which I was born has been reduced to a day clinic. There is no longer a movie theater. Yosemite still has a public grammar school, but its existence is threatened as employees move out of the Valley.

Conflict between the Government and the Concessioners (Postwar to 1963)

At the same time that Yosemite Park & Curry was awash in postwar business and visitation rose to unprecedented levels, tension between the federal government and all concessioners in national parks also rose to unprecedented levels.

Within Yosemite Valley the Park Service and the concessioners were getting along. The problem developed at higher levels of the federal government. What was new at this time was that another government agency, the General Accounting Office, decided that the government was not exacting a sufficient fee from the concessioner for the privilege of doing business on public property, which the concessioner did not own. Some members of Congress joined in this effort.

One of my father's pet peeves was the franchise fees that the government charged for doing business on public property. He pointed out repeatedly that the concessioner had no option other than passing the franchise fees on to the visitor in the form of higher costs for lodging and services. Thus, the effect was to make a visit to Yosemite more expensive to the public who own the Park. It amounted to an additional levy on the taxpayers who owned the Park. Increased franchise fees also placed the concessioner at a disadvantage with competing businesses, located just outside the park, which did not have to pay the franchise fees.

During the Truman administration Secretary of the Interior Harold Ickes determined that these problems might go away if the government took over running the concessions in national parks. This obviously did not sit well with concessioners, who did not relish the idea of being forced out of business. Ickes became a swearword among concessioners. The concessioners banded together to form the National Park Concessioners Association to lobby in Washington with friendly politicians to protect their mutual interests. Yosemite representatives were in the forefront of these efforts, because the Yosemite Park & Curry Company was the largest concessioner in the national park system.

A parallel problem was that concessioners, who did not own the facilities that they operated, had no collateral to finance capital improvements. At this time the Park Service was still friendly toward constructing or upgrading facilities.

Into this quagmire of unresolved problems stepped my father, who originated two legal concepts that assured the concessioners the ability to operate and expand for a period lasting thirty to forty years. These concepts were incorporated into a law known as Public Law 89-249. It became the revered Holy Bible and Constitution of the concessioner.

The first concept was a preferential right of renewal, which meant that a concessioner who had performed satisfactorily in the eyes of the Park Service had a preferential right to renew its contract to operate. The second was a possessory interest, which meant that if the government forced out a concessioner, or if a new concessioner came in, the retiring concessioner had to be reimbursed for its investment. These legal tools tended to give a concessioner a monopoly. However, the tradeoff was that the Park Service could dictate the prices charged for all goods and services. What emerged was in effect a regulated monopoly similar to a public utility. While these changes were being incorporated into concession contracts, the idea of government operation of concessions faded away and has never been raised since.

These efforts culminated in a 30-year contract for the Yosemite Park & Curry Company, entered into in 1963 after protracted and seemingly endless negotiations. One unfortunate fact about bureaucratic government is that it often lacks a sense of urgency about completing negotiations. It is not uncommon for concession contracts to continue for years after expiration under the same terms, as in a lease. The story on the 30-year contract is that after all terms had been agreed and the contract drafted, it sat in a stack of papers on a desk in Washington, D.C., awaiting signature by the appropriate official for an extended period. Finally, an exasperated Hil Oehlmann travelled to Washington and haunted the office of the official, saying he would not go home until the contract was signed. Hil returned home bearing the contract. He verified the truth of this story later.

These experiences prompted my father to coin the often-reiterated remark, "I never had anything against government until I had to deal with it."

Ironically, the contract, fought for so tirelessly, proved to be the undoing of the original Yosemite Park & Curry Company. Emerging conglomerates were eyeing concession contracts entered into under Public Law 89-249 as potentially profitable monopolies. They figured out that to get around having to buy the business and pay for the possessory interest, they could buy a controlling interest in the stock of a corporation which held the concession contract and be in the same position as if they had purchased the assets of the concession. This is exactly what happened with three successive operators. And so it came to pass that the concessioner in Yosemite remained the Yosemite Park & Curry Company in name only.

Affirmative Action in the National Parks
A Brief Effort

Members of the National Park Concessioners Association encompass operations that range from serving Mt. Rainier mountain climbers to serving customers at the Statue of Liberty Gift Shop. The National Park Service is charged with administering the same diverse set of operations.

Of course, being a massive bureaucracy, the Park Service had the goal of administering these diverse concessions under a single set of policies. The results were often ridiculous and sometimes laughable. For example, during the Johnson administration I was invited to attend a meeting on affirmative action with a newly appointed director assigned to oversee affirmative action initiatives.

The man was a vibrant African American who set the tone for the meeting by playing some Dick Gregory tapes offering rhetoric that sounded like something like Stokely Carmichael. The man had obviously been a political appointee, and had been given the position by a bureaucracy that was willing to exchange wisdom and experience for the appearance of racial diversity and racial balance.

To the man's credit, following the end of Gregory's ethnic jingoism, he said to us, "I will level with you guys. I don't know anything about national parks. Tell me your experiences with affirmative action."

Operators of concessions in some of the more remote park areas in the West said that they had made efforts to recruit African Americans. However, they were unable to attract or keep many of them because many of the prospective employees were urbanites unaccustomed to living and working in isolated areas.

Operators from some parks in the Southwest told the man that they had hired Native Americans but had a problem with inter-tribal hostilities. When they tried to solve the problem by limiting their hiring to a single tribe, members from the other tribes would claim that they were being discriminated against.

Another concessioner claimed that 80 percent of his employees were African Americans.

"Where is your concession?" the man asked him.

"In the Virgin Islands," he responded.

After further discussion of that kind, a number of the concessioners offered to finance tours of their facility for the ostensible purpose of giving the director the opportunity to see conditions for himself. The man accepted with enthusiasm and brought his girlfriend along for the trip.

It was a win-win situation, since the people in the Department of the Interior could reassure themselves that they had taken bold action to promote affirmative action. The bureaucrat was thrilled with his all-expenses-paid vacation. And the concessioners were especially delighted with the fact that they never heard from the man again. In their opinion, satisfying that bureaucrat with a few steak dinners and a several nights in a visitor facility was a bargain.

The man didn't know anything about national parks, but he obviously knew how the American system of government worked. Perhaps it is more accurate to say that he knew how to work the American system of government.

This is a typical example of what happens when another agency of the federal government decides to get involved in national park management without knowing what they are doing.

USNR AND SHASTA
A HOSTILE TAKEOVER

The 1960s ushered in other changes in the concessions. The comfortable family-like atmosphere of the Yosemite Park & Curry Company began to unravel when a conglomerate company called USNR acquired a 38% share of the outstanding stock in the Yosemite Park & Curry Company. USNR acquired stock by offering financial inducements to employees, former employees and other stockholders, creating a conflict of loyalties.

USNR severed important connections with the past when they replaced CEO Stuart Cross with Alan Coleman, from the Stanford Business School, who had no prior experience in Yosemite. Stuart had been a long-time friend of our family, and had been working in Yosemite throughout the term of his predecessor, Hil Oehlmann, Sr.

USNR was itself acquired by another conglomerate named Shasta, which eventually succeeded to a controlling interest in the Yosemite Park & Curry Company. Don Hummel became CEO; he had owned other concessions in national parks and been mayor of Tucson, Arizona. He had been president of the National Park Concessioners Association. He was an outspoken champion of private operation of national park concessions.

The little community in Yosemite Valley experienced a great loss when Mary Curry Tresidder passed away in 1970. There was an exodus of other management employees, many of them nearing retirement age. With her passing, a long-standing connection between Yosemite and Stanford University began to unravel. During that same year another beloved resident, Dr. Avery Sturm, retired from medical practice (see page 154) and left the park, ending the era during which Yosemite would be managed by a concession run as a benevolent family business, staffed by overqualified but dedicated individuals who formed a unique Yosemite community.

During its years of operation the original Yosemite Park & Curry Co. had become known as a training ground for hotel management executives. Since there was not too much room at the top in Yosemite, many went on to careers in other places.

Keith Whitfield, who was my boss as head bellman at Camp Curry, went to Sun Valley as an executive. Wayne Whiteman, another friend and fellow employee, went to Hilton Head. Bob Maynard, a management executive in Yosemite for many years, wound up as head of operations in Aspen, Colorado.

Roger Hall spent time working in Yosemite before returning to take over the family operation at Mesa Verde National Park, Colorado. Roger's father, Ansel Hall, had worked as a naturalist in Yosemite, and introduced Ansel and Virginia Adams. Roger later went on to a career in the Navy and teaching. These few examples illustrate another way in which experiences in Yosemite influence lives.

MCA ERA

In 1973 Music Corporation of America (MCA) acquired a controlling interest in Yosemite Park & Curry Company. The name stayed the same. MCA, headquartered in Los Angeles, was principally in the business of publishing music, booking acts, operating a record company and distributing television productions.

For virtually all of my living memory many writers in the media have delighted in reporting that Yosemite was being systematically ruined by overcommercialization by profit-hungry concessioners. Environmental purists have joined the rallying cry and supplied eloquent rhetoric to support it. These folks had a field day when MCA acquired the Yosemite Park & Curry Company.

MCA was accused of planning to create another artificial tourist attraction like Disneyland in Yosemite, complete with Las Vegas–style convention facilities and a new ski resort at Tuolumne Meadows. I came across a letter written on August 30, 1974, by Jay Stein, vice president of MCA, to Hil Oehlmann, after Hil had retired and moved to Palo Alto with my mother.

In this private communication, Stein defended the intentions of MCA against its critics. He stated that MCA did not plan to build a new hotel at Glacier Point to replace the hotel that burned down in 1969, but intended only to replace a gift shop and restaurant at the request of the Park Service. Stein stated that MCA had suggested keeping the Tioga Road open all winter as a suggestion to ease the then-energy crisis and abandoned the suggestion when he learned the Park Service viewed it with disfavor. Stein further stated that keeping the road open to Tuolumne Meadows to facilitate cross-country skiers had been a suggestion of the Park Service, and that MCA had never had any intention of creating downhill skiing facilities at Tuolumne Meadows.

With regard to the charge that MCA was planning to transform Yosemite Valley into a convention center, Stein responded that no extension of existing facilities was planned, and that the practice of providing accommodations for meetings in a natural environment for groups which did not often exceed 100 would continue during the off-season, when rooms were not in as much demand. Neither MCA nor its successor, DNC Parks and Resorts in Yosemite, a subsidiary of Delaware North (DNC), has attempted to create facilities for conventions in Yosemite Valley.

DNC has acquired a modern convention facility, ideal for smaller conventions, five miles outside the Park boundary, known as Tenaya Lodge. Tenaya Lodge was built by another developer who did not operate any concessions within the Park. Tenaya Lodge now serves a need for those desiring to hold a convention within easy access of Yosemite. Other hotel accommodations, suitable for larger groups, are located just outside the Park in El Portal. They were not built or operated by either MCA or DNC.

MCA was accused of upgrading tent cabins without baths in Camp Curry in order to increase profits and exclude visitors of modest means. The upgrade was under consideration by the Park Service before MCA came along, utilizing cabins designed by the Park Service, because demand for the tent cabins had been steadily declining. Mr. Stein pointed out that at the time 59% of overnight accommodations in Yosemite Valley rented for under $4 per person double occupancy. What has happened since then is that tent cabins remain, although their number is steadily decreasing. Tent cabins now rent for over $100 per night.

The Park Service regulates the price of all overnight accommodations in Yosemite Valley, theoretically based on comparability. It is difficult to find anything comparable to tent cabins without baths outside Yosemite. Visitors can now occupy campgrounds in much greater comfort, bringing with them all the comforts of home in motor homes. Regulation of suitable, appropriately priced overnight accommodations is a challenge.

The most controversial project that MCA did undertake was the television series "Sierra," depicting the life of rangers. The Park Service approved the project and supervised it. Crews were accused of trampling meadows. The most notorious incident that did occur was the painting of rocks for technical reasons, which made front-page news. Stein stated that only nine square yards of rock were painted with a water-soluble solution, which was easily removed with no damage.

Mr. Stein quoted an unidentified park superintendent as explaining to a visitor, "On the positive side, we hope that this series will convey the spirit of the National Park System, some of the beauty of the national parks and, we hope, will eventually instill an awareness and appreciation of national parks and their values in a great number of American citizens.... Frankly, we want Americans to see our national parks, to appreciate them, and to recognize a park ranger for what he is and what he stands for. We hope that young people especially will be turned on to the park ranger, will be anxious to talk to him and be more receptive to our programs and policies."

The Sierra Club threatened to sue to stop the program, which was eventually discontinued by MCA. I watched the program, and I enjoyed it. I particularly enjoyed an episode that showed Yosemite native and my childhood friend Charlie Castro climbing a giant Sequoia to put out a fire 200 feet off the ground (more on Charlie in Chapter 23). I leave it to the reader to determine whether the "Sierra" program was a desecration of Yosemite or a worthwhile educational endeavor. I come out on the side of Stein and the unidentified superintendent.

A principal accusation made against MCA is a genuine bum rap. MCA was accused of planning and designing a tramway to Glacier Point. The truth about that project, according to respected Yosemite historian Hank Johnson, is that a tramway was first proposed in 1913, but the idea was not pursued.

The idea was introduced as a serious proposal in 1929 by the Yosemite Park & Curry Company under Don Tresidder and presented to the Department of the Interior. An actual design of a tramway similar to what is commonplace in the Alps, designed in such a way that the cables and superstructure could not be seen, was presented. The proposal received some support in Congress, but was opposed by the Sierra Club, the Yosemite Committee of Expert Advisors under Frederick Law Olmstead, Jr., and the then-superintendent Charles J. Thomson. Horace Albright, who was then director of the Park Service, opposed the idea but said he would send it on to the Secretary of the Interior if requested to do so. The tramway was considered in the 1980 Master Plan but not implemented.

Harry Chandler, publisher of the *Los Angeles Times*, expressed support. The Secretary of the Interior, Ray Lyman Wilbur, never requested that the proposal be sent to him, and it died from lack of action. The Company lost interest as the Great Depression deepened. The proposal became a dead issue. MCA did no more than express interest in this long-abandoned project, but did not attempt to implement it. According to Mr. Stein, MCA abandoned the idea when they learned the Park Service would not consider it a viable project.

My personal opinion has always been that the tramway would have been less invasive to the environment than the roads and parking lots that have existed and now exist. In any event, the tramway was no more than a suggestion by MCA which went nowhere after a bit of sound and fury.

Any notion that Yosemite would be managed by a Hollywood promoter was dispelled when Ed Hardy become the one and only chief operating officer to preside over the Yosemite concession on behalf of MCA. As previously mentioned, Ed grew up in Palo Alto and was my high school classmate. After designing and operating the Almaden Country Club in San Jose, Ed operated the Riviera Country Club in Los Angeles.

Ed did not seek the position of chief operating officer in Yosemite. While at Almaden Ed taught swimming to the children of Don Stevens and became a close friend. Stevens felt that Ed would be the perfect person to manage Yosemite for MCA and lobbied MCA executives. Ed was not sure he wanted the job. He was happy managing the Riviera Country Club and living in Malibu. When offered the position, Ed hesitated, consulted his family and finally accepted. He and his family did not regret the decision and soon caught a lasting case of Yosemite glad tidings fever that still persists.

Ed proved to be an astute businessman who knew how to cultivate political connections. He set out to determine when accommodations were not being fully utilized and to look for ways to fill them. One of his first projects was to be instrumental in helping fund the Yosemite Institute, a naturalist program for young people, which drew participants and parents to Yosemite. Ed would make daily calls to the entrance station advising as to what overnight accommodations were available. The MCA executives in Los Angeles gave Ed considerable latitude in managing Yosemite, satisfied that the bottom line was in good hands. Ed entertained Queen Elizabeth, and she reciprocated by entertaining him at Buckingham Palace.

Ed was enterprising. Knowing that the Park Service had a tendency to try to phase out and not replace damaged cabins, he had a local contractor from Mariposa available to come to Yosemite on a moment's notice, sometimes in the middle of the night, to repair a cabin damaged by a tree falling on it before the Park Service could phase it out.

At times Ed chafed at Park Service regulations he felt were too restrictive, such as prohibiting pizza or ice cream cones. When the Park Service suggested that a barber and beauty shop was not appropriate in Yosemite, Ed successfully resisted, pointing out that he wanted his employees well groomed and that they should not have to make a 70-mile round trip to Mariposa for a haircut.

Ed genuinely loved and venerated Yosemite and wanted to make it a place that visitors could enjoy in comfort. One of his striking characteristics was that he took a personal interest in every employee working under him, down to the most menial, and would frequently stop to ask how they were doing. He was often helpful with employees' personal problems. He was truly a benevolent boss. Employees loved him. Even now, twenty years after he left Yosemite, I have personally observed Ed stopping to chat with employees still working there.

In this respect Ed differed from previous CEOs who were more distant. He more resembled my father, who had hired many of the employees and also took a personal interest in them. When I was working in Yosemite many former employees would tell me how much they appreciated my father's attention to their personal concerns.

ENTER AND EXIT THE JAPANESE
HOW THAT CHANGED DOING BUSINESS IN YOSEMITE

The story of how MCA departed and DNC entered as the concessioner, because of the involvement of a Japanese company, is generally known. The details are not exactly as reported in the press.

Here is the story, as explained to me by Ed Hardy; Dan Jensen, who worked for MCA during the transition and is now CEO of DNC; and Kevin Cann. Kevin was deputy superintendent of the Park Service under five superintendents, and is now retired from the Park Service and a Supervisor in Mariposa County.

The story starts before Matsushita, a Japanese company, acquired an 80% interest in MCA. Mike Finley was brought in as superintendent in part because it was felt that the concessioner under Ed Hardy was asserting too much influence over Yosemite. This tension was nothing new and has gone on between superintendents and CEOs of concessioners as long as I have followed it, to a greater or lesser degree. CEOs of concessioners generally remain longer. superintendents are in Yosemite for a shorter period, often as little as two years, and often have to leave just as they are acquiring a grasp of management issues. Park Service employees at the level of superintendent must go where assigned like military personnel.

The Yosemite contract was viewed as a virtual monopoly, which it was. The Yosemite contract was coming up for renewal in 1993, and the Park Service saw a golden opportunity with the Matsushita acquisition of 80% of MCA to get rid of the possessory interest of MCA and a preferential right in a new contract.

Matsushita had little or no interest in the Yosemite contract. It just came with the package they acquired. Their representatives barely visited Yosemite. Ownership of a Yosemite concession by a Japanese company was politically very unpopular. Japanese companies had acquired Pebble Beach and Rockefeller Center, and some feared Japan would take over the country. Matsushita wanted no part of this political fallout for an asset they never wanted. Secretary of the Interior Lujan saw an opportunity to be a hero by disposing of the Japanese.

When MCA learned that a proposed new contract would contain no possessory interest and preferential right, they decided that they did not want the contract. The Park Service thought there would be many interested parties, but discovered less interest than anticipated in the watered-down contract. They miscalculated that large hotel chains would want the contract. The Park Service did not realize that large hotel chains were not interested in an operation where the price of everything down to a candy bar was regulated. Further, large hotel chains like to advertise their identity, but renaming the Ahwahnee Hotel the Hyatt Yosemite would not be acceptable. Moreover, a new operator would have to buy out the possessory interest held by MCA under the old contract.

There was an attempt to form a nonprofit corporation to bid on the Yosemite contract. However, an entity with no experience in the hotel business that would have to raise the capital to buy out the possessory interest of MCA proved to be impossible to find.

Secretary Lujan persuaded another nonprofit to put stock in escrow while the Park Service looked for a buyer for the possessory interest of MCA for substantially lower than its market value. This was a greatly undervalued price, according to Ed Hardy; however, MCA, under Japanese ownership, wanted out. The Park Service got rid of the possessory interest for a bargain price. The price paid for the possessory interest was estimated by Ed to be half of market value (assuming there was any market). Everyone was happy except Ed, who was out of a job he loved.

Secretary Lujan was not motivated by the goals of preservationist reformers. His primary motivation was to make more money for the government. He is quoted as saying candidly, "We're not looking to break anyone or be unreasonable. I am very happy with the system; I just want a greater return."

The Park Service set out to find a bidder who would accept a contract without a possessory interest or preferential right and found an unlikely prospect, Delaware North Company, a family-owned Fortune 500 company out of Buffalo, New York, who owned concessions in baseball parks and racetracks, the Boston Bruins, and other varied assets. Delaware North was eager to venture into uncharted territory for them, but territory that looked promising for a company eager to diversify.

One of the terms in the negotiation was to substitute, in part, a capital improvement fund for the franchise fee. The latter was seen as more beneficial to the concessioner than simply paying the federal government for the right to do business, something that had always been a thorn in the side of the concessioner. Thus, there was born a new way of doing business in Yosemite. Ed Hardy was initially offered a position to stay on with DNC, but it did not materialize. Why it did not depends on whom you ask, so I will say no more, other than to note that Ed followed the path of all previous CEOs who moved out of Yosemite before they really wanted to.

THE DELAWARE NORTH ERA

DNC entered Yosemite with a turnover of management employees, which is not unusual with a change of operators. Several CEOs presided, modifying Ed's unique relationship with the Yosemite employees. Eventually, the present CEO, Dan Jensen, returned to Yosemite. Dan had been an employee of MCA and a key player during the Matsushita negotiations.

Both Delaware North, the parent company, and DNC, the subsidiary, were quick to establish good relations with the Park Service. Employees had been unionized under MCA, so the change from college students and young people who were looking to find themselves had shifted to career hotel employees, many of them older than their younger counterparts. This did not originate with DNC, and has continued to this day.

No dramatic changes in visitor accommodations have been proposed. The average visitor likely would not have noticed a difference. In fact, overnight accommodations in Yosemite Valley, both campgrounds and hotel units, have declined. Due to supply and demand, the prices have risen considerably for hotel units in the Valley. Visitors have been, and are likely to be, willing to pay a premium for staying in the Valley, in some cases in older and more rustic accommodations than are available in more modern motel units just outside the Park, only a ride of a half hour, more or less, from El Portal. Resistance to any upgrading of units in the Valley is to be anticipated.

There have been temporary interruptions in service to visitors due to natural occurrences such as fires, floods and rockslides. The Park was also closed in 1995 during a budget crisis. The three-month closure of Yosemite Valley in 1997 due to a flood was the longest closure in its history. These events have clearly impacted profitability, but DNC has persevered and been able to operate successfully. The parent company, Delaware North, obviously likes to operate national park concessions because they have sought rather aggressively to acquire concession contracts in other national parks and some state parks.

DNC currently operates without a preferential right or a possessory interest. They hope to be able to renew a contract on that basis at the expiration of the present contract.

Dan Jensen pointed out to me in a recent conversation a major problem with the loss of the possessory interest and preferential right. There is less incentive to maintain buildings if the government owns them lock, stock and barrel, and the concessioner is entitled to no return if the concessioner is replaced. DNC is required to contribute to a fund for capital improvements that has millions of dollars in it. However, the Park Service must approve the proposed improvements. Priorities may vary, or the fund may sit there for an undetermined period of time until the Park Service decides what to improve. This problem is compounded by pressure from those who want infrastructure removed rather than improved. This problem will manifest itself in the next three years when a new master plan is developed, as is later discussed.

Another aspect of this problem is illustrated here: Suppose a roof leaks. It can be continually repaired, but it might be more cost effective to replace it. DNC can continue to pour money into the former, but the Park Service must approve the latter. Meanwhile, the roof leaks continue. My observation is simply that there must be a better way to do business for the benefit of the visitor.

If I had a crystal ball, my prediction would be that DNC will be around for a while and that major changes in the concession operation are unlikely. However, nothing has been certain in concession operations.

HEALTHCARE SERVICES IN YOSEMITE VALLEY

Roger Hendrickson, M.D. Photo by Patricia Hamilton, 2009.

I am indebted to Roger Hendrickson for tracing the evolution of health care services in Yosemite from the full service hospital in which I was born to the day clinic that now exists in Yosemite. Roger practiced medicine in Yosemite from 1960 to 1979.

The first hospital in Yosemite was built by the War Department near the old Yosemite Lodge in 1913, transferred to the Interior Department in 1914 and remodeled in 1915. In 1928 Congress granted the funds for the construction of the existing facility, which was named after W.B. Lewis, a superintendent.

The hospital opened in 1929 with Dr. Hartley Dewey in charge. He held a concession contract until 1943, when the Navy doctors from the Ahwahnee temporarily took charge.

Dr. Avery Sturm joined Dr. Dewey in 1935 and stayed in Yosemite for 36 years. After military service he returned to Yosemite in 1946 and held a concession contract. During succeeding years he hired several second doctors, including Roger Hendrickson and Dr. Jim Wurgler. With Dr. Sturm at the helm, the Lewis Memorial Hospital provided much-needed and highly advanced care.

The remote nature of Yosemite required medical services over and above what was required in a typical small town practice due to exposure to unexpected hazards and ski injuries. During Dr. Sturm's tenure the hospital provided surgery, obstetrics, cardiac care and orthopedics—in short, full service. Because of his expertise in treating ski injuries, Avery was summoned to help in the 1960 Winter Olympics at Squaw Valley. He and his wife Pat were gracious and caring people, much loved by the locals.

After Avery retired in the early 1960s, Doctors Roger Hendrickson and Jim Wurgler continued to operate the hospital. They began to see hints of inevitable changes. In 1967 Medicare came into existence accompanied by a proliferation of administrative details, multiple meetings and staff commitment. They joked that every meal or cup of coffee in the lounge needed to be a "staff meeting."

Medical insurance with multiple providers became a bigger issue as the hospital served an itinerant population. Insurance premiums skyrocketed as dramatic concerns about malpractice claims escalated, particularly in California.

Medicine itself was experiencing intense growth in specialization and complexity. The hospital staff now had the option of evacuating patients by helicopter to outlying hospitals. Because they ceased to perform more complicated procedures, hospital usage was decreased, and income was decreased while costs simultaneously increased. All of these changes, no one single issue, formed a "perfect storm" of signs of the times and intensified. It became increasingly obvious that the feasibility of maintaining a fully accredited and self-supporting hospital was questionable.

After long hours of discussion, debate, financial review and consideration of various options, it was decided that the goal should be to continue to make use of a fine facility and skilled medical professionals, but to do so in other than an official hospital setting. This meant eliminating overnight stays, obstetric care and major surgical procedures, converting Lewis Memorial Hospital into an extended day care facility which could continue to offer 24-hour emergency care as well as bed and breakfast facilities for patient stabilization. The bulk of visitor and community medical services could be provided in this office setting.

Thus, Lewis Memorial Hospital ceased to be a full service hospital in 1975 and since then has been known as the Yosemite Medical Clinic, continuing to provide 24-hour emergency physician care along with daily medical attention for Yosemite guests, employees and employees' families.

The current contract to operate the extended day clinic has expired, and there were no takers for a new contract. Thus, the Park Service had no option but to take it over and staff it with its own personnel.

One consequence of all this is that it is no longer possible to be born in Yosemite, except by accident.

Best's Studio in the original location, circa 1910. Now site of the Ansel Adams Gallery. Courtesy of Adams Family Collection.

ANSEL ADAMS GALLERY
A SURVIVING FAMILY BUSINESS IN THE NATIONAL PARKS

There were several pioneer photographers in Yosemite prior to Ansel Adams, who managed to produce images with the cumbersome equipment of the time. That equipment had to be transported with considerable effort, a far cry from the point-and-shoot cameras in use today. These early photographs, along with the wealth of artwork that features Yosemite as its subject, were instrumental in attracting widespread attention to Yosemite and permitting a viewer to visualize what even the eloquent words of John Muir could not convey.

When I was born in 1934 there were three photographic studios operating in Yosemite: Best's Studio, Foley's and Boysen's. A fourth, operated by Arthur Pilsbury, burned down before I was born. Only one, Best's Studio, survived and avoided being absorbed by a larger concession. All were originally located in the Old Village but moved to the area near the post office, museum and visitor center, on either side of where the Ansel Adams Gallery is located.

The original Best's Studio, now the Ansel Adams Gallery, has continued in operation for over 100 years by four generations, a feat unequalled anywhere else in the National Park System, to my knowledge. The concession contract

Harry Best in his studio. Courtesy of Adams Family Collection.

with the federal government was renewed in 2010 for another 10 years.

Ansel Adams did not start the business. It was a going concern when he married Virginia Best, the only daughter of the founder, Harry Best, in 1928. When Ansel married Virginia he was still debating whether to pursue a career as a concert pianist or a career as a photographer.

Ansel never managed the business on a day-to-day basis. He was too busy taking photographs and perfecting the artistry that would make him world famous. After Harry Best died in 1936, Virginia was the manager, sales person and bookkeeper for the business. The Adams family lived in a building that was part of the studio, up a flight of stairs, until Ansel and Virginia moved out of Yosemite Valley in 1962. This was the childhood home of Michael and Anne, whom I visited frequently.

Harry Best was born in Ontario, Canada, on December 22, 1863. He and his brothers came to California via Portland, Oregon, in 1887. He was both a political cartoonist for the *San Francisco Post* and a fine artist. He first visited Yosemite Valley in 1901 with some fellow artists and, like many others, fell in love with Yosemite. He also fell in love with a Yosemite visitor, Ann Rippey, from Los Angeles, who spent summers in Yosemite.

Ansel Adams as a boy, with his family. 1916. Courtesy of Adams Family Collection.

On July 28, 1901, they were married beneath Bridalveil Fall following a whirlwind courtship. The following year the young couple decided to seek their fortune in Yosemite and started the first Best's Studio in a tent, later moving it to various locations. At this time Yosemite was still administered by the state of California, before there was any National Park Service.

In the early days of Best's Studio, the business operated only in the summer, and the Bests moved out in winter. Virginia, the only child of the Bests, was born in 1904. A three-year-old Virginia sat on the lap of Theodore Roosevelt and asked him about his family. The Rough Rider responded by sending Virginia a photograph with a note which said, "For little Virginia with best wishes for the future from Theodore Roosevelt November 12, 1907." Little did Teddy Roosevelt know what an interesting future Virginia would have.

Although she had no formal education past the high school from which she graduated in San Diego, she was a cultured lady, instrumental in supporting the Bach Festival in Carmel. Virginia was a mountaineer in her own right while growing up in Yosemite, claiming some first ascents of peaks in the Park. She was best known for her gracious hospitality. I remember the Adams home above the studio as having always being full of interesting people, suitably entertained. The Adams home beamed with parties, celebrations, highjinks, music, poetry, photography, political discussions and jokes, welcoming anyone who was ready for fun.

By the time Harry Best died in 1936, the studio had been established as a year-round operation in Yosemite with a concession contract with the National Park Service. Virginia and Ansel took over operation of the business. Ansel and

Ansel Adams. *Virginia and Ansel Adams. Courtesy of Adams Family Collection.*

Virginia decided early to sell only quality merchandise, even though it was more profitable to sell junk.

Ansel had been attracted to the Southwest to explore his photographic pursuits, and Virginia became interested in buying native American handicrafts to sell at Best's Studio. Virginia and her longtime cobuyer, Ernie Johansen, became experts at detecting quality in the merchandise. Mike Adams reported that other buyers of Indian handicraft would just buy it in bulk, whereas Virginia would go through it item by item and pick only items of the best quality. There were little or no comparable handicrafts from Native Americans living in Yosemite.

Although Southwest Indian handicrafts did not have a connection with Yosemite, the National Park Service encouraged their sale in national parks to help Native Americans. The National Park Service allowed exemptions on the payment of a franchise fee to the federal government for sales of Native American handicrafts.

The business became more than an art and photography gallery as photography workshops were added. The tradition of selling only quality merchandise has continued.

In the 1960s and 1970s another generation took over running the business. Michael Adams and Jeanne Falk were married in 1962 at the Yosemite Chapel. Ansel and Virginia moved out of Yosemite Valley in 1962 to Carmel Highlands, where a benefactor had gifted them property in Carmel Highlands overlooking the Pacific Ocean. They sold two homes in San Francisco that Ansel had inherited and built a home and darkroom. The home was later gifted to Friends of Photography in 1982, with Virginia retaining a life estate. Mike and Jeanne later acquired the home and now spend a good part of their time there.

Until 1971 Mike was in medical school and in a flight surgeon program in Germany. Jeanne Adams started accompanying Virginia on buying trips to the Southwest. When Mike and Jeanne returned from Germany, Mike went into medical practice in Fresno, and Jeanne stepped into Virginia's role as CEO of the business, by now much more than a gift shop and photography studio. An associated publishing business named 5 Associates was bequeathed to Anne. It could be carried on outside the Park. During this period Anne had lost her first husband, Chuck Mayhew, and had three small daughters. She did not wish to move back to Yosemite.

The gallery retained the exclusive right to sell first-edition Ansel Adams prints, which have now become very valuable. The original work product of Ansel is owned by a trust administered by three trustees. One trustee is Bill Turnage, a longtime financial advisor to Ansel. He played a major role in helping Ansel to convert his talent and reputation into financial gain—something many artists have been unable to accomplish.

Jeanne Adams has a background in political science and history with a Master's degree in education from Stanford University. She has taught high school. When Mike and Jeanne took over active operation of the gallery in 1971, the gallery progressed from manual to digital. It became more of an educational and environmental advocacy organization, continuing and expanding the photography workshop programs, with increasing emphasis on the importance of photography as the technology constantly changed, and continuing to raise the quality of merchandise.

Jeanne has participated, and continues to participate, in conferences on sustainability of ecosystems and awareness of the same. For eight years she served as the informal citizen liaison to the California Resources Agency. She served as a trustee on boards fostering cultural and environmental interests, all during the time she was overseeing the management of the business.

In 1972 Best's Studio was renamed the Ansel Adams Gallery. In 1975 Ansel commented on the contributions to the enhancement of the gallery by Mike and Jeanne:

> The Gallery stands alone in the Parks.... This fact is known and appreciated more than you realize. We represent a potent force of opinion that, in a sense, justifies for me all the work I have done in

30–40 years. I never considered the Studio—and now the Galler—as a place of casual fun and relaxation. It is a dead serious symbol of a constructive Park ideal. Everyone concerned therewith should accept this fact; in addition to making the business function well, they also have a certain responsibility to see that the National Park ideals are supported.

Truly the Gallery has become a nurturing place for the artistic interpretation of Yosemite, and a force in promoting environmental thinking, education, and encouragement of resource protection and National Park Service ideals.

In 1989, George Hartzog, a former National Park Service director, commented on the Gallery as follows:

Together, Best and Adams created a world-renowned legacy of paintings and photographs and forged a partnership with the National Park Service to present the majesty and interpret the meaning of Yosemite that is unique in the annals of public land management. This tradition of cooperative interpretation of America's heritage still flourished under the leadership of the children and grandchildren of these remarkable artists. It is a great delight in celebrating the lives, the art, and the commitment to public service of this illustrious family.

Now the fourth generation has taken over management. Sarah Adams, daughter of Mike and Jeanne, is a graduate of New York University with a major in art history. Sarah is an art appraiser. In 1996 the Ansel Adams Gallery purchased the historic 76-year-old Mono Inn on the shores of Mono Lake, across the Tioga Pass on the east side of the Sierras, and established a gallery and world-class restaurant at that location, opening in 1997. For five years Sarah served as Director of Fine Art for the gallery. The Mono Inn operation was terminated after the birth of Sarah's two children.

Matthew Adams, the son of Mike and Jeanne, is now CEO of the gallery. He holds a master's degree in business administration from Washington University St. Louis. Matthew brings an international flavor to the gallery. Before rejoining the family business he advised businesses in Russia and the Ukraine. He is married to Ming Zhu Hu Adams, a native of China who operates a worldwide medical supply business. Matthew is pioneering the sales of Ansel Adams digital prints on the Internet, and also is carrying on the gallery in Yosemite under a new contract with the Park Service. Matthew is an expert at recognizing genuine original fine prints. There has been some misrepresentation in selling these in the secondary market. The gallery controls the primary market exclusively but cannot control the secondary market.

The Ansel Adams Gallery owes its longevity and continued success to the fact that it has become an institution rather than just a business. As testimony to this, neither the Yosemite Park & Curry Company, under its varying management, nor the present concessioner has ever attempted to acquire the Gallery. In the recent contract negotiations, no one bid against the Gallery for the concession contract.

I am privileged to serve on the Board of Directors of this venerable institution.

CHAPTER 18

MASTER PLANNING

Master planning can be defined as an attempt by an empirical process to determine the wishes of the public, which owns Yosemite Park. Any such plan is severely hampered by the reality that not all members of the public want the same thing.

MISSION 66—THE FIRST PLAN

Mission 66 was the first attempt by the Park Service to redefine and relocate infrastructure in Yosemite, which had changed little during many years preceding. It was first conceived in 1956. Projects included the much-needed widening of the Tioga Road, the winterization of the Wawona Hotel, the building of a new Yosemite Lodge to replace the old lodge that had been built by the cavalry, the relocation of the Old Village, the building of a new general store and construction of 20 new Park Service units in El Portal.

Most of the Mission 66 improvements were undertaken during the two years that I was serving Uncle Sam in Europe. I returned to find a transformed Yosemite Valley. The improvements were planned and completed in the absence of the extensive public hearings that would later characterize master planning.

ACQUISITION OF EL PORTAL PROPERTY

In 1958 Congress authorized the secretary of the interior to acquire from the U.S. Forest Service 2000 acres just outside the boundaries of Yosemite National Park for, among other purposes, an administrative site. This instituted a process of relocating infrastructure outside of Yosemite Valley.

The area is adjacent to the community of El Portal on the Merced River, approximately fifteen miles west of Yosemite Valley. El Portal is the former terminus of the Yosemite Valley Railroad, which ran until the 1940s. The land was the first suitable land outside Yosemite Valley for any infrastructure, since the road between El Portal and Yosemite Valley follows the Merced River up a steep canyon. The land was acquired by a transfer from the U.S. Forest Service.

A sewage plant was built on the land, rather than being added to the Yosemite Valley infrastructure. Some housing for employees in Yosemite Valley has been built. From the time this land was acquired, the Park Service has encouraged transferring functions deemed to be administrative to El Portal. The concessioners have generally resisted this trend.

One victim of this program was our beloved cabin, which was bulldozed to make way for a trailer park to house employees working in Yosemite Valley. One of the cabin renters joined a survey crew in a futile attempt to gerrymander the boundaries in order to save the cabin.

1980 General Management Plan

A general management plan (GMP) for Yosemite Valley was initially proposed in 1980. Most of it has not been implemented, initially because resistance by the Reagan administration, coupled with subsequent lack of appropriations. Reagan's view of environmentalism has been characterized by his famous comment, "If you've seen one redwood, you've seen them all."

Reagan's secretary of the interior, James Watt, earned a reputation as history's most environmentally insensitive holder of that office. When his tenure ended, environmentalists danced in the streets.

There was little enthusiasm for funding the improvements recommended by the 1980 GNP. One primary recommendation of the plan, which never materialized, had been a goal advocated by a number of environmentalists: Since the advent of the automobile there had been advocacy for the removal of private automobiles from Yosemite Valley. The 1980 GNP proposed doing exactly that.

A gas crisis in the late 1970s had people waiting in long lines. Gas prices skyrocketed. It was anticipated by some that public transit would become the norm in the United States and that Yosemite could become the norm. In anticipation of the change, the Park Service removed parking places estimated to be as many as 6000, creating the problem of drivers looking for a place to park. This problem persists.

The concessioner (MCA) at the time was accused of blocking the plan. They were not enthusiastic about it. However, my opinion is that they needed simply to sit back and witness the inaction of the Reagan administration. The 1980 General Plan languished in a state of suspended animation and was not funded.

THE YOSEMITE VALLEY PLAN (YVP)

In 1997, during the friendlier administration of President Clinton, a massive flood closed Yosemite Valley for three months, washed out a main access road and severely damaged infrastructure located in the flood plain of the Merced River, which flows through Yosemite Valley. Funds for restoration were appropriated.

The Park Service correctly determined that if damaged facilities were rebuilt in the flood plain, the same damage would likely occur again, given the recurring pattern of floods. The Park Service further determined that this was an ideal opportunity to revive the moribund 1980 GNP, rather than reinventing the wheel, in an effort to repair flood damage. The subsequent Yosemite Valley Plan (YVP) went beyond the repair of flood damage and addressed some perceived neglected needs.

The YVP was drafted in 2000 after extensive public hearings and the required environmental studies. Predictably, the plan was challenged in a lawsuit, largely upheld by the federal district court, but later invalidated by the U.S. Ninth Circuit Court of Appeals, as explained in the next chapter.

Several years ago I reviewed a copy of the draft YVP at the request of Congressman Sam Farr. Even though I am a lawyer, I found the plan to be a difficult document to understand. It's hard to imagine that a layperson, particularly one who wasn't already aware of the problems and issues, would be able to understand it at all. These issues are now moot, since the YVP has now been scrapped due to a court ruling later explained.

I spoke with Yosemite officials about the plan and attended public hearings that were conducted as part of the approval process. The broad general outlines of the plan are acceptable to the great majority of the public. They include:

1. Reclaim priceless natural beauty.
2. Allow natural processes to prevail.
3. Promote visitor understanding and enjoyment.
4. Markedly reduce traffic congestion.
5. Reduce crowding.

It is difficult to quarrel with these broad objectives.

One of the good things that the master plan did was to consider and then to reject suggestions put forth by the environmental extremists, a small but vocal minority that would destroy the visitor experience for millions. The suggestions of members of this group include:

1. Remove all visitor accommodations from Yosemite Valley.
2. Remove all campgrounds from the Valley.
3. Remove all private automobiles from the Valley.
4. Require all overnight visitors to be transported into the Valley by bus.
5. Remove all employee housing and the school.
6. Remove historic buildings.
7. Provide no parking for day use visitors.

Only an extreme environmental purist would defend these guidelines. There is no question that, if the views of the extremists were adopted, it would substantially impair, if not destroy, a quality experience for most Yosemite visitors.

Following this exercise, a series of public hearings was held to determine the wishes of the public. Alternatives, many of which were highly controversial, were proposed. They included mandatory bussing from parking lots—one of which was in the Valley, others outside the Valley—for day-use visitors; reduction of facilities catering to low-income visitors; removal of historic bridges which were thought to interfere with the natural flow of the river; blocking off one of the two access roads in and out of the Valley (reducing access to a single two-lane road); and the reduction of parking spaces in the Valley from 1,622 to 550. Many of these measures, in my opinion, were overkill.

Severe traffic congestion occurs only during a few peak periods. For these times a reservations system seemed to me to be an obviously less expensive way to deal with traffic congestion. However, this alternative was rather summarily dismissed. I wondered if I was missing something, so I asked Dave Mihalic, superintendent at the time of the 2000 Yosemite Valley Plan. He responded as follows:

> The reservation system had several issues as well—where do the people wait for a car to drive out so they can drive in? How do you deal with vacationers who drive from outside California or fly in from Europe and rent a car, only to learn that "you can't get

there"? I realize there are lots of answers to these two questions, but the planners had to consider all that, plus get the gateway communities to buy into these solutions. Not impossible, mind you, but the 'planners' just plan—they don't always think of the consequences which the public pointed out during the 22 public meetings across California and 4 more around the nation.

The YARTS system (existing public bus transportation from gateway communities to Yosemite), which was supported, gave the public the option of getting on a bus in the gateway communities, leaving their cars in their motel parking lots (already built and not by the government) and taking the bus into the Park for the day, returning that night (and thus adding a second night's stay to their motel bill). The gateway communities somehow believed that if the public "had to" do it this way—the same argument against a reservation system, by the way—then the public wouldn't come!

David Mihalic also suggested that the 2000 Yosemite Valley Plan was not designed to guide the Park Service in how to manage Yosemite. It was designed to withstand a legal attack. A legal attack on an environmental impact study is usually based on the agency's not having considered all aspects of a proposal affecting the environment. In this case, the attackers found a missing detail that the court held not to be properly addressed, as is more fully explained in the next chapter.

CAMPGROUNDS

I expected that the loudest voices at the planning hearings would be those of environmental purists wanting to "restore" Yosemite to something it never was. I was surprised. Recommended reduction in campgrounds was the recommendation most strongly opposed. The opposition was from people of modest means and labor unions who felt the workingman was being excluded from Yosemite. Many had fond memories of camping in Yosemite. Their pleas reached George Radanovich, the congressman representing the district in which Yosemite is located, who put pressure on the Park Service to restore some reductions in campgrounds. On this issue the voice of the visitor was heard— although the issue is not yet resolved.

EMPLOYEE HOUSING

Since the YVP has been invalidated by the court, I will not dwell on most of its recommendations. However, one deserves some attention because it has been a continual source of controversy. Efforts to move on-site housing for Yosemite employees out of the Park have been advocated for many years. When I was a child most park employees lived in Yosemite Valley. As a result, park residents constituted a solid community of people whose lives were intertwined with shared experiences of working, living and playing together. Today the community of Yosemite employees is fragmented, because workers commute from towns that are located up to 40 miles from Yosemite in every direction.

The residences for Park employees were scattered around the Valley so people could live near the places where they worked. Because no one could own a home in Yosemite, many employees purchased homes outside the Park where they could build equity and retire.

Employee population during the peak season is estimated to be about 1,500, of which 89% work for the concessioner, 8% for the National Park Service and 3% for others. The number of concessioner employees varies from 800 to 1,200. The number of National Park Service employees remains relatively constant.

My recollection is that these numbers have changed little during the 75 years of my life. There has not been a significant increase in park employees since the 1940s, just as there has not been an increase in overnight visitor accommodations in Yosemite Valley during that time.

Most of the concessioner employees are housed in dormitories and in tent cabins. There are some single-family homes and apartments, which are occupied largely by management employees. Most of the lower-paid employees are single. One employee housing area known as Camp 6 was destroyed in the 1997 flood and will not and should not be rebuilt. Some employees have been housed for several years in unsightly "temporary" structures brought into the area and placed behind the post office without notice to the adjacent concessioner, the Ansel Adams Gallery.

Until the 1960s and 1970s many concessioner employees were college students working during summer vacations. Now that the season has expanded, this is no longer the case. Tent cabins, which tend to be hot in summer and cold in winter, are obviously far less appropriate for permanent employees than for summer college students. Some permanent housing for Park Service employees is available in Yosemite Valley.

The concessioners have been resisting the effort to move employee housing out of the Valley, but some employees have voluntarily moved, since there is not enough housing in the Valley.

In the 1970s another government agency, the General Accounting Office, compounded the problem for Park Service employees by determining that rents in government-owned housing were too low, and, by raising them, they created a financial strain on low-paid Park Service employees.

Employees who are commuting into Yosemite Valley to work must travel long distances, sometimes as much as 40 miles in each way to El Portal, Mariposa, Groveland or Oakhurst. These lengthy commutes are over winding roads that are occasionally closed by storms and rockslides.

Commuting employees add to the traffic congestion. Most of them commute in private vehicles because work hours are not coordinated among the employees, especially concessioner employees, and because their housing is not centralized.

Some administration offices have been moved out of the Valley, so employees do not need to commute. Some functions, notably reservations, have been relocated.

Bob Binnewies, the same superintendent who was instrumental in creating the Yosemite Fund, made the case for removal of employee housing in a letter to Stan Albright, the superintendent in 1989, in which he recommended that removal of employee housing be made a condition in the 1993 renewal of the concession contract.

The decision will be whether a lucrative private business monopoly will be allowed to continue to dominate Yosemite Valley or whether the natural and scenic qualities finally will take precedence.... Many YP& CC employees could live and work outside the Park. Most modern corporations provide executive and administrative services that are distant from product delivery points. Even within Yosemite, the YP & CC executive and administrative staffs are distant from the Wawona Hotel and Tuolumne Meadows, yet The Company's product is delivered at those locations. An executive/ administrative/logistical concession function located outside Yosemite

Valley is a practical option to the many structures, houses and attendant traffic that accompany these functions in Yosemite Valley.

Some employees are required to be on hand to aid visitors in case of emergencies. The reality is simply that, unless Yosemite Valley is turned into a completely unpopulated wilderness, there will always be a need for some onsite housing for Park employees in Yosemite Valley.

One proposal recommended that The Row, where I lived as a child be "restored to a mosaic of mixed conifers and riparian communities." Areas fitting this description are all over Yosemite Valley, to be observed by visitors without the necessity of tearing down employee housing.

I have never felt the removal of employee housing from Yosemite Valley to be warranted. Such removal has caused and will cause more problems than it will solve. The benefits, both tangible and intangible, of housing employees near where they work outweigh any burdens that may be imposed on the visitor experience.

One way to test this hypothesis is to compare removal of employee housing with the five broad goals of the YVP:

> The amount of priceless natural beauty that could be reclaimed is negligible, as are the natural processes being allowed to prevail. There is no more impact on these factors from employee housing than there is for visitor accommodations, which the YVP retained.
>
> The housing of employees in Yosemite Valley does not adversely influence promoting visitor understanding and enjoyment. If anything, the improvement of employee morale and sense of community, as well as the improved attraction for highly qualified workers, will only serve to enhance visitor enjoyment.
>
> Housing employees in Yosemite Valley will clearly reduce traffic congestion, because they will not have to drive or be bussed in and out of the Valley to work.
>
> Housing employees in the Valley will not increase crowding. The employees have to be in the Valley whether they live there or not.

Before further efforts are made to reduce employee housing in the Valley, further study is required and a better reason offered than the goal of "reducing the human-built environment," which is no more than a collection of buzzwords.

There is a "dog in the manger" process at work on the part of some of the opponents of employee housing. Perhaps some spokespersons are annoyed that they can't live in Yosemite Valley and wish to deny anyone else the opportunity to live there.

THE TRUE MEANING OF THE YOSEMITE VALLEY PLAN

David Mihalic, retired Yosemite superintendent, was entrusted with the duty of finalizing the Yosemite Valley Plan before the expiration of Bill Clinton's term. He succeeded in doing so. The plan was finalized in 2004. After the tumult, shouting and misinformation circulated from the public hearings, the YVP was presented in a 900-page document—in contrast to the 1980 GMP, which was fewer than 100 pages and much easier to understand.

Rather than reading and digesting the 900-page document, commentators would conduct exit polls from people emerging from the public hearings after they had pushed their own agenda. This resulted in misinformation and unfounded rumors.

Secretary of the Interior Bruce Babbitt announced the passage of the YVP with great fanfare at an event that I attended.

David Mihalic, who completed his assignment in pushing through the plan, later characterized the plan:

> Part of the problem in the whole plan is "dueling environmentalists." You have one group who wants to "save" Yosemite by implementing the YVP. And you have another group who wants to "save" it even more, contending the YVP doesn't go far enough! You have very few people who understand the true ramifications of what will occur to the average American park visitor when the YVP is finally implemented.

I agree with another observation Dave Mihalic made, that, in the final analysis, the average visitor to Yosemite, whom the plan was designed to benefit, was largely shut out of the decision-making process.

Mihalic summarized his view on the YVP, which he was charged with promoting:

The plan has turned into one to discourage visitors. The plan has turned Yosemite from a place we want to share with people, to one where people have become the problem. The Park was set aside for the benefit and enjoyment of people, to explain the wonder of the place and instill in them values that they would take with them when they left, and that would help them to better understand the world in which they live. The focus is "How many people?" It has become one of numbers and carrying capacity. "Carrying capacity" is a concept to manage grazing animals, cattle and sheep on a piece of pasture. Parks aren't pastures, and people aren't cattle. The YVP in essence says people aren't the visitors, they aren't the customers, they are merely "the problem" to be tolerated for as little time as possible, and to get in and get back out as quickly as possible. Except for the elite who can afford the Ahwahnee, of course. They have more political juice than those in Camp Curry. It's always been that way, so they get to stay!

David Mihalic's philosophy on the management of Yosemite was captured in a question and answer session with Bill Stall of the *Los Angeles Times* on January 9, 2000:

Stall: "The Yosemite planning process has been going on since the late 1970s. How will you get a new Valley plan in effect by the end of the year?

Mihalic: Well, we haven't been able to do it up to now. It's actually easier to do it this way, to make it in a crisis. You know, one of the best things the Park Service does is to rise to a crisis. If someone falls off a rock around here, we can do a bang-up job of rising to the crisis. If there is a flood we can do a bang-up job. If there is a fire, we can do a bang-up job. The emergency kinds of things are what we do best.

Stall: What is so special about Yosemite Valley, and, therefore, such a problem?

Mihalic: It is a magnet. The Valley was the core. It was the Old Faithful of Yellowstone, the Crater Lake of Crater Lake. As a result, over 100 years ago, as this place became better known, the development was concentrated in the Valley. The Park was so isolated, and it's still relatively isolated, it took some time to get here. People would come, and they'd stay a week. All the stuff inside the

Valley—the campgrounds, the overnight accommodations—people came and stayed a week. I'm told that in the 50s and 60s, about 80% of the folks who came to the park stayed at least one night. The average was around three nights. Now that's reversed. 80% come for the day. That's one of the reasons we're confronted with an infrastructure that was set up and developed and designed over time to serve visitors who spent the night here.

Stall: Doesn't that reduce the need for lodging in the Valley?

Mihalic: It certainly reduces the need. It may not reduce the demand. The fact is, if you have less supply, you'll have more demand. So what you have to do is manage the demand. It would be horribly difficult to try to add more overnight accommodations. But, if there are people staying in destination communities, they can come in for the day. That's the visitation pattern. That's a good thing, because it is dispersing the demand on the Valley part of this great park. Because many times when people talk about Yosemite, they're talking about the Valley.

Stall: Some argue that a more natural experience, meaning less development, is the better experience.

Mihalic: That's saying you've got to enjoy the world the way I enjoy it. I've got black coffee. I don't begrudge the fact that your coffee has something else in it. There is nothing in the 1916 law that says only if you suffer can you really have the experience. There is nothing that says these places have to be the way one class of people sees them.

Stall: The Valley is seven miles long and only a mile wide. How many visitors can you accommodate without affecting the resource? Is that the crux of the planning process? The number of visitors has doubled since 1980.

Mihalic: In my mind, it's not (so much) the numbers of people as the management of them. Carrying capacity studies work great when you are talking about sheep and pasture. But this certainly isn't pasture, and people are not sheep. It's not so much what they tolerate—like white rats in a maze experiment—but what they prefer. So we're trying to get to the point where we could manage the experience, and the quality of the experience, and help people choose the right thing.

Stall: Your job is to reconcile differences among people to the greatest degree so you can accommodate all?

Mihalic: This is my life's work, so maybe I feel a little more emotional about it. To me, one of the special things about Yosemite National Park is the beauty of the place and how it inspired people. It was so important at the time it was set aside that one of our great presidents, Lincoln, took time when our country was trying to rip itself apart... to set aside Yosemite for the people. Just in its genesis the Park is special. I think this place is so special for so many reasons. It is more than just a place; it is a sacred place. And what we do here, we have to do for the common good, not just for the shrillest or the loudest voice who thinks their way is the best way. Does it mean it's a place where anybody can engage in a particular pursuit just because it can be done here? I don't think it is, because it is not a recreation area. It's the most special of places. That's why we are not a land-management agency. We manage our nation's heritage, our nation's patrimony, and the things that define us as people.

Stall: But you do have to manage future development in the Park.

Mihalic: Sure. The 1916 act didn't say set these places aside but don't do anything with them. The 1980 general plan at least preserved it until today. Maybe we haven't gotten it right yet. But at least it's improved, and almost 50% of that general-management plan has been implemented. We're still working at the hard stuff, but this place is worth the effort.

Stall: A transit system is still critical?

Mihalic: The flood of 1997 [which washed out roads and campgrounds)] offered us an opportunity and also just increased the complexity of the challenge. It would have been wonderful if we could have just stopped the world, closed the park, and then fixed it and opened it up again. But we didn't have that luxury. We have people who want to visit while we are doing it. There's the short-term stuff we have to deal with while we are crafting a long-term fix. The transit portion has to be more effective. We have to do a better job to move people around.

Stall: You can't please everyone.

Mihalic: Everybody who feels they have the right answer for this place—that actually makes me feel better because we have the luxury of having customers who are committed to what we do and who care very much. At least we know that people share our values, and it gives us a common point from which we can all begin. I'm not sure we can satisfy them all. It's not a bad thing to have public controversy. It means the public cares and wants to have a say, and I think that's a good thing. The idea is that you have this spectacular place that can inspire so many. There are people who came here for a summer and stayed their whole lives. There are people here who have learned an ethic, whether it's the environment or wilderness, and they have taken it with them.

If that meant having a campground here, or a lodge, or even an Ahwahnee Hotel [which opened in 1927], and that's the hook to get somebody in here and let them park on some pavement so they get the value of this natural splendor, and they take it back to their home in an enlightened way, then it doesn't matter whether we have paved over a couple of extra parking spaces in the Valley. What we have done is made an investment in terms of values to instill in people that those people can take with them.

If people come here and leave the better for it, then that's our challenge. But if they come here and have a bad experience, a congested experience, and they only think it was a bad recreation experience, then we have failed those people."

We the people are not Yosemite's problem. The Park Service must not come to regard us as nuisances to be discouraged from visiting Yosemite at all, or, if we must come, to make our visit short and as bereft as possible of any conveniences or facilities that would otherwise make our visit more enjoyable.

Dave Mihalic's assessment of the 2000 YVP proved to be prophetic. The "dueling environmentalists" who thought the plan did not go far enough decided to sue. A lawsuit was brought by environmentalists who were so extreme that long-established conservation organizations, notably the Sierra Club and the Wilderness Society, did not join them. They were the group of radical local extreme environmentalist purists, "Friends of Yosemite Valley." My reaction as a visitor was to ask, "With friends like this, who needs enemies?"

I wholeheartedly agree with Dave Mihalic. Planning has not benefitted the visitor, which it is supposed to do. I am not a fan of master planning as it has been conducted. I come close to agreeing with academics and environmentalists who state that trying to make planning decisions based on a perception of what the public wants is futile. There is nothing close to consensus. The loudest voices tend to be heard. There is no assurance that the recommendations of planners will be funded. There is always someone out there with his or her own agenda looking for a way to challenge a plan in court if they don't like it.

The visitor is better served by relying on the judgment of Park Service professionals, working in cooperation with concessioners, who are professionals in the hospitality industry, and nonprofit organizations dedicated to trying to improve the Yosemite experience for the visitor.

Stoneman Bridge, from which Peter parachuted in a mattress cover. Courtesy of Yosemite Research Library.

CHAPTER 19

MERCED RIVER LITIGATION

THE WILD AND SCENIC RIVER
THAT IS ONLY PARTLY WILD AND SCENIC

In 1987 Congress chose to amend the Wild and Scenic Rivers Acts (WSRA) of 1964 by including 81 miles of the Merced River within its provisions. A substantial portion of the 81 miles is within Yosemite National Park. The Wild and Scenic Rivers Act of 1964 is aimed at protecting free-flowing rivers in wilderness areas from development. There are three designations within the act: "wild," "scenic," and "recreational." It was obvious to anyone at the time that the designation "recreational" applied to the Merced River in Yosemite Valley. The designations of "wild" or "scenic" would have made most, if not all, of the infrastructure in Yosemite Valley in violation of the act. The "wild" and "scenic" designations allow very little development. However, Yosemite Valley has been a recognized recreational area for over 100 years. At the time the Merced River in Yosemite National Park was designated a wild and scenic river, no one recognized the unintended consequences this would have.

WSRA requires a separate plan for the river to be prepared within three years to address the requirements of the act. The Park Service failed to recognize this and allowed the three-year deadline to pass without any plan. No one objected.

The Park Service continued to ignore the requirement of a plan until 1997, when the flood occurred. At that time, with funds appropriated to repair flood damage in Yosemite Valley, the Park Service decided that this was an ideal opportunity to revive the 1980 General Management Plan. Someone woke up and realized that the Park Service had neglected to do a plan for the river.

If a plan for the river had been done, as required, Yosemite Valley could have been designated as a recreation area. The Park Service would then have completed the Yosemite Valley Plan without having been concerned with requirements of WSRA.

The Park Service was now faced with a requirement of doing two plans, one for the river and one for Yosemite Valley. They elected to finish the river plan first, before the Yosemite Valley Plan, so the Yosemite Valley Plan could incorporate the decisions made in the river plan into the Yosemite Valley Plan.

Through this process the Park Service inadvertently created a smoking gun for a tiny group of local radical environmentalists with a declared agenda of removing visitor accommodations from Yosemite Valley. This group, calling itself the "Friends of Yosemite Valley," hired environmental lawyers who succeeded in undoing the Yosemite Valley Plan and postponing needed repairs of infrastructure in Yosemite Valley. Funds intended for repair of flood damage had to be diverted to payment of attorneys' fees. After hours of wasted effort and mountains of paperwork, the Park Service had to start over again.

In defense of the Park Service I would argue that an agency charged with the significant responsibility of looking after Yosemite had more pressing matters to attend to than to search the Federal Register for little known ramifications of a harmless looking directive which received no publicity when enacted.

BIOGRAPHY OF A RIVER—FROM GLACIAL SNOW MELT TO THE U.S. NINTH CIRCUIT COURT OF APPEALS

The Merced River originates with glacial snowmelt high in the Sierras, over fifteen miles by foot from a road. It flows through alpine meadows and forest until it passes its first brush with tourist accommodations at the Merced Lake High Sierra Camp. The Merced Lake High Sierra Camp is the first and largest of a string of seven walk-in tent facilities open to hikers in the summer. It was built in the 1920s. One must hike or ride horseback for 14 miles following the river from Yosemite Valley to reach this destination. At Merced Lake High Sierra Camp the traveler may enjoy the comfort of beds, meals and showers, staffed by a crew of summer employees. The High Sierra Camps are immensely popular. The demand greatly exceeds the supply.

From Merced Lake the Merced River gathers strength as it flows through a labyrinth of granite, forming miniwaterfalls and placid pools. It then flows into Little Yosemite Valley and lazily meanders past a garden of meadows and trees. Little Yosemite Valley is four miles from Yosemite Valley and fairly easily accessible to hikers. It is a jumping-off point and frequent overnight destination for those ascending Half Dome. Little Yosemite is a popular destination for backpackers. Little Yosemite is but a small foretaste of what the Merced River will encounter when it meets civilization head on four miles and a 2,500-foot descent downstream in Yosemite Valley.

At the foot of Little Yosemite Valley the entire Merced River plunges over 500-foot Nevada Fall in a torrent. During most of the summer months Nevada Fall mist drenches hikers ascending the Mist Trail, a steep route up the cliff immediately adjacent to the fall. This is a dramatic and exciting hike, a favorite of many, placing them very close to the power of nature. For those desiring an easier ascent, there is a longer horseback trail away from the river and the falls.

At the base of Nevada Fall, the Merced River winds its way between rocks to a pool appropriately called Emerald Pool, and across a sheet of granite known as Silver Apron. These are favored resting spots for sunbathers, river watchers and exhausted, footsore hikers. Then the Merced River plunges over a wider and lower Vernal Fall for 300 feet, which can be seen from a bridge below the fall. The bridge is only a one-mile walk from a road head, the most popular walk in Yosemite.

From Vernal Fall to Yosemite Valley, the trail is almost always full of throngs of hikers. The obese and out of shape huff and puff their way to the bridge, amid backpackers heading far off into the wilderness. Small children follow their parents, asking, "How much farther, daddy?" Women in high heels can occasionally be seen. For many Yosemite visitors, this is their only venture beyond the end of the road.

The Merced River enters Yosemite Valley at a place known as Happy Isles, where the land becomes flat, rimmed by 3,000-foot cliffs. Happy Isles is so named because when it reaches the flatland, the river spreads out around several tree-covered islets. There is a visitor center and a snack bar at Happy Isles. There once was a fish hatchery here. This is the first place where the Merced River encounters people who can reach its shores by motorized transport, although not by private vehicles. Since the 1960s the upper third of Yosemite Valley has been closed to cars. However, it is accessible by shuttle buses and bicycles, as well as by foot.

From Happy Isles the Merced River flows through Yosemite Valley with very little elevation decrease. It becomes somewhat wide and lazy, bounded by trees and meadows. The river encounters roads and bridges, and many visitors. It passes campgrounds where people stay in tents or bring the comforts of home with them in RVs. At many points in the Valley visitors can walk along its placid shores, and, in some places, see reflections of the granite walls towering above Yosemite Valley. In some places sandy beaches can be found along its shores.

At the lower end of Yosemite Valley the Merced River begins its descent into the Merced Canyon down a boulder-strewn course with many rapids. The all-year highway follows the river to the boundary of Yosemite National Park.

There are many spectacular views of the plunging tumbling waters along this road. Below the Park boundary the Merced River passes some outside-the-park motels with modern amenities and the small town of El Portal. El Portal was once the terminus of a railroad that ran along the river from the city of Merced in the Central Valley. A railroad museum preserves some of this heritage.

This part of the river is also designated under the WSRA. Below El Portal the Merced River flows along side the all-year highway toward Mariposa past a few more tourist facilities. It is joined by the South Fork Merced River at the site of Major Savage's trading post. This is the point from which the Mariposa Battalion set off in search of hostile Indians and discovered Yosemite Valley. Upstream the South Fork flows past the Wawona Hotel, at the southern boundary of Yosemite National Park, then through a roadless area, mostly outside the Park until it joins the main Merced River.

The Merced River in the Merced Canyon does not flow precipitously. It bounds around rocks and forms small rapids and wide flat pools, ideal for river rafting, which takes place on this part of the river. The Merced Canyon is scenic, but it cannot compare to Yosemite Valley. Driving through Merced Canyon on the way to the Valley gives one a slight taste of what is to come. As one drives out of Yosemite Valley, the Merced Canyon is an anticlimax.

At Bear Creek the all-year highway (State Highway 140) turns away from the Merced River toward Mariposa. The Merced River flows on through the foothills of the Sierra into what was once the Gold Country. Eventually, when the Merced River has almost reached the flat Central Valley, it is dammed for the first time, by the Exchequer Dam, one of the older California dams. The Merced River flows on across the Central Valley into the San Joaquin River, a muddy vestige of its former self.

The Merced River flows all year and takes on a different character in different seasons. In spring, as the snow pack melts, the water is high and torrential, pounding over the rocks with great force. It is ice cold. As summer approaches, the water becomes more placid, warm and perfect for a bracing swim. In fall the river gets slower as the fall colors reflect in its waters. Unlike Yosemite Falls and Bridalveil Fall, Nevada Fall and Vernal Fall continue to flow but with much less power. There is no mist on the Mist Trail. In winter the water is dark and cold. Then another season begins.

The Merced River occasionally floods Yosemite Valley, sometimes destructively. As much as 11 feet of water has been known to cover most of the Valley at the crest. When this happens, large trees are uprooted and debris piles up along the banks. Nearby meadows are muddy swamps. It is not a pretty sight.

Over the years the Merced River has known contact with various types of human beings. Yosemite Indians lived near it in Yosemite Valley for at least 1,000 years. Gold miners panned and dredged its waters in Merced Canyon and below. Thousands swam and rafted it the summers in Yosemite. Mist-drenched hikers on the way to Nevada Fall have been rained on by it.

Many backpackers have cooled themselves in the Merced River while visiting the High Country. Most of these visitors can be called "friends" of the Merced River. Until recently I have not been aware that the Merced River had any enemies.

Recently the Merced River acquired a new group of self-appointed friends and protectors who initiated litigation in the federal courts to protect the river. This set off a new round of controversy in the never-ending conflict between preservationists and visitors seeking enjoyment. The National Park Service is caught up in it, cast in the role of the enemy of the river. Does the Merced River care? I doubt it. While the litigants sweat and strain, the river just keeps on rolling along.

ENJOYING THE RIVER

During my early years in Yosemite, and well into the later years, I believed that the Merced River belonged almost entirely on the enjoyment side of the traditional dichotomy between enjoyment and preservation. I did not believe the Merced River was threatened or needed protection or preservation. My viewpoint has not changed much.

The Merced River flowed in front of our house at the end of The Row. As early as I can recall I was wading and swimming

Peter, enjoying the river.

in it during the summer. I do recall that water came across the road and up to our doorstep in the 1937 flood, when my parents were out of the Valley and a baby sitter was looking after me.

During my first summer working in Yosemite we held on to four corners of mattress covers and parachuted off Stoneman Bridge, near Camp Curry. The sandy beach below El Capitan where the employees and some visitors gathered to swim and sunbathe was always crowded in summer. There is no swimming there today. Yellow markers indicate areas of riverbank restoration. The main form of evening entertainment for summer employees used to be beach parties along the Merced River, where revelers gathered around fires and played guitars, and couples cuddled. This form of recreation has died out. Campers in campgrounds sought campsites close to the river. A row of tents along the river in the Housekeeping Camp was the premium accommodation, in great demand. Visitors lined up to switch to them when I was a desk clerk. I enjoyed rewarding nice families when I could. Now, after the 1997 flood, campgrounds have been moved to higher ground.

When I was an employee it was illegal to float down the river in rafts. We used to do it at night to enjoy the spectacular sight of a full moon on the cliffs above Yosemite Valley. Now rafts can be rented and can be seen dotting the river, so the river still provides recreation, but of a different sort.

When I worked in Yosemite Valley, our favorite swimming hole was a place called Steamboat, about halfway down Merced Canyon toward the Park entrance. A couple of giant boulders dominated a perfect swimming hole about ten feet below. We lay around in the sun on top of the rocks and dived off them on countless afternoons off. There was a rather difficult route up one side of the larger boulder, and we used to try to ascend it without falling off into the pool. We had parties out on the rock at night with portable radios. Steamboat was lost as a recreational mecca by a natural event, a rockslide that left a gash on the slope above and deposited debris into the perfect swimming hole. Also, a wall now blocks off access from the road.

During the summer months thousands of visitors have partaken of the bracing, refreshing waters of the Merced River. Many others have walked along its shores in all seasons and enjoyed the river as a backdrop to the mountains above. Its waters are clear, and the sandy and rocky bottom is visible in most places. The Merced River in Yosemite Valley has many moods, from torrential rushing to lazy meandering. The river can be destructive in floods, but, for the most part, it cleanses itself of any debris that falls into it. I do not recall ever seeing anything I would describe as pollution. One would see leaves and branches floating in the river and pollen collecting in eddies, but these are natural phenomena.

The Merced River is such a mighty, dynamic and prominent feature of Yosemite Valley that few traditionally thought much about it in terms of preservation or regarded the river as threatened in any way. Anyone who claims that the Merced River in Yosemite Valley is anything other than recreational is ignoring reality and history.

A spokesman for the "friends" was quoted in the media as complaining, "Yosemite is being loved to death," suggesting that a federal court can resolve that problem.

Dave Mihalic responded to this comment: "I used to say that 'loved to death' was a disingenuous term. I love my wife; I love my kids. I don't love them to death, and if I engage in actions harmful, I change. I love them 'to life.' But the answer in the parks is to remove the lover! Who benefits from that? Why, only those whose view of the world is better than mine, even though I 'love' Yosemite!"

THE PARK SERVICE BLINDSIDED
BY THE U.S. NINTH CIRCUIT COURT OF APPEALS

In 2007 I became interested in the litigation that had been filed by the Friends of the River. As an eyewitness to 75 years of action by the Merced River I considered myself a percipient witness who perhaps could be of some service. I have seen floods, and I have seen infrastructure relocated from areas near the river. I have seen restoration of river habitat. I have seen removal of the Old Village Store, the movie theatre and Degnans to locations away from the river, the removal of employee housing in Camp 6 adjacent to the river, and the closing off of El Capitan Beach, the most popular swimming hole in Yosemite Valley in my day as an employee. None of this was done because the Merced River had been designated wild and scenic. It was done because it was considered the right thing to do from the standpoint of reasonable park management.

I learned that Federal District Judge Ishii upheld most of the YVP, but there had been an appeal to the Ninth Circuit Court of Appeals, and the plan had been sent back for revision in 2005. I learned that there was further litigation and another appeal. I learned that mainstream environmental organizations such as the Sierra Club and the Wilderness Society were not supporting the Friends of Yosemite Valley. I learned that the Yosemite Fund had enlisted the support of other environmental organizations in filing an amicus curiae brief in support of the Park Service.

I learned that an injunction had been issued halting the Park Service from repairing some of the flood damage, authorized in the YVP, and impacting some Yosemite Fund projects. The Friends of Yosemite Valley were quoted in the media as saying they were trying to stop further "commercialization" of Yosemite Valley. I was somewhat surprised at this because the trend during my lifetime has been away from what I would call "commercialization," despite vastly increased visitation.

I wondered by what logic a tiny band of self-appointed "saviors" could bring the Park Service and the Yosemite Fund to a halt in the master planning process and prevent the Park Service from completing needed projects to repair damage caused by the 1997 flood. What could the Park Service have done to deserve such a fate?

In February 2007 I accepted an invitation to sit in on a planning session mandated by WASA pertaining to the Tuolumne River, which flows through areas of Yosemite National Park less developed than Yosemite Valley. The Park Service was attempting to avoid the problems encountered with the Merced River.

Among the participants in this meeting were two of the members of the Friends of Yosemite Valley, George Whitmore and Bridget Kerr. George Whitmore was one of the original climbers of El Capitan. Bridget Kerr was a young lady employed in the Park. I asked them what they were trying to accomplish in the litigation. They stated somewhat vaguely that they were trying to force the Park Service to follow the law. I asked why they wanted emergency road repairs and sewer repairs enjoined. They said they had no objection to emergency repairs.

I asked Mike Tollefson, then the superintendent, why there was a dispute over emergency repairs if the plaintiffs did not oppose them. He responded that repairs included upgrades to avoid future emergencies. Mike Tollefson said later that he believed that the plaintiffs simply wanted to stop anything the Park Service was doing as part of their declared goal of reducing visitation in Yosemite Valley.

I detected animosity between the plaintiffs and the Park Service. I asked the plaintiffs if they would consider mediation to resolve the dispute so visitors would not be caught up in litigation not of their making. The plaintiffs said they would welcome mediation. Mike Tollefson said that in all attempts to resolve the problem, plaintiffs had been totally uncompromising. I went away with the clear impression that the plaintiffs and the Park Service were on totally different wavelengths. I resolved to find out by what logic an appellate court had found in favor of plaintiffs. The result made no sense to me. I then gathered all the briefs and rulings and waded through them, a guaranteed formula for a migraine.

The smoking gun employed by the attorneys for the Friends of the River was a requirement in the WASA, which is not in the Organic Act of 1916, which entrusts management of national parks to the Park Service. That requirement is that any plan required by the WASA must "assess user capacity" for a wild and scenic river. This applies even to a corridor that has been designated "recreational." The Park Service has never been required by law to "assess user capacity" along the Merced River corridor within Yosemite Valley, or within Yosemite National Park. No court has determined what "assess user capacity" means, particularly when applied to a designated wild and scenic river within a developed area of a National Park.

Judge Ishii's initial ruling held that the Park Service had complied with the requirements of WASA by adopting a qualitative standard rather than a quantitative standard. In my opinion, the evidence overwhelmingly supported this finding.

The method used by the Park Service is known as the Visitor Experience and Resource Protection (VERP). The Park Service views management of user capacities as a proactive ongoing educational process which must be continually monitored under changing conditions, under the dual guidelines of the National Park Service Act, enjoyment and preservation. Many actions used by the Park Service to restrict and control excess visitor use were cited. The philosophy underlying the VERP approach is that if people appreciate and are educated about scenic values, they will neither denigrate nor despoil. The mantra of this approach is the slogan "Leave no trace."

Unfortunately, the U.S. Ninth Circuit Court of Appeals did not accept Judge Ishii's ruling. The reviewing court held in effect that the Park Service was required to add on to the VERP program a quantitative standard as to maximum visitor capacity. Stripped of its legalese, the reviewing court held that the Park Service must determine how many visitors can enjoy a river without degrading it. The Park Service contended that it could not do this without evaluating how the VERP program was working on an ongoing basis. The court stated that assessing user capacity...

> ...does not mean that NPS is precluded from using the VERP to fulfill the user capacities requirement...but that the VERP be implemented through the adoption of quantitative measures sufficient to ensure its effectiveness as a current measure of user capacities... it may be able to comply with the user capacity mandate in the interim by implementing preliminary or temporary limits of some kind. [348 F2d at p 9 of 15)

My legal mind fails to grasp what this means.

In a gigantic display of overkill, the reviewing court went on to enjoin improvements to flood damage in Yosemite Valley until this elusive question was resolved. In addition to that, the court invalidated the entire Yosemite Valley Plan, which had been upheld except for the "assess user capacity" requirement, and one other minor issue.

I pondered the question, "How is the Park Service supposed to comply with this directive as a practical matter?" The visitor use simply cannot be addressed quantitatively without being arbitrary. The number of visitors in the Merced River corridor changes by the hour, if not by the minute, every day. There is no practical way of enforcing any restriction. It cannot be assumed that the mere physical presence of any given number of people will denigrate the river or destroy the visitor experience of others. It depends on what the viewers do. If people throw trash into the river or ride dirt bikes over meadows, a very small number can create environmental damage. What about the time-honored custom of skipping rocks in the river? Should this be prohibited?

The reasoning of the U.S. Ninth Circuit Court of Appeals, which I consider to be seriously flawed, is that the court stated expressly that WSRA did not require a quantitative standard as to the number of viewers who could look at a river without degrading it. However, they sent the case back to the District Judge to impose one, anyway.

In my opinion the U.S. Ninth Circuit Court violated the cardinal principle of administrative law that a court cannot substitute its judgment for the judgment of an administrative agency having jurisdiction unless the action of the administrative agency is arbitrary and capricious. The U.S. Ninth Circuit expressly determined that the Park Service did not act arbitrarily or capriciously. The court clearly substituted its judgment for that of the Park Service that a qualitative standard under VERP could address user capacity without imposing a quantitative limit on visitors. In my view, the opinion was a blatant act of judicial activism.

David Mihalic points out that the Park Service did consider quantitative limits and even suggested one in the 1980 General Management Plan, which has never been invalidated by a court, but considered VERP a preferable management tool. I did not note that this was brought to the attention of the court.

Whatever other effect the ruling may have, a new buzzword has been invented—"visitor capacity"—which we are likely to find preached by the purists. To my mind this is just another way of saying the visitor is the enemy.

The court ruling was not expected by the Park Service, which felt their diligent efforts in crafting the extensive Yosemite Valley Plan would be upheld. The ruling left the Park Service with a bad choice. Appealing the ruling to the U.S. Supreme Court was not an option, because this decision was up to the Justice Department, not the Park Service. The Justice Department no doubt figured it had more pressing matters to be resolved than how many people can view a river without denigrating and destroying the experience for others.

So the Park Service embarked on its only real perceived option, back to the drawing board, another attempt to reconcile WASA with the Organic Act creating the Park Service, with the result likely to be challenged in court again.

A DUBIOUS COMPROMISE

On September 29, 2009, a settlement agreement and stipulation were entered into, which resulted in the dismissal of the lawsuit. The parties reached the settlement through the court-authorized mediation process authorized by Magistrate Judge Sandra M. Snyder.

The settlement authorized the Park Service to continue certain maintenance projects that had been enjoined. The settlement authorized continuing mediation in the event of further disputes, while reserving the right of the parties to go back to court if the mediation should fail, since mediation is a voluntary procedure in which neither party is obligated to accept the recommendations of the mediator.

The settlement also directed the Park Service to redo the 2000 YVP, despite the fact that the court had previously approved most of the recommendations in the plan.

In the settlement the Park Service agreed to pay $1,025,000 to the attorneys for the plaintiffs. Mike Tollefson, superintendent of the Park Service during the litigation, philosophically observed, "I thought it would be more."

What did the National Park Service do to deserve this penalty paid by taxpayer dollars? They failed to please everyone. That was a given from the start.

A purist would say that the attorneys were appropriately rewarded for their role as saintly saviors, rescuing Yosemite from the evils of "commercialization." A cynic, on the other hand, would regard the attorneys as environmental ambulance chasers and would suspect that the million dollars is only a down payment on the next lawsuit.

Readers may draw their own conclusions.

What did taxpayers get for their million dollars? They got three years of uncertainty concerning the future of Yosemite, forcing the park service to restart the planning process. The plan that had been challenged in only one respect had to be thrown out completely.

A visitor/taxpayer/beneficial owner of Yosemite might well ask, as I asked, wouldn't the million dollars be better spent on repairing the Yosemite infrastructure that had been damaged by the flood? The attorneys' fees came from a fund that was intended for flood damage repair.

WHAT NEXT?

The planning process has started all over again and will take three years at a cost that would seem enormous to anyone other than people spending taxpayer dollars. The Park Service personnel charged with the project will go on stoically doing as directed.

Because of the reasoning of the court, the focus of the new plan will likely shift to protecting the river rather than to maintaining the infrastructure of Yosemite Valley.

As of this writing we do not know the end of the story. Not only do we not know the particulars of the plan that will be created, but also, in these economically difficult times, we do not even know whether or not the plan will, in fact, ever be funded. In the meantime, the Merced River, the nominal real party in interest in the litigation, will be indifferent to the outcome.

The most important party of interest in the litigation, the American taxpayer, park visitor and beneficial owner, was not represented in the litigation. In the ensuing, as in the last, planning process, their voice will likely be drowned out by the louder voices of the dueling environmentalists.

A POTENTIAL FUTURE CONCERN

This potential future concern is expressed from a Park Service perspective by Dave Mihalic:

> The new plan will focus on the "outstandingly remarkable values" (ORVs) identified for the Merced River. The total length of the Merced River is 81 miles, but the plan will focus on the 7 miles in Yosemite Valley that is not designated as "wild" but is likely to be treated as such. As a result, the policies for a general park management plan will focus on the river, rather than on Yosemite Valley as a whole, under the Wild and Scenic Rivers Act, which will trump other laws and considerations. This will devalue the National Park designation. The Wild and Scenic River designation is now being viewed as equivalent to any Yosemite Valley master plan.

> This is the rationale behind negotiating away the Yosemite Valley Plan. The government has agreed to a position that flies in the face of established practice and planning policies and congressional intent in declaring Yosemite to be a public trust. There are huge ramifications, many of which are unknown. However, what it seems to say is that the requirement of the 1916 act establishing the Park Service that use of Yosemite be balanced between enjoyment and preservation is secondary to the requirements of preserving the "outstanding remarkable values" dictated by the Wild and Scenic Rivers Act. If this happens it will be a huge government betrayal of the public trust which the National Park Service is entrusted with administering.

It remains to be seen whether this dire prediction will come true. The plan has yet to be approved and implemented. More litigation may follow. It is certainly arguable that if the act establishing the Park Service is to be trumped by WSRA, Congress must do it. It cannot be accomplished by a settlement in which the public, the beneficial owner, is unrepresented. I would be very surprised to see legislators elected by people rather than rivers make such a statement. In my view, saying that WSRA trumps the public trust is saying that rivers are more important than people.

WHAT WILL BE THE IMPACT ON THE AVERAGE VISITOR?

For the next three years the planning process will be reinstituted, resulting in scoping sessions (public hearings culminating in a lengthy summary) which probably will be indigestible to most people. While the process is ongoing, rumors will fly and the media may engage in exit polls at the public hearings which will generate misinformation. The usual loud and strident voices of the environmental purists will be heard.

However, as in the last public hearings, the voices of people of modest means who do not wish to be shut out of Yosemite may speak with a louder voice. There will be no consensus. Some are certain not to be satisfied. There may be more litigation. The mediation process in the settlement agreement might make it less protracted, and, in a best-case scenario, it could produce a result that warring factions can at least live with. At best, the process will be tedious.

There will be a greater focus on protecting the river. There is likely to be a user capacity lid placed on day use visitors to Yosemite, based on what so-called experts say. If I were in the position of either the Park Service or the concessioner, I would bite the bullet, accept the pressures being brought to bear, accept a reservation system for day use as the least undesirable and least expensive option, fine-tune it and try to make it work. Only in times of peak visitation will it even be needed. As a visitor, I could live with it.

The Friends of the River would like to see all visitor accommodations removed from Yosemite Valley. The court decision slowed down Park Service efforts to make needed repairs in Yosemite Valley but did not stop these efforts. The Park Service will very likely again reject the drastic solution of removing all visitor accommodations or even significantly reducing them, as they have consistently recommended. If the Park Service were to recommend drastic reductions in visitor accommodations in Yosemite Valley, there would be a public outcry heard 'round the world, which would surely be heard by politicians in Congress. It is hard to imagine Congress appropriating funds for such action in a time of massive deficits. I just don't think it will happen.

I do not believe a court has jurisdiction to order the removal of all visitor accommodations in Yosemite Valley or even to order a drastic reduction, in opposition to a Park Service recommendation against doing so. Surely a decision to maintain the status quo by the Park Service cannot be regarded as arbitrary and capricious by even the most activist of courts. The Ninth Circuit came nowhere near ordering this in the recent litigation, which did not even address visitor accommodations.

When the dust settles after the plan is completed and considerable money and energy expended, a difference may not be readily apparent except to a sophisticated visitor. The river waters cannot speak to the quixotic efforts by their "friends" to protect the river, unless perhaps the continuing rush of water is laughter.

Tent camping in the meadow was appropriate at one time.

Chapter 20

What Is Appropriate in Yosemite

There has been a recurring dispute during my lifetime as to what activities are appropriate and inappropriate in Yosemite, and in Yosemite Valley in particular. The debate has intensified as there are more visitors, and as the pendulum of Park Service management philosophy swings more toward preservation and away from enjoyment. Historically there was not as much of an issue, because the Park Service wanted to encourage visitation in order to protect Yosemite from miners, loggers and sheepherders. Therefore, the Park Service was more tolerant of enticing visitors with entertainment and amusements that could be found in other resorts.

There are varying schools of thought. On one extreme there are those who believe that nothing should be allowed except activities directly related to appreciation of nature: hiking, biking, naturalist talks, slide shows, etc. On the opposite extreme are those who would allow the concessioner to provide any kind of activity the guests enjoy, as long as it does not damage the environment. There are shades of opinion in between, with very little agreement.

I have presented this quandary at a talk I was giving, and listed activities that have been carried on in Yosemite in my lifetime. I asked for a show of hands as to which activities were considered appropriate. There was universal disagreement. Some activities that have no relationship with nature, such as the Bracebridge Dinner, have been grandfathered in because they are traditional and have no direct impact on the environment. Others, like the fire fall, have been phased out because they are considered man-made attractions.

A colloquial way of asking the question as to appropriateness would be: "If Yosemite is regarded as a natural cathedral, is there anything wrong with playing bingo in the parish hall?"

As a starting point only an extremist would agree that basic comfortable lodging and food are not appropriate. Only an extremist on the other end of the spectrum would consider gambling casinos, strip malls and theme parks appropriate. All manner of guest services in between the extremes are subject to potential controversy. How is the Park Service, the regulatory agency in charge, supposed to make these judgment calls?

The activities of the concessioner are regulated down to what can be charged for candy bars and served for meals. Profits are limited by what can be charged. For this reason major hotel chains are not interested in operating in national parks. Not enough profit can be made, and operators of major hotel chains chafe at restrictions imposed on what guest services they can provide.

There are guidelines and standards imposed by Congress, as part of what has been called the 1998 Omnibus Management Act. The latest act is entitled Public Law 105-391 and can be found in Title 36 CFR 51. The trend has been to tighten up standards. The basic standard is what is necessary or appropriate, considering that the Park is being set aside so the visitor can enjoy its natural beauty. A superintendent has considerable discretion but cannot be totally arbitrary.

Superintendents may disagree and have disagreed. As a general rule a concessioner must demonstrate some relation between the proposed activity and the enhancement of the appreciation of the visitor for the natural attractions of the Park, or some necessity apart from that.

One example concerns the placing of television sets in rooms at the Ahwahnee Hotel. Superintendents in other parks had considered it inappropriate for a visitor to come to a national park and sit in a hotel room and watch television. On the other hand, when Superintendent Dave Mihalic considered this he concluded that television could be a tool for informing visitors about Yosemite and getting across the message the Park Service wanted to get across. He also felt that if someone had hiked all day and wanted to watch a favorite program at night, there was nothing seriously wrong with that. Thus, not only did the superintendent exercise some discretion, he left some discretion to the visitor, who could watch Oprah instead of viewing Yosemite Falls. The same discretion rests with a visitor in an RV in a campground.

An example of the necessity side of the coin is the wine tasting seminars held in the Ahwahnee. At first glance these may seem inappropriate, and some of my friends have asked me why they are allowed.

The justification is that the guidelines stipulate that the concessioner is entitled to make a profit. At the same time the concessioner is required to stay open in the off-season when there are not enough visitors to justify staying open if the concessioner had a choice. Also, being able to keep employees year 'round is considered a benefit to the visitor. Therefore the concessioner is allowed to hold some events in the off-season to attract visitors. All this needs to be monitored as conditions change. There is far less of an off-season now than there was when I was growing up. Skiing was established at Badger Pass almost a century ago to attract visitors to Yosemite in winter and has now become a tradition.

One additional example involves a music festival called Vintage Days that has now been discontinued, to my regret. Tom Bopp, a popular Yosemite musician and historian (see Chapter 22) persuaded the Park Service to allow the event because it featured the music that was popular when the Ahwahnee was built and thus had historical significance. It was held on weeknights in winter, so it also satisfied the necessity requirement because visitation was slow at the time.

In my opinion the existing system works reasonably well. Someone must make the judgment calls about appropriateness. The superintendent is the logical person to exercise discretion, assisted by a staff on the scene. Obviously these decisions should not be made by bureaucrats in Washington, D.C.

Those who believe that the people are the enemy, or those who believe that nothing should be done to "market" Yosemite, may well disagree with the approach that Congress has selected. However, anyone who has read this far must realize that these folks and I dance to a different drummer.

Many visitors believe that the National Park Service has always been providing oversight in Yosemite. They are unaware of all the politics, passion and controversy that have brought us to where we are. Most visitors tend to accept somewhat passively any restrictions that the Park Service imposes, even if they disagree with them.

As Ken Burns noted, "For the first time in human history great sections of our natural landscape were set aside—not for kings and noblemen or the very rich—but for everyone for all time." Yosemite is part of an experiment, ongoing and still recent in history. Those who conceived the idea of national parks would not have conceived the reality of 3,000,000 to 4,000,000 visitors a year.

The granite walls, domes, spires and waterfalls will endure. Visitors surely will not damage them permanently by just gathering to gaze at them. The Ahwahneechees who lived in Yosemite had many legends about the natural features and assigned human personalities to some of them. If these human personalities could express themselves they would no doubt be amused at the swirling debates about what is right for Yosemite.

Humans are puny by comparison to the natural features. While the debate goes on, the Park Service, concessioners and nonprofits will do the job of day-to-day management as best they can. The words of Abraham Lincoln, who first signed the proclamation setting aside Yosemite to the people, will resound, somewhat paraphrased. "You can please some of the people all of the time. You can please all of the people some of the time. But you cannot please all of the people all of the time."

It is virtually certain that many visitors will want to continue to come to Yosemite to receive the "glad tidings." For some it will be a first visit. For others it will be a return visit. Many will put up with some inconvenience in order to be able to visit Yosemite Valley. Many will be willing to pay a premium to stay overnight in Yosemite Valley, instead of staying outside the Park and being bussed in or driving in under restrictions. They will relish the experience of waking up to the magnificence of Yosemite or watching the sunset as it climbs up the granite walls. These visitors will want to experience Yosemite in their own way. Others will say it is too crowded, or too inconvenient, or too expensive, or there is not enough to do, and they will go elsewhere. So be it.

Foreign visitors are likely to continue to flock to Yosemite to see one of the wonders of the world. Already the many languages heard in Yosemite Valley cause the Valley to sound like the Tower of Babel. Excessive, heavy-handed restrictions on visitors could have international repercussions.

All in all I see no need for drastic changes in Yosemite Valley, based on someone's notion as to what is appropriate, nor do I see any reason for any visitor to bewail the loss of anything vital. The essence remains, and can be found with a little effort, education and direction.

CHAPTER 21

OFF AND ON RELATIONSHIP WITH THE SIERRA CLUB

The Sierra Club has an identity in the minds of many larger than itself. To some the Sierra Club represents the premier organization fighting for preservation of the environment. To others it is an obstructionist group of elitists trying to stop progress with litigation.

The Sierra Club is a very large organization that has always been characterized by internal disagreements among its leaders and members. Although the Sierra Club, under the leadership of John Muir, was a prime mover in opposition to the dam at Hetch Hetchy, a considerable number of its members at the time, including some prominent members, supported the dam. Ever since John Muir, the founder of the Sierra Club, and Gifford Pinchot, the founder of the U.S. Forest Service, split rather decidedly over their differing views on conservation of natural resources, their respective missions have at times clashed. Throughout its history the Sierra Club has never spoken with a single voice.

As a child of a family involved in concessions in Yosemite I grew up with a negative view of the Sierra Club. Concessioners tended to equate the Sierra Club with opposition to recreational services they wanted to provide for visitors, regardless of the source of the opposition. At the same time Ansel Adams was a prominent director of the Sierra Club (albeit he had his share of disagreements with other directors), and, as an admirer of Ansel, I concluded there must be some good in the organization if Ansel was part of it. Thus, I grew up and have always been somewhat schizoid about the Sierra Club.

I have twice joined and twice resigned from the Sierra Club. At present I am not a member. Some find this incongruous, concluding that anyone who grew up in Yosemite must be a Sierra Club camp follower. It is not so.

In 1913 the Sierra Club acquired private property inside Yosemite National Park at Tuolumne Meadows adjacent to Soda Springs from a homesteader, John Lembert, and owned it for over 50 years. Parsons Lodge, an imposing stone structure, was built on the property in the 1930s and maintained by the Sierra Club, who kept a caretaker on the property. The Sierra Club also maintained a campground on the property, which they utilized to launch popular outings into the nearby Yosemite backcountry. The Sierra Club campground, in the meadows along the Tuolumne River, was a favorite camping spot for our family. We camped there every year for a number of years. I confess that my first selfish reason for joining the Sierra Club was to be able to camp in this premier campground.

In the late 1950s or early 1960s, the Sierra Club deeded the campground and Parsons Lodge to the federal government. The Park Service promptly closed the campground. I am unclear why the Sierra Club made this decision, and I do not really care. I consider it a very ill-advised decision, then and now, to give up such a prime parcel of real estate, even to a National Park held in a public trust. With

Typical Sierra Club outing in the wilderness. Courtesy of Adams Family Collection.

the campground closed, I saw no reason to continue being a member of the Sierra Club, and I resigned.

I moved to Monterey County in 1962, the same year that Ansel and Virginia Adams moved to Carmel Highlands. I was invited to a meeting at Ansel's home to form a new chapter of the Sierra Club. I became a charter member, largely out of deference to Ansel. I remained a member for a number of years and participated in some hikes and activities. We took the boys on a couple of Wilderness Threshold trips operated by the Sierra Club, but gradually became less active. I watched what I perceived to be a growing number of urban types becoming involved in development issues having nothing to do with the Sierra. I watched the club become more political and litigious. In my mind the Sierra Club was straying from its original purpose. Finally, I resigned again and have not rejoined.

During his summer as manager of Sunrise High Sierra Camp, my son Vince encountered a number of arrogant Sierra Club members, by no means typical, but who sometimes give the Sierra Club a bad name. These people would act as if they owned the mountains, ask for free showers and ask that their garbage be hauled out, and would sometimes act as if they deserved special treatment for causing Yosemite to be set aside as a public trust. The Sierra Club, under the leadership of John Muir, played a role, but by no means was the exclusive cause.

On issues pertaining to Yosemite the Sierra Club seldom takes a unified position. The club consists of different chapters that often take differing positions. Individual members often hold widely divergent viewpoints and range from purists to supporters of visitors and concessioners. No individual truly speaks for the Sierra Club as a whole. The Sierra Club is not normally critical of the Park Service in general, but some chapters and individuals sometimes disagree on particular issues.

Kevin Cann, deputy superintendent in Yosemite under five superintendents, reported that MPR arranged a "debate" between the Park Service and the Sierra Club, anticipating a spirited argumentative session. The spokesmen expressed agreement on most subjects, disappointing those who arranged the program. Kevin best characterized the position of the Sierra Club toward Yosemite as "amorphous," which authenticates my perception.

In the letters of Ansel Adams I noted an estrangement from the Sierra Club at higher levels somewhat parallel to mine. In 1968, after a meeting at Clair Tappan Lodge which Ansel described as "the blackest day in the history of the Sierra Club," Ansel considered resigning as a director and wrote to the other directors:

> The hatred which the actions, and chiefly the attitudes of the Sierra Club have engendered in ever-widening circles in the outer world will be a long time healing. The opposition is not necessarily evil; perhaps only lacking the education and the motives for more conservation thought and action. We should first try cooperation, then persuasion; then we will have to fight. But to begin an episode with the conviction that the 'other side' is evil, crooked, predatory and dishonest is to lose half the battle to begin with. I hear sickening, vituperative, paranoid statements about people we have to deal with, and I am ashamed (and startled) with the logic and tactics involved. I am certain that if we are to be effective in the future we will have to consider the entire human 'picture' and attempt some compassion-ate understanding of attitudes and requirements other than ours.

This statement was brought about by a situation in which the Sierra Club

Log enclosure at Soda Springs Tuolumne Meadows, on land the Sierra Club gave away. Courtesy of Yosemite Research Library.

had opposed the location of a nuclear power plant to be built by PG& E at Nipomo Dunes, and agreed not to oppose an alternate site at Diablo Canyon if PG&E would choose the alternate location. Ansel felt that this was a milestone in cooperation, and that cooperation was not compromise. Some directors and members of the Sierra Club disagreed and felt that both locations should be opposed after PG&E had acted upon a perceived deal. Ansel's view prevailed in a vote by the membership.

The tendency to be uncompromising, to be more litigious and to regard opponents as evil brought about my resignation from the Sierra Club. Ansel continued as a director and continued to try to sell his viewpoint. This brought him into conflict with his long time associate and friend Dave Brower. Dave Brower became increasingly more uncompromising, dictatorial and prone to act without authority of the Board of Directors. Ansel was forced to lead a group calling for the dismissal of his longtime friend as executive director of the Sierra Club. Dave Brower went on to leadership positions in other conservation organizations where his uncompromising style caused him trouble again.

However, the relationship with the Adams family apparently healed. I attended social functions at the Adams home after Brower was dismissed as leader of the Sierra Club. There was a convivial atmosphere. On a personal level I found Dave Brower to be a friendly, cordial and interesting person.

In 1971 Ansel resigned the position he held as a director of the Sierra Club since 1934, stating in his letter of resignation, "It is imperative that the governing body—the directors—be composed of experts in the important fields of law, politics, science and finance. I do not fit into any of those categories; my contributions have been (and will continue) in the fields of creative photography and the interpretation and aesthetic appreciation of the natural scene."

Since Ansel's resignation I have observed a continuation of attitudes that Ansel criticized in 1968, and a perpetuation of the idea that compromise is capitulation. I am not at all sure the leadership has been as recommended by Ansel in 1971. However, as I noted above, the Sierra Club is truly amorphous.

Jeffrey Pine Cones. Della Hoss print. Courtesy of Creative Offsprings.

CHAPTER 22

THE MUSE IN YOSEMITE

ART IN YOSEMITE

Artists have been drawn to Yosemite since visitors have come to Yosemite.

The work of early artists was instrumental in attracting visitors to Yosemite, as have been the words of John Muir and the photographs of Ansel Adams and other photographers. Much of the artwork of early artists can be seen in Yosemite, in the Ahwahnee Hotel, Yosemite Lodge, and the Museum and Visitor Center.

There are too many leading Yosemite artists to mention. If I attempted to do so, I would risk omitting someone significant who put his or her individual stamp on Yosemite art. For anyone interested in Yosemite artists, there are many better sources. I will therefore limit my comments to those artists with whom I have personal acquaintance, outside of my immediate family. My mother, Della, was, of course, a recognized Yosemite artist, who did Ahwahnee menus for many years, in addition to the linoleum block prints in *Trees of Yosemite*, which have been mentioned elsewhere in this book.

I did meet Chiura Obata, one of the artists recognized in the Visitor Center, who contributed art with a distinct Japanese flavor. He was a Native American Japanese who taught art at University of California Berkeley, but this did not prevent him from being sent to an internment camp during World War II, now recognized as perhaps one of the most unforgivable civil rights violations in American history. Chiura Obata was a delightful and humble man. He was a devoted baseball fan. He wore a hearing aid that had a built-in device that allowed him to tune into baseball games when conversation bored him.

Chuck Eckart is a shirttail relative and old friend. We have the same stepfather, Hil Oehlmann, Sr. Chuck has created art in many different mediums, and has done distinctive art in Yosemite.

Kay Pitts, whose exploits have been reported elsewhere in this book, has also earned a spot in the Visitor Center. Kay is instigator of an annual competitive exhibit and an artist-in-residence program called Yosemite Renaissance.

Kay described the start of the Yosemite Renaissance: A Woman of Immense Proportions (WIP) served as the executive director of the Mariposa

County Arts Council, which was the umbrella organization for the Renaissance nonprofit status. "The county is going to give money to the arts," the woman told Kay. "Let's make a joint presentation." Kay helped put the presentation together; the WIP presented it and then told Kay the good news that the Mariposa Arts Council and her Yosemite Renaissance were to split a $15,000 grant. The Renaissance used the money to hire an executive director and hired the WIP as an interim director. When the new hire assumed the position, The WIP waged war against the man, routinely writing 10- and 12-page diatribes against him.

Everything came apart when Kay ran into a member of the Board of Supervisors. "How are you using the $15,000?" the man asked her. "We only are using the $7,500," Kay replied. He then told her that the Yosemite Renaissance was supposed to get the whole grant.

When Kay contacted her for the rest of the money, the WIP said that she was going to destroy the entry slides and thus destroy Yosemite Renaissance. At first the board told Kay there was nothing they could do to help, but Kay said, "You don't know me. I'm a relative stranger to you. What you don't know is that I am personally acquainted with the people running things in Sacramento. If you let this woman destroy Yosemite Renaissance, I assure you that I'll shut the Mariposa County Arts Council right down."

She got the slides back, the WIP got fired, and what turned out to be a pattern of malfeasance caused the State of California to shut down funding to the Arts Council. Then Kay showed what a quality person she was by going to bat for them, explaining to the people in charge in Sacramento that the Board members were victims not perpetrators. The Mariposa County Arts Council got their funding restored.

The Yosemite Renaissance thrived under Kay's direction as president and especially under the leadership of Bob Woolard, the executive director who, I'm told, the WIP had opposed with apparent malice. Her service has earned Kay a position among the preeminent artists on display in the Yosemite Visitors Center.

Kay creates acrylic paintings.

WRITERS ABOUT YOSEMITE

There has been more written about Yosemite than anyone can read.

I will mention only a few writings that have been meaningful to me. I will no doubt bypass some good writing.

First, any of John Muir's many writings will be likely to evoke a strong passion for Yosemite. John Muir captured its essence most eloquently in the written word.

For those who would like to know more about Ansel Adams, his autobiography does a good job of chronicling his many accomplishments. If a reader is interested in how Ansel's creative thought process evolved, and how he felt about many subjects, the best read is *Ansel Adams: Letters, 1916-1984*, published by Little, Brown and Co. Ansel was prolific letter writer and communicated his ideas and thoughts to friends on a regular basis. A reader will feel they know Ansel well after reading this work.

As noted in Chapter 23 and elsewhere in this book, any of Shirley Sargent's many books are the best way to learn about the people who shaped Yosemite and the Yosemite experience. Shirley writes in great detail after thorough research.

Another book that will describe what it is like to live in the Yosemite community is *My Heart and Home* by Marian Woessner, wife of Yosemite dentist Charlie Woessner (Fithian Press, Santa Barbara, 2002). This book covers the time period from 1951 to 1998, after the time my family moved on.

In 1928 my uncle, Frank J. Taylor, a well known writer of his time, collaborated with Horace Albright, one of the founders of the National Park Service, to write a book about rangers of that era entitled *Oh Ranger* (Stanford University Press, 1929). The book was illustrated by my aunt, Ruth Taylor White, a talented cartographer.

Then there is, of course, the book entitled *Trees of Yosemite*, written by Mary Curry Tresidder and illustrated by my mother (Stanford University Press, 1935).

For a description of some famed Yosemite characters whom I never met, and a good history of Yosemite, *Yosemite, Its Discovery, Its Wonders, and its People* by Margaret Sanborn is a good read (Random House and Yosemite Association, 1981 and 1989).

For a hilarious cartoon characterization of Yosemite, it is hard to improve on *Fur and Loafing* (Yosemite Association, 1999) by the late Phil Frank, who created the cartoon character Farley. In this delightful satire you will meet bears who move to San Francisco in the winter to watch the Giants, the ranger Stern Grove, who presides over Asphalt State Park, and Mrs. Mellmac, who vacuums pine needles from her campsite, because "Mother Nature is a slob."

Finally, any of Hank Johnson's books contain accurate historical information and good stories about Yosemite. Hank was a long time resident of Yosemite.

These books all illuminate the human side of the Yosemite experience and the personalities who have contributed to it. They illustrate a point that I have been trying to emphasize throughout this book: that people are an integral part of the Yosemite experience. The human presence demonstrates that the Yosemite experience is about more than just viewing spectacular scenery.

This brings me to a final discussion of another book about Yosemite. I was amazed to find a book about Yosemite by an author who shares with me a genuinely passionate feeling for Yosemite. However, I disagree with him on almost every major point. The book is entitled *Yosemite: The Embattled Wilderness* by Alfred Runte (University of Nebraska Press, 1990).

Alfred Runte is identified on the book cover as an environmental historian based in Seattle, Washington, and a leading authority on national park history and management. In the acknowledgment on page xi, Runte points out that his management experience in Yosemite is limited to "beginning in 1980, work seasonally in Yosemite Valley through 1983, giving walks, campfire lectures, and seminars as a park naturalist." He goes on to state, "My knowledge of park history, I admit, was sometimes uncomfortable for management personnel, who expected history to vindicate their actions rather than suggest a possible need for critical review."

My disagreement with Runte starts with the title of his book: *Yosemite, The Embattled Wilderness.* I have put forth the view in Chapter 16 that Yosemite Valley is not now and never has been a wilderness by any current definition. Runte's book is largely about Yosemite Valley, not the 95% of Yosemite National Park that comes much closer to the definition of wilderness.

The battle that Runte characterizes is one in which Runte and his followers hope to turn a prime recreational area into a wilderness. The opposing forces, which Runte characterizes as "commercial," want to retain Yosemite Valley as a prime recreational destination. The latter forces are in control. Runte must realize that his forces are greatly outnumbered by 3,000,000 to 4,000,000 annual visitors who are willing to accept Yosemite Valley as it is, even if some of them would like to see some changes.

He must realize also that the Park Service, which manages Yosemite Valley, does not share his vision for Yosemite Valley, which he acknowledges. Runte and his followers cannot hope to win the battle by direct action. Instead they must resort to chipping away at the enjoyment of the visitor by guerilla warfare, if conflict about the future of Yosemite Valley is deemed to be a battle.

I see the current conflict much differently than Runte sees it. When Abraham Lincoln designated Yosemite Valley as a place to be enjoyed by all of the public, he set in motion a social experiment, radical at the time, which is still ongoing. He did not envision a battle akin to a civil war between the public, for whom Yosemite Valley is held in trust, and Runte's small band of revolutionaries, who want to dictate to the public how they must enjoy Yosemite Valley, if at all.

In the first ten chapters Runte traces environmental history of Yosemite quite accurately, purposely deemphasizing the human side of the history of Yosemite, as he explains. He credits the accuracy of much of the research to two ladies from the Yosemite Research Library who I have known personally, the late Mary Vocelka, wife of a concessioner executive, and Linda Eade, currently in charge of the Yosemite Research Library. I will second Runte's praise for the Yosemite Research Library, which is gold mine of information on the history of Yosemite.

Runte unfolds his vision of what he believes is the highest and best use of Yosemite Valley. That vision is for the Valley to become a nature sanctuary where scientists can study ecology and biodiversity in a natural setting as little undisturbed by human intervention as possible. According to Runte, all activities not focused on this vision should be prohibited. I do not question the idea that this vision should take place somewhere, but I do question that it be accomplished by displacing the many visitors who have come to know Yosemite Valley as a prime recreational destination. To me it would seem better, and surely less controversial, to place Runte's nature sanctuary in an area that has never ceased to be wilderness.

Mr. Runte may not be aware that the Park Service in Yosemite maintains a large staff engaged in research, scientific and interpretive studies. I talked with several of these researchers, and they all advise that their studies and the present level of visitation are not mutually exclusive; the visitors do not interfere with ongoing research and scientific studies. It is neither necessary nor appropriate to banish or limit visitors in order to continue scientific research.

In the later chapters, Runte joins the "visitor is the enemy" crusade with great zeal, although he reserves his greatest animus for the concessioners. He poses this question: "What potential effect would pandering to the tourists have on the long-term integrity of the Park and its resources?" He characterizes the concessioners as profit-driven operators to whom "the natural features of the Park were just something more to be sold."

I do not take this and other derogatory comments about the integrity of family and many friends personally. It is simply that Runte has never known any of the concessioner executives personally, as I have known them. If he had known them, he would have realized that most, if not all, of them came to Yosemite because they love the natural features of the Park as much as Runte, and that they have been just as committed to preserving its natural features, but for a different purpose, so that the public, not just environmental scientists, can enjoy them.

To Alfred Runte, what Ken Burns describes as America's Best Idea is a management failure in need of drastic corrective measures. I searched Runte's tome for signs of humor, humility and humanity and found little if any. Could I as a visitor pass the litmus test put forth by Runte and his followers, even though tainted by past and present association with concessioners? If I were to be allowed to return to my roots by visiting the reconstituted natural sanctuary Mr. Runte and his followers would like to see, I don't think it would be much fun. I don't think I would enjoy it much or see many of my friends.

MUSIC IN YOSEMITE

Tom Bopp can be found playing the piano at Wawona five nights a week and singing anything from old Yosemite songs to almost anything written from 1920 through 1940. He knows most of the lyrics. He can also be found occasionally playing at the Ahwahnee during the winter. Tom is also an historian of Yosemite, particularly Wawona. He was kind enough to contribute the article on music in Yosemite, page 209, he being the ultimate authority. In my judgment he has earned the designation Icon.

Tom grew up in Southern California and learned to play the piano early in life. He earned a degree in music theory and composition at UCLA. He worked briefly as a piano tuner before landing a job at an establishment known as Joanne's Chili Bordello, which advertised "17 varieties of chili served in an atmosphere of sin." When Tom told the owner he could only play a half hour of ragtime, the owner told him, "Don't worry about it. Just repeat. No one will notice."

In 1983 Tom was hired as a substitute piano player at Wawona for a week, then a second week, then the summer. He was rehired for three additional summers and returned to JoAnne's in the winter, moving from the sublime to the ridiculous. Finally Tom was hired permanently and moved to Oakhurst, with his wife, Diane, a teacher. Tom later moved to Fish Camp, which Tom referred to as an upgrade. Since then Tom has found his niche as musician and historian and become a Yosemite institution. But for a chance gig at Wawona, Tom might be a piano tuner playing part time piano in a chili bordello, a waste of talent for sure. That is how it sometimes goes with chance visits to Yosemite.

Tom describes his experience as follows: "I had two ambitions as a kid—to live in the mountains and get a job playing the piano. When I got the Wawona job, I fulfilled two life ambitions in one shot. That was it. I reached Nirvana."

"Music And The Yosemite Experience"
by Tom Bopp

"Vintage Songs of Yosemite," a project to discover and preserve Yosemite's musical heritage, got its start when curator David Forgang ran across a few copies of old Yosemite-related sheet music in the Yosemite Museum Collections. Forgang knows I enjoy performing obscure old songs as pianist at Yosemite's Wawona Hotel (my job since 1983), so he made copies for me. His idea was to have me record the songs for inclusion in the 1990 Yosemite Park Centennial exhibit. Before then, I was but dimly aware that Yosemite had any musical heritage at all. Now, after years of concerted digging, it turns out that there is far more Yosemite music than perhaps anyone had ever imagined, and that this charming aspect of cultural history has a poignant and relevant message for Yosemite's visitors and protectors.

> ...Each day from dawn to dawn,
> Only the merry song,
> Is ever heard here in Yosemite!
> — *From the 1954 song, "Yosemite," by Harry Mabry.*

10,000 years ago, a warming trend began to melt Yosemite's glaciers, creating "Lake Yosemite," which had to fill with silt before any land animals could move in. The first human habitation in the area dates to this period, suggesting that we are no less indigenous to Yosemite Valley than any other land animal, no less a part of Yosemite's ecosystem. With the arrival of the first plan life and animals, lightning fires and bird songs animated the early Yosemite environment. Likewise, the combination of campfire and song very likely accompanied the first human visitors, thousands of years ago.

Myths, songs and rituals, essential to human nature, would be composed and linked to Yosemite, just as the birds would import their songs. Designs, unique to Yosemite, would be woven into headdresses and baskets, just as animals would import their own nest designs.

> ...and 'round the campfire at night, the entertainment's
> just right—
> There's everything that mortal tongue can tell!
> — *From the 1915 song, "Toot Your Horn For Camp
> Curry," by Glenn Hood*

Song and dance around crackling campfires—these are perhaps the oldest and most venerable of ongoing cultural activities in Yosemite. Though the early peoples may have been singing and dancing for reasons different from those of current visitors, from a distance the activities of these two groups are strikingly similar and indeed ancient. "Yosemite Musicology" may be a pretty small field of study, but, much like the fire fall, it is very telling of the human experience in Yosemite. It also makes for a fine analogy with which to assess a proper place for human culture in Yosemite.

The little that remains of Yosemite Indian music history has yet to be studied, but much remains from the more recent past. Of all the cultural artifacts preserved by the Yosemite Museum Collection, some of the most delightful are the colorful pieces of sheet music, dating as far back as the 1870s. Just the cover art is captivating—a collection of period pieces evoking each decade's peculiar tastes—but to hear the music come alive is to step through a time warp. The immediacy of freshly performed old music creates the magic of time-travel, a sort of emotional rerun of the feelings of performers and listeners of past times. Through music, one can empathize with Yosemite visitors through a means that is more direct than written language; this is why it is so important to preserve and encourage the arts in such places, for without them, we would leave a poor and inadequate account of our time here.

> "In the Sierra I sang and whistled [the songs of Robert Burns] to the squirrels and birds, and they were charmed out of fear and gathered close about me." — John Muir

In reading the words of John Muir, we may learn his mind, but to stand out on a rock in Tuolumne Meadow and sing "*Ca' The Ewes*" (1794, Robert Burns) is to experience *being* Muir in some partial sense, as he likely sang that shepherd's song to his flocks there at the end of the 1860s. Close your eyes and sing "*In The Big Yosemite Mountains*" (1933, adapted by C.A. Harwell) or "*Yosemite, O Land of Cliffs and Waterfalls*" (1934, adapted by Carsten Ahrens), and you'll find yourself transported back to a sweet, long-past campfire, harmonizing with the late Yosemite Naturalist Carl Sharsmith, who learned those songs as a young man.

Dr. Carl Sharsmith giving a ranger-talk in Yosemite in 1994. Watercolor "The Last Leaf" by Diane Detrick Bopp.

Detail from "The Last Leaf."

Listen to the 1949 recording of Dick Jurgens' orchestra playing "The Bridge by Yosemite Falls" (1945, by H.L. McMillen), and as decades melt away, you're back dancing under the stars at Yosemite's Camp Curry.

"Dreaming of the mountains, winding trails throughout the hills, Eternal waters falling, in a land of a thousand thrills."
— *From the 1921 song "Yosemite, God's Wonderland," by Phil Patterson*

It is more than just an exercise in sentimentality; music brings us a bit closer to others' feelings about Yosemite. It is through culture that people feel and value Yosemite and express themselves. Yosemite is to us a cultural entity— not a disconnected ecosphere that we stand back and observe, but a system of which human nature is a part. We cannot see Yosemite but through our own individual culturally tinted glasses. The arts and crafts, even souvenirs, teach us about the nature of our connection to the park.

I feel a kinship with my many predecessors who have shared the music tradition in Yosemite, and enjoy sharing their stories with our guests at the Wawona Hotel. Little anecdotes link specific songs to Yosemite; one of my favorites was told to me by Wawona Washburn Hartwig (named after the Wawona Hotel, where she was born in 1914). In 1885, Wawona's newlywed grandparents, Estella and hotelier John Washburn, took up residence in the front room off the Wawona Hotel lobby. In the adjoining parlor, Estella would play her piano and sing along with invited guests; at that time the parlor was a private room, separated from the main lobby by folding doors. I asked Wawona what songs her grandmother played, and after some thought she hummed me a tune and said, "Gram [Estella] used to sing this one all the time, puttering around the house or out in the garden." I recognized it as *"Love's Old Sweet Song"* (1884 by G. Clifton Bingham and James Lyman Molloy), probably the most popular song of the year Estella married; for decades after her husband's death in 1917, it remained Estella's favorite. *"Just a song at twilight, when the lights are low, and the flick'ring shadows softly come and go..."* Singing it now with guests in the hotel—same song, same sounds and feelings within the walls of the very same room—the intervening century becomes almost inconsequential, and there is a sense of sharing the room with those long-ago people, barely separated from us by the invisible but otherwise impenetrable wall of elapsed time.

Homemade music was heard in dimly lit parlors all around Yosemite in the late 19th century. Just up the river from the Wawona Hotel, Azalia Bruce might be singing one of her favorites, *"The Last Rose Of Summer,"* at her reed organ, while in Yosemite Valley Elvira Hutchings, perhaps accompanying John Muir and herself on her guitar, might be harmonizing Burns' *"My Love Is Like A Red Red Rose."* Long before the arrival of the passive entertainments of television, radio, and phonograph, the participatory and expressive pastimes of singing and recitation, whether by elegant parlor fireplaces or outdoor campfires, were essential to any gathering.

> "Oh, I'm Strong For Camp Curry because there's no worry,
> No hurry, no flurry is there;
> The location's immense,
> There's no bound'ry or fence,
> It's all common sense,
> And the life is in tents!"
> — *From a 1915 recording of* "I'm Strong For Camp Curry," *by Walter DeLeon*

In the early years of the 20th century, Camp Curry featured musical entertainment provided by guests around the campfire. Founded in 1899 by David and Jennie Curry, the venerable assemblage of wood-floored tent-cabins and cottages remains a popular place to stay in Yosemite Valley. In a 1912 brochure, proprietor David Curry proclaims, "No attempt is made at systematic entertainment of guests, though the evening camp-fire has furnished many an impromptu entertainment of merit. Camp Curry has a piano, and guests are invited to bring other musical instruments." Evidently, the guests obliged the invitation, perhaps too enthusiastically, forcing the Currys to shift their policy in the interests of good business. By 1922, the Currys were printing programs for the evening entertainment, with dinner menus on the flip side. On one of these, it says, "The program is under the personal direction of Carol Weston, and the cooperation of our talented guests is cordially invited (auditions gladly arranged by appointment)." To this day, they lock the pianos in Yosemite hotels.

From these printed programs, along with early souvenir phonograph records (sold by Curry), we learn that campfire entertainment was not the domain of guitar-strumming folk singers; on the contrary, the Yosemite campfire was an extension of the salon. Two recordings, circa 1919, feature Curry campfire musicians Carol Weston (violin) and Edith Benjamin (soprano), performing "By the Waters of Minnetonka" (published in 1914 by J.M. Cavanass and Thurlow Lieurance) and "Fiddle and I" (by Frederick E. Weatherly and Mrs. Arthur Goodeve). Their plaintive music, singing through the aural patina of an antique phonograph record, matches perfectly the black-and-white images of early Yosemite visitors dressed in black skirts, shirtwaists, and wool suits. It also speaks across the years to us of a sweetly romantic attachment to the outdoors.

> Let the Fire Fall,
> Hear the Ranger call,
> Glowing stars will fall from above,
> As they play our old song of love.
> — *From the 1951 song "Let The Fire Fall," by Sidney Miller*

There is evidence of some rather serious attention given to the subject of musical entertainment in Yosemite in past decades. In a long article for the *San Francisco Examiner* (July 9, 1927), esteemed music critic Redfern Mason laid out his vision for the aesthetic development of Yosemite. Writing that " … sooner or later, it will dawn on the federal government that the administration of this lovely pleasure ground of the people has an aesthetic side," Mason suggested that "all it [Yosemite] needs is some genius, begotten in the image of a Wagner or a Beethoven, to realize its possibilities as a temple of the god of music." He goes on to suggest music to accompany the Fire Fall:

> "…what would we not have given, if a fine trombone player had sung the great motive from 'The Flying Dutchman,' or if a chorus of women's voices had sung 'Lift Thine Eyes' from the 'Elijah,' or a sonorous bass had chanted the Zuni Hymn to the departing sun. . ."

Mason also had some choice words about jazz: "Much of the music now heard, it is true, is not worthy [of Yosemite]. Jazz is a profanation; the art of the vaudevillian is an affront to the genius of the place." He concludes, "Here is the spot chosen by manifest propriety for the Bayreuth of California. The very remoteness of Yosemite is in its favor. If thousands can resort to a little town in Bavaria to hear "Tristan" and "Parsifal," why should not we Californians emulate their example and build ourselves in this magic vale a place of musical pilgrimage that will be to the Golden State what Bayreuth is to Europe?" Alas.

In a letter dated April 16, 1910, park superintendent William W. Forsythe wrote to J.B. Cook, the manager of the Sentinel Hotel in Yosemite Valley, "Answering your recent inquiries on the subject of musicians, there is no desire to impose any restrictions on you in regard to them, further than to require that they be competent musicians. Those you had last summer were incompetent." While Redfern Mason sought to impose his elite taste in music upon the Yosemite cultural scene, Forsythe was, to his credit, a bit more democratic in not wanting to "impose any restrictions."

> Oh, charming valley of the high Sierras,
> Yosemite, the handiwork of God,
> Your whisp'ring pines, your babbling brooks are calling,
> And 'long your paths the wild flow'rs nod.
> — *From the 1947 song* "Yosemite," *by Alfa Hardy*

In the ongoing and sometimes heated debate about how to protect Yosemite, purely cultural elements often sneak in and color decisions about what to keep or discard of the Yosemite experience. Jazz, pizza, souvenirs, dancing and theater have all been questioned as to their appropriateness, perhaps because they appear unrelated or even contrary to Yosemite—but outward appearances often belie the depth of a connection. A simple campfire song from years past may elicit rolled eyes from one listener, but tears of emotion from another. One may as well rate the appropriateness of bird songs in Yosemite based upon their aesthetic merits.

One of the lessons in the study of Yosemite music is in the process of suspending one's prejudices to the many different styles. For many listeners, the older the tune, the more strangely detached it may seem to be from its subject. In the late 19th century, Yosemite music took the form of Victorian waltzes, mazurkas and marches. By the first two decades of the 20th century, we find pseudo-Indian music (e.g. *"Spirit of the Evil Wind, Pohono, a Lullaby,"* pub.1910 by Allan Dunn and H.H. Stewart). In 1915, singer Glenn Hood introduced his

ragtimey song "*Toot Your Horn for Camp Curry*" with the eyebrow-raising lyrics, " …toot in the morning, toot at night, toot every chance you get with all your might . . ." hoping to encourage more people to drive cars into Yosemite. By the late 1940s, visitors were dancing to big-band ballads like "*The Bridge by Yosemite Falls*," and thrilling to "*Indian Love Call*" during the nightly Fire Fall. Yosemite stores now sell New-Age music with Yosemite titles, certain to become just as dated in coming years as other Yosemite music.

The rippling sound of a 19th century waltz may seem entirely unrelated to a cowboy song from the 1950s, until you realize in listening that the waltz evokes the glistening spray of a waterfall (as in "*Falling Waters*," 1874, by J.L.

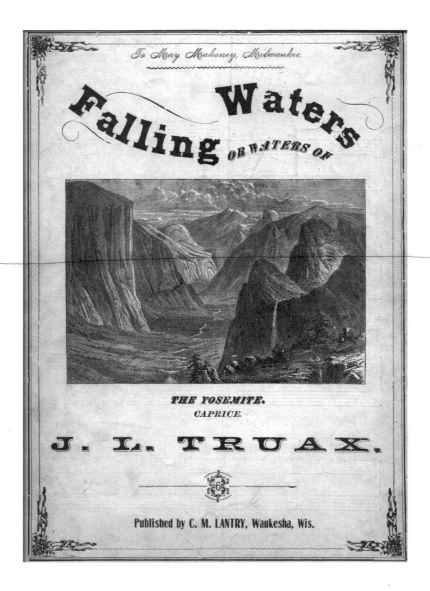

Truax), and the cowboy song reminds you that "…here in Yosemite, fair nature's wondrous gem, our hearts o'erflow with peace and joy and love …" (from "*Yosemite*," 1954, by Harry Mabry).

Though stylistically at opposite ends of the musical spectrum, and separated by 80 years, these two pieces were once a cherished part of somebody's Yosemite experience (and may still be), and their message of attachment to nature links them to the hearts of thousands of years of Yosemite's visitors.

Down by the old Merced River,
Where campers are thicker than fleas,
Along about twelve o-clock midnight,
You'll hear this refrain through the trees:
Bring back, bring back, oh bring back my bacon to me,
to me. . .
— 1950s Yosemite campfire song, aimed at bacon-stealing
bears.

An article entitled "*Yosemite Valley and Our Changing Values*," printed in the Summer 1999 issue of the *Yosemite Guide* (published and distributed by the National Park Service), addresses the gradual elimination of human impact, on Yosemite Valley over the years. Among those listed are hotels, stores and residences that once "degraded" Sentinel Meadow, the practice of car-camping along the Merced River, the "Indian Field Days" rodeo in Leidig Meadow and bear feedings. The same article states, "Over the years many entertainment-oriented events and attractions occurred in the park, most of which had little or nothing to do with Yosemite's natural wonders. The motivation behind such activities was simply to attract more visitors to the Valley and encourage them to stay longer." Of the Fire Fall, the article says that "it was halted amid a growing trend to eliminate artificial, man-made attractions, and to end massive nightly traffic jams, crowding, and exodus that drew visitors from throughout the Valley to the best viewing sites in the east end."

These telling excerpts illustrate a subtle, but critically prevalent, mindset that tends to undermine support for our efforts to preserve Yosemite. Yosemite's early human inhabitants weren't singing and dancing to "attract visitors" any more than latter-day campfire singers. Certainly Yosemite is the attraction, and not any of the activities that visitors entertain themselves with once they are in the Park. Moreover, it is essential that we intentionally bring our cultural activities to places that inspire us—where we can learn to more deeply express the connection between the humanities and nature itself.

This is the point: Yosemite music is representative of the best of human nature, of the cultural identity that all people inevitably bring with them wherever they go, and of the means by which they interpret what they experience. Our efforts to preserve Yosemite focus not only on controlling elements that are destructive, but also on encouraging elements that are constructive. Non-destructive elements that appear to be "artificial," "man-made," or "have nothing to do with Yosemite's natural wonders" may turn out to be valuable after all. Expressions of judgmental scorn over these sorts of things don't help our efforts to garner support for preservation.

National Parks are to preserve culture as well as nature, so our challenge is to weigh the value of cultural activities against their impact. The historic Yosemite Chapel remains to "impair" an otherwise pristine Yosemite meadow, but in today's cultural climate we value its presence enough to tolerate its environmental impact. For many, cultural events within the Park enhance and deepen the meaning of the Yosemite experience. Hotels, camps, roads and trails remain to "degrade" Yosemite Valley, but their impacts are balanced by their value as portals through which many come to learn to love and protect Yosemite. To deny or subdue our identity while in Yosemite is to miss the point that human nature is part of Yosemite's nature, and that the clash between them is often merely illusion.

> …Yosemite, though fate may lead us far away,
> We'll count the moments lost we spend away from you.
> *From the 1934 campfire song* "Yosemite" by Carsten Ahrens

— Tom Bopp, 2010

PART 3

Personalities, Adventures and Misadventures

Herman Hoss.

Chapter 23

Personalities

Family Members

Herman (1894–1971) and Della Hoss (1900–1997)

My father, Herman H. Hoss, was born in the small rural town of Earlville, Illinois, due west of Chicago. His father was the local banker. When Herman was in high school, his father decided to move the family to Southern California, for health reasons. He bought an orange grove near Corona, California, when that part of Southern California was mostly orange groves, a fragrant paradise with a mild climate, bearing little resemblance to what it is today. Unfortunately the business venture was not successful and my grandfather went broke in the Great Depression.

Herman graduated from high school in Corona in 1914. Like many others of that generation, Herman contracted tuberculosis and was incapacitated for a year. He recovered, but his lungs were weakened, and he suffered from respiratory problems the remainder of his life and opted for a slower moving demeanor, avoiding stress if possible, projecting a calm and low-pressure presence. However, he did not give up smoking.

Herman attended USC in 1915 and 1916 and transferred to Stanford in 1917. He worked in Yosemite for the Curry Camping Company while going to college. I have uncovered records of this era. Despite the fact that Herman was a prolific letter writer, I did not find anything to tell me what or who caused him to go to Yosemite in the first place, and I do not remember asking him.

Herman was supposed to be drafted into military service in World War I, but he was deferred while his health was investigated. He tried to volunteer but was rejected for physical reasons. This was somewhat of a disappointment, since in that era young men were eager to join a war "to make the world safe for democracy," which now seems like a cruel bittersweet slogan.

Herman graduated from Stanford Law School in 1920 near the top of his class. He demonstrated superior ability to analyze legal issues. He worked one more summer for the Curry Camping Company as chief clerk at Camp Curry. He remembered the job fondly. He enjoyed putting the advance reservations in cubbyholes, housing the guests in the proper places and being the first to greet them, more of a challenge than it may seem. I can say this from my own experience as a room clerk.

The prominent Wall Street law firm Sullivan & Cromwell hired Herman. He went to New York in the fall of 1920 and stayed eighteen months. The high-pressure atmosphere and elitism did not suit him. There was talk of sending him to the Philippines, where he did not want to go. He decided to return to his job at Camp Curry while he contemplated his next career move.

This would be regarded by some as a giant step in downward mobility, but it turned out to be a blessing for all concerned, particularly me, not even a gleam in his eye at the time. A position of part time federal commissioner (later called a magistrate) opened up. There he could exercise legal skills while working his way up in management positions in the Yosemite Park & Curry Company, becoming personnel manager and eventually secretary-treasurer, third in the chain of command. The company did not have a corporate counsel per se, but Herman dealt with legal issues that arose. He found the appropriate career path and would have stayed in Yosemite until retirement but for World War II, which turned everybody's life upside down.

Herman was tall, angular and thin. He had to wear special shirts and coats. He had the type of metabolism that allowed him to eat or drink anything without gaining weight. He had a great sense of humor and loved jokes, either to tell them or listen to them. He had a great empathy for others, and would go out of his way to help people experiencing difficulties. He loved to discuss any issue and debate about it. He would listen to both sides thoughtfully. If one could hold his or her own in a discussion with Herman, one really felt good.

Herman lived the Golden Rule and taught it, without accepting Christian theology, although he loved to debate religious issues. He was not a fan of clergymen, with the exception of Al Glass, a resident minister in Yosemite, whom he greatly respected. His mother had been president of the Women's Christian Temperance Union and induced him to sign a pledge at the age of eight that he would never partake of alcoholic beverages. However, his legal mind told him that a contract signed by a minor was unenforceable. He loved the cocktail hour, but never showed signs of overindulgence. Herman was a well-recognized expert in mixing dry martinis. I remember visiting a special place in Wawona where mint grew, and gathering mint for mint juleps.

With his calm temperament, Herman seldom raised his voice or showed anger, although some anger dwelled within him. He could be critical of others without demonizing, belittling or bullying them. I never saw a trace of racial or ethnic prejudice in him.

Herman often dressed rather formally, with a vest and a Phi Beta Kappa key. I don't recall ever seeing him wearing shorts, except tennis shorts, or wearing a cowboy hat. A friend once remarked that Herman was the only man he had ever seen who would wear a tie to haul refuse to the dump.

In addition to his role as the parson in the Bracebridge Dinner, Herman participated in theater in Palo Alto. His most famous role was Jonathan, the unsavory character in the classic play "Arsenic and Old Lace."

Due to his fragile health Herman did not travel outside the United States, except to Canada and Mexico. Herman was a skilled poker player with friends, but never visited casinos. He was a prolific reader and loved high-level conversation on any subject, from his favorite chair at home.

Herman would have been out of place at a country club, and I never knew him to venture on a golf course, even in Yosemite. His intelligence was universally respected, and he was often asked for advice. I recall very few, if any, enemies. He was an avid Stanford football fan, and was particularly antagonistic toward University of Southern California. I was an adult before he confessed that he spent his first college years at USC.

After he left Yosemite, he took a low-pressure job as corporate counsel for Schwabacher Frey, a printing and lithography business and department store run by a prominent and benevolent San Francisco family. Schwabacher Frey printed ballots, and Herman became an authority on election law.

After he retired, he was somewhat bored. Two of my contemporaries with a prosperous law firm in Sunnyvale hired him as a senior advisor and called him "our secret weapon." They put his name on the letterhead. Herman was noted for undervaluing his services and was never motivated to make big money. He would have made a brilliant law professor or judge, but he did very well at what he chose to do.

Because of his compromised health Herman was not able to introduce me to the mountains personally, as many fathers do. I never went on a backpacking trip with him. I had to seek out the glad tidings on my own.

My mother, Della, was born in Harvey, Illinois, the youngest of five

Della Taylor Hoss, around the time of Peter's birth.

Della's siblings as Easter bunnies, left to right: Kay (Mrs. Frank) Taylor, Della Taylor Hoss, Frank Taylor, Ruth Taylor Day, and Bernice Taylor FitzGerald ("Aunt Skinnay").

siblings. When she was very young, the family moved to Oregon and then to Los Angeles, where Della spent most of her formative years. The family was of modest means. Della's brother, Frank J. Taylor, was a writer for the *Saturday Evening Post, Readers Digest* and other publications. Two sisters were artists. All attended Stanford, in the days when only 500 women attended and tuition was affordable. About the time Della left for college, her parents divorced, unusual in those days. She had little contact with her father. I do not recall meeting him. My grandmother lived with other members of the family in her later years.

After college Della learned etching and wood block printing in a commercial art studio in San Francisco. Later she studied in Seattle under Mark Tobey, who taught her rubbed graphic drawing. She came to Yosemite on a temporary assignment arranged by her brother, Frank and met my father there. They were married in 1928.

Della was a talented artist. She collaborated with Mary Curry Tresidder, illustrating a book on trees in Yosemite, with linoleum block prints. Trees were her favorite subject. She described herself as a "tree person." After *Trees of Yosemite* was out of print, my sons, at the urging of their mother, reprinted twelve woodcuts from the linoleum blocks. They are now sold in the Ansel Adams Gallery under the name "Creative Offsprings." The original 34 linoleum block prints from the *Trees of Yosemite* have been donated to the Hunt Institute for Botanical Documentation at Carnegie Mellon University in Pittsburgh, Pennsylvania.

Above, left: Della and grandson Martino.
Above, right: Della on her 80th birthday.

Left: Della and Peter, 1970.

Below: Patti Hoss and Della, print show with
Martino at Ansel Adams Gallery, 1996.

When Della was over 70 years old she travelled to the bristlecone pines in the White Mountains, east of the Sierra. The bristlecone pines are the oldest known trees on earth, some over 4,000 years old. They grow only inches a year, at a very high elevation under conditions hostile to any growing thing. Della drew pencil drawings of the pines, which have been reprinted by a digital process by Creative Offsprings. Della said of the bristlecone pines, "The story told in the bristlecone cycle has become a form of religion to me. I shall probably go on trying to capture some of the mystic significance of these trees the rest of my life—the life-death struggle, always present in nature."

Della also drew menus for the Ahwahnee dining room. She did some writing and loved to invent limericks. She loved to entertain my friends in her home in Palo Alto. There was nothing pretentious about Della.

Della was a petite and winsome five foot two. Herman towered over her, a foot taller. She was as right-brained as my father was left brained. They were quite a combination. I inherited my father's left-brain. My mother's right-brain passed on to my son Martino, who is a fine artist. Della loved her grandchildren and encouraged them in their endeavors.

Della did not wear fancy or expensive clothes. However, she did not allow me to wear jeans to school, which upset me at the time. She had no interest in becoming socially prominent, and treated everyone equally. Some part of her humble background remained with her. She was easy to talk with, warm and friendly, and took an interest in what other people were doing, and in what I was doing. She encouraged me in many endeavors and wanted me to be my own person. Della liked to cook wholesome homey meals. Her favorite she called "Hoss hamburger," diced hamburger on a baked potato.

Della was not much interested in politics, as Herman was, but I recall she was a great fan of "Ike" Eisenhower because she identified more with his personality than his politics. She once received a form letter bearing his signature. She treasured it, showed to everyone and insisted that he signed it personally.

Our little house in Yosemite was often filled with classical music. Some compositions filtered into my brain have remained with me, and remind me of childhood. My parents never raised their voice to each other or to me, even when annoyed. It was always a soft-spoken rebuke. Since I had no siblings to quarrel with, the lack of bickering and bombast contributed to an unusual childhood.

My mother was a deist. When she needed to, she went directly to God, without any ecclesiastical intermediaries. It was quite remarkable how often God agreed with her petitions.

Many young people lived with Della after Herman and Hil died, and she encouraged them. She managed some foreign travel in her later years with friends. Herman's health discouraged him from this. Della travelled some with my family, always waiting patiently with her little suitcase while we got organized. In her later years, one doctor described her as "a prototypical little old lady."

Della and Hil Oehlmann, Sr.

She managed to stay in the house she loved in Palo Alto until one night, at the age of 96, when she went peacefully to sleep and did not wake up, just as she had wished.

Patti Hoss (1935–2001)

Patti was born in Ogden, Utah. She was raised in a Catholic family amid the surrounding Mormon culture. Her father, John Kozicki, worked as a timekeeper up and down the Southern Pacific Railroad.

The family moved to Sacramento when Patti was 15 years old. She was the youngest in her family and the first to attend college, since her father believed that his daughters should aspire to nothing better than being married off, especially to railroad men, if that were possible. She was in the first graduating class at Sacramento State.

Patti always regarded family as more important than career. In fact, she didn't begin to pursue her own career until our sons were in junior high, so that she could be at the door to greet them.

Patti worked as a speech pathologist. She was involved as a volunteer in many community activities, and became the only female director

Patti and Peter Hoss at her 60th birthday.

Martino and Vince Hoss, at Vince's wedding in Yosemite, 1995.

(at that time) of the Monterey Jazz Festival. Our son Martino's classmates referred to Patti as "Mrs. Rowdy" when she interrupted Martino's high school graduation with a singing telegram.

Following her death we conducted a Celebration of Life in her honor that was very well attended. I remember that Vince said that his mom was the best mom anyone could have. My cousin Byron commented at her Celebration that she had a smile that would light up a room. Patti had a wry sense of humor, a talent for thinking up offbeat activities, and a cheerful, positive attitude. She encouraged me to undertake activities and adventures I would not otherwise have done.

Martino Hoss and Maura Murphy Hoss

Martino is my older son. His given name was Martin Lyell, the middle name after the highest peak in Yosemite. He was born when I was in the service in Vicenza, Italy, hence the name Martino, which the Italians fastened on him, and which stuck. We left Italy when Martino was three months old. He had the option of Italian citizenship until he was 21, which he declined.

Martino grew up in Salinas, California, where he attended public schools. He had little choice about being exposed to Yosemite and visited Yosemite from infancy. The family took annual camping and ski trips to Yosemite all during his school years. Martino accepted Yosemite as part of growing up.

Martino showed an early talent for art and started drawing Christmas cards for us when he was in grade school. His grandmother Della encouraged his art interest and was a major formative influence. Martino attended University of the Pacific (UOP) and graduated with a degree in Fine Arts. He worked five summers at Tuolumne Meadows in Yosemite while in college and

Martino with his wife, Maura, daughter, Taylor, and son, Burke, hiking in Yosemite High Country, 2009.

one year afterward, becoming somewhat of a fixture.

After college Martino travelled around Europe on a Eurail Pass and met his future wife, Maura, a student at UC Berkeley, on a train travelling between Stockholm and Copenhagen. He returned home, somewhat unfocused, not sure of what he wanted to do for a career. What he wanted to do at that time was work another summer at Tuolumne Meadows and be near Maura in Berkeley.

One day, without a job and with no serious prospects, he came to me and said, "I think I should marry Maura." I said, "I think that would be a good idea." It turned out to be exactly that. Maura, a motivator throughout their entire marriage, encouraged Martino to enroll in the prestigious Art Center College of Design in Pasadena, California, and worked to put him through school. Martino initially contemplated a career in advertising. He started his career across the street from where I started mine in Fresno, California. We each lasted one year in Fresno.

Martino determined that he wanted to pursue a career as a fine artist, and he and Maura moved to Seattle, knowing virtually no one. He has been successful, both artistically and financially, in this very chancy career. He produces mostly natural scenes using serigraphs, pastels on copper, wood blocks and other media. He has painted murals. He sells most of his own work and has attracted a following, and now works largely on commissions.

Martino is gregarious and funny and enjoys zany pursuits. He is a born salesman, a somewhat unusual combination for a skilled fine artist. He and Maura have two children, Taylor, born in 1993, and Burke, born in 1999.

The family makes annual visits to Yosemite. Martino is encouraging his family to explore the trails with him, with some success. Taylor enjoys singing, dogs, school and friends. Burke excels at sports and in school and has a great way with people. He has a highly developed sense of fairness. His Aunt Anne calls him "Mr. Truth and Justice."

Maura grew up in Pasadena, California, in a very close family of four highly motivated daughters and two highly motivated sons, all very successful. She was a competitive tennis player in high school and has now taken up running and has run the Big Sur, Goodwill Games and New York marathons. She attended Outward Bound in the Pecos wilderness and considered it a life-changing experience. Maura has led nature hikes at the UC Berkeley summer camp, the Lair of the Bear. Maura and her sisters all graduated from the University of California, Berkeley.

Maura's family did a lot a camping, and she has happy memories of Yosemite as a child and pre-teen and is naturally attracted to the outdoors.

Maura has pursued various careers since marrying Martino: advertising in Los Angeles while putting Martino through Art Center College of Design in Pasadena, commercial real estate in Fresno and Seattle, and marketing and consulting in Seattle. She has a master of science degree in communication management from the Newhouse School of Public Communication at Syracuse University. Maura has been employed by Microsoft for seven years and is now Director of Communications for the Legal and Corporate Affairs group.

As mentioned, Maura is a motivator. A favorite expression: "Be a player."

Vincent Whitney Hoss and Wendy Thomson Hoss

Vince is two years younger than Martino. He grew up in Salinas, California, and attended public schools. He showed an early interest and talent in drafting and anything mechanical. As a child he watched repairmen to see how they fixed things, a talent surely not passed on from his father or grandfather. Another natural attribute of Vince is direction-finding. Once he has been somewhere, he can find his way back—even years later.

Vince attended University of Oregon and obtained a degree in architecture. In his early years after graduation he was an associate in a firm that pioneered the CAD system, utilizing computers in design. He joined a firm, BGFC, with offices in Bakersfield, San Luis Obispo and San Jose, California and served as its information technology director for eleven years, becoming an expert in buying, brainstorming and educating co-workers in the use of computers. He is a LEED certified professional with a strong commitment to sustainable design practices. BGFC has now merged with a Canadian-based firm with more than 70 offices worldwide; Vince is moving from computer technology into project management.

Vince's wife Wendy, son Chris, Vince, son Teddy, and Peter. Wawona Tunnel entrance. Photo by Patricia Hamilton, 2009.

Vince worked three summers at Sunrise High Sierra Camp in the Yosemite High Country, the last year as manager. He has hiked and cross-country skied extensively in the Yosemite High Country, having made twelve trans-Sierra ski trips with the Yosemite Winter Club. He met his wife, Wendy, through Yosemite friends. They are the only family members to be married in the Yosemite Valley Chapel, where they were married in 1995.

Vince and Wendy live on twelve acres between Bakersfield and Tehachapi. They have two sons—Teddy and Chris. Teddy and Chris are both interested in animals of any size and are collectors. They both love the outdoors. Teddy has scientific interests as well as the ability to pick up shells on a beach and sell them to passersby and to sell drawings at public events. Chris is a born fisherman and cannot look at a rock without climbing it.

Vince is quieter than his brother but readily participates in zany pursuits and establishes solid relationships. He can always be counted on to be helpful in many ways.

Wendy is from a fourth generation farming family from Kern County. Her two brothers are engaged in farming. She has always had a passion for horses, and Vince and Wendy now own horses.

Wendy has early and happy memories of Yosemite and worked with the Yosemite Institute while in college. The Yosemite Institute provides environmental education for high school students who come for a week of immersion in nature study. Wendy attended University of California, Berkeley, and UC Davis School of Law and now practices transactional law in Bakersfield. There is at least one other attorney in the family.

Wendy retains a strong interest in nature. She is very devoted to Teddy and Chris as well as to Vince. The family visits Yosemite often, and spends a lot of recreational time in the outdoors. Wendy has been on many of the winter club trans-Sierra cross-country ski trips with Vince.

Wendy's family owns a large beachfront home between Santa Barbara and Carpenteria. She is a tireless, gracious hostess. Vince and Wendy entertain many friends at the beach house as well as at their home at Hart Flat where friends gather for some relief from the summer heat and winter fog in Bakersfield.

Wendy is known for her warmth, friendliness, and compassionate spirit.

Hil Oehlmann, Sr., and Hil Oehlmann, Jr.

Hil Oehlmann, Sr., came to Yosemite in 1916 as a porter for the Curry Camping Company, with Don Tresidder. For more than five decades Hil served as an executive with the Yosemite Park & Curry Company. He succeeded Don Tresidder as CEO during World War II. He managed Yosemite throughout World War II and into the postwar years with wisdom and energy. He oversaw the dramatic postwar growth of visitors to Yosemite that eventually swelled into numbers that wouldn't have been considered possible in the years preceding the war.

Hil and Else Oehlmann skiing at Badger Pass. Courtesy of Bob and Nancy Eckart.

Hil was my father's closest friend. The two of them worked together on many projects including federal government contracts and with the National Park Concessioners Association, in which I eventually became involved.

Hil's life was marred by tragedy. His first wife, Helen, died at a young age in a freak accident. Hil married to Else in 1946. His son, Hil Oehlmann, Jr., was six years older than I and became something of a mentor to me. He was a promising student at Stanford Law School, vying for top honors with two other students—Bill Rehnquist and Sandra Day O'Connor (both destined to become justices of the U.S. Supreme Court); I spent an afternoon visiting with all of them, in my parents' house in Palo Alto, when in high school.

On the night of my high school senior prom, Hil, Jr. was tragically killed in an auto accident, along with four sailors. The sole survivor of the accident was the driver, a fraternity brother of Hil, Jr., who had a reputation for drinking too much. Ironically, several days before the accident, Hil, Jr. was overheard to say that he was going to stop riding with this driver. To this day I wish that he had done so. He held such great promise. Who knows the heights to which he might have climbed if his life hadn't been cut short in such a tragic fashion?

Hil, Sr., maintained a stoic attitude toward the world and continued to pursue life following the two tragedies. He had an air of outward calm, concealing from others whatever might have been weighing upon his spirit. Hil and Else became close friends with my parents. Each year they traveled to the Conference of National Park Concessioners Association by train across the United States, enjoying warm fellowship.

Following the death of Else and my father, Hil and my mother were married, as previously reported.

Hil was a private person. Even though I knew him all my life, I never knew him very well until reading his memoirs with him. His long struggles with the federal government caused him to become an outspoken political conservative. He was an astute businessman with great personal integrity. Hil overcame adversity without losing his sense of humor. He had a love for music and unstoppable intellectual curiosity. He was a consummate gentleman and a connoisseur of the good life, having spent considerable time in 5-star hotels. He was a longtime member of the Bohemian Club, enjoying camaraderie with the rich and famous, entertaining many of them when they visited Yosemite.

While living in Palo Alto, every day he would get in his Cadillac at noon and drive to a favorite restaurant, where he would dine by himself and enjoy a martini and lunch served by a favorite waitress who greeted him at the door as "Mr. Hil."

Hil enjoyed friendly discussion on almost any topic. He and my father enjoyed endless rounds of discussions; it was a taste that I picked up myself.

Bob and Chuck Eckart

Bob and Chuck are sons of Else Oehlmann and the stepsons of Hil Oehlmann. They are both about my age, and we were friends in Yosemite while I was in high school. We became shirttail relatives when my mother married Hil; at that point we shared a stepfather.

Chuck Eckart at Della's 80th birthday party.

Chuck is a successful fine artist and lives in Point Reyes Station, California. He has used a variety of media and subjects—it's impossible to classify or pigeonhole what he has done.

Bob is a retired banker. He spent two-thirds of his banking career in the San Francisco Bay area and the balance in Mariposa. He was a thirteen-year board member of the Yosemite Association. He enjoyed rock climbing in Yosemite. He married Nancy Moe, the daughter of a Park Service family from Yosemite and a prime mover in the second annual Yosemite Grammar School reunion in 1993.

Mary FitzGerald Beach

Mary is my first cousin on my mother's side. I'm the youngest of the cousins, and Mary is the second youngest. Therefore, at family reunions we would seek out each other's fellowship.

Aunt Bernice (Aunt Skinnay) resting at top of Nevada Fall. Courtesy of Mary FitzGerald Beach.

Mary grew up in Pasadena, graduated from the University of Colorado, and has three children. In 1968 she moved to Monterey and became a long-time docent at the Monterey Aquarium and at Point Lobos.

Mary is a talented artist and photographer. All of her life she has been a frequent visitor to Yosemite. She mastered the art of getting reservations in advance. She would learn the first date that the reservations were available, would call as soon as it was possible, and remain on the phone until she got the reservations she wanted.

YOSEMITE ICONS

A few people I have known have made an impact on Yosemite that reached far beyond the boundaries of Yosemite.

Ansel Adams at Glacier Point, shooting from atop his station wagon, 1943. Courtesy of Adams Family Collection.

Ansel Adams

Ansel Adams captured for the world Yosemite's ineffable beauty through photographs that conveyed the sweeping majesty of Yosemite as well as other areas of scenic beauty.

Ansel was a leader in the movement that would turn photography into an art form. He would form a vision in his mind of the image he wanted to create, take a picture, and then work tirelessly in the darkroom until he had produced the image of his vision. The photographic medium of black and white was perfectly suited to this approach.

To reach the vantage points from which to take photographs, Ansel had to carry large equipment and glass plates, sometimes over long distances. He mounted a platform on top of a Pontiac station wagon from which he could take his photographs. This vehicle became a familiar sight around Yosemite and elsewhere in the West wherever there were scenic pictures to be taken.

Ansel Adams, 8 months old. Courtesy of Adams Family Collection.

Ansel spread his vision to others, teaching many workshops and leading many fledgling photographers in the art. Many tried to master his talent; only a few have approached it.

Original Ansel Adams prints, particularly signed ones, command a very high price. Exhibitions of his works have been shown around the planet and always attract enthusiastic reviewers. A recent show of his works proved to be

Ansel, circa 1930. Courtesy of Adams Family Collection.

the most popular exhibition ever shown at the San Francisco Museum of Modern Art. People lined up for blocks to see it. I noted the viewers, many of them obvious urban types who perhaps had never set foot in the mountains. They represented all lifestyles from every imaginable background. Each of them wanted to savor Ansel Adams photographs.

I concluded that Ansel accomplished with images what John Muir had done with words. Both of them managed to capture the essence of glad tidings, the spiritual quality that attracts visitors to Yosemite and to the mountains that they loved, opening up a vision of Yosemite

Top, right: Ansel with darkroom enlarger.

Below, left: Ansel with his grandchildren, Sarah and Matthew.

Below, right: Ansel with his wife Virginia and son Michael.

Courtesy of Adams Family Collection.

Valley and the High Country to many who have never seen it and never will.

Personal comments on Ansel come from two sources—personal acquaintance and reading his letters from 1916 to 1984 published in a book entitled *Ansel Adams: Letters, 1916–1984,* collected and published after his death. These letters trace Ansel's thought process as his career unfolded.

My recollection of Ansel during my childhood is that he was somewhat of an eccentric mountain man, the father of a childhood playmate and a photographer, yet to become world famous. As I grew up and Ansel became more famous, I came to know him as a genial host, a talented pianist, a witty raconteur who loved to tell jokes and listen to them, a very creative person, an outspoken environmentalist and a gregarious man who loved a party.

It was fun to be around Ansel. Although Ansel held strong views on many subjects, he did not resort to demeaning comments about those who disagreed with him. His disagreements with the Park Service and concessioner executives were without any perceptible personal animosity. Any animosity that Ansel harbored would be directed toward those individuals he considered destructive. I detected no arrogance in Ansel. I saw less of him after he became world famous, but when I did see him it was like old times. I traded jokes with him over the years, and he was always cordial and took an interest in what I was doing.

Another side of Ansel is that he was deadly serious about the art form he was creating. A favorite word of Ansel's was "integrity." He respected anyone who he believed had integrity and was turned off by anyone he believed did not have integrity. He did not like artwork or souvenirs that were of poor quality. He retained a passionate interest in protecting the natural environment. Like John Muir, he wanted everyone to be able to partake of the glad tidings and draw spiritual enlightenment from that experience. He was not an elitist; he did not want to preserve the enjoyment of Yosemite for himself or a select few.

Reading Ansel's letters reinforced and embellished this view of Ansel. He wrote frequently to his trusted friends and associates in an honest, clear way, sometimes impassioned, sometimes tired, sometimes discouraged, sometimes elated, always striving for the ideals he was trying to achieve. These sentiments were echoed in the words of a *New York Times* reviewer:

"Adams was a splendid, rumbustious writer, overflowing with jokes, puns, expletives and exuberance.... Never were letters less deliberately composed; he wrote when exhausted and distracted, on the spur of the second, in bits and fragments..... His letters to close friends are warm and wonderful, reading them one frequently feels (as one doesn't often in reading printed letters) what a marvelous thing it would have been to have him for a friend."

I am privileged to count him as a friend, even if from a different generation.

Ansel met Presidents Johnson and Ford. He did a portrait of Jimmy Carter. As a lifelong Democrat he was critical of the politics of President Ronald Reagan. In a letter written to seven Democratic senators and representatives in 1982, when he was 80 years old, Ansel described the Reagan administration as "the most dangerous in history." He was adamantly opposed to the policies of James Watt, Secretary of the Interior under Reagan, commonly referred to as the most environmentally insensitive person ever to hold that office.

Ansel Adams in his home studio in the Carmel Highlands. Courtesy of Adams Family Collection.

In July 1983 Ansel received a phone call from Michael Deaver, a Reagan aide, stating, "The President would like to meet you and discuss why you dislike him so much." Ansel accepted the invitation and conversed with Reagan for 50 minutes without either convincing the other to change any views. Ansel described the meeting as "the vacuum hitting the fan," although he acknowledged that Reagan was hard to dislike on a personal level, no matter how much you disagreed with him.

Ansel died in April 1984, believing that the reelection of Reagan would be a monumental disaster and would be likely to lead to a nuclear war with the Soviet Union. It is perhaps a blessing that he was spared the result of the 1984 election, as well as the irony of seeing the tearing down of the Berlin Wall and the disintegration of the Soviet Union and the end of the Cold War instead of his prediction.

Peter Hoss speaking to a large gathering at the Nic Fiore Memorial at Yosemite. Photo by Patricia Hamilton, 2009.

NIC FIORE (1921–2009)

For decades, Nic Fiore was a Yosemite icon, teaching generations of people how to ski and managing the High Sierra camps almost as a fiefdom.

Nic was a French Canadian who came to Yosemite after World War II, and remained for over five decades as director of the Badger Pass Ski School during the winter. He taught skiing for 58 years. In 1958, over the course of only 21 days, Nic once taught more than 200 people to ski, including some celebrities.

I was one of the thousands of people that Nic taught to ski. I'm a slow learner. He spent a decade teaching me in an episodic fashion. We would run across each other somewhere and he would say, "Come to Badger and we'll run down the hill together; I'll show you some things." Each time he would show me something new or improve my technique.

Much of what follows is gleaned from reminiscences at Nic's Celebration of Life, which took place in December 2009.

Nic was a man who demanded excellence from the people who worked for him. We were told that his daughter, Cindy, worked with him for a while, but the job was never secure. She would do something to irritate him, and he would fire her. However, his wife Midge would go to bat for her daughter that night and make him hire her back.

Nic had a kind heart and a genial personality. In overseeing the High Sierra camps during the summers, he treated his employees with a paternal attitude, regarding them as members of an extended family. He was very careful in his selection of those who worked for him. They were required to work in close contact with each other in isolated areas, removed from the distractions of ordinary life, so it was essential that the High Sierra crewmembers get along well with one another.

Nic exercised several functions in Yosemite. He had the task of welcoming guests as they arrived at the Bracebridge Dinner for more years than anyone could remember. Nic's wife, Midge, was an important person in Yosemite Valley in her own right. She worked quietly out of the limelight. I saw Nic many times over a period of 50 years and have scant memory of seeing Midge.

Nic is especially remembered as a man of good humor and enthusiasm. His most famous quote came after he first came to Yosemite in the middle of a dark night. When he came out of his lodging the next morning, he looked up at the towering walls around him. "This is really beautiful," he said. "But where are the beginner's slopes?"

Nic was filled with infectious enthusiasm for life. He had great physical stamina. On days off he would ride a bicycle up to Glacier Point and back. He always said that he had the greatest job in the world. Nic created the job and his role in Yosemite. He mentored generations of High Sierra camp summer employees, including my sons.

For decades Nic was a familiar figure on the Badger Pass porch and throughout the Yosemite High Country, speaking in a distinctive French Canadian accent. Whenever requested to do so he would launch into a full-throated rendition of his beloved *Alouette*.

Nic passed away in March 2009 at age 88. On December 12 that year, more than 850 of his family members, friends and admirers gathered at the Curry Village Pavilion to celebrate a life well-spent, laughing at the stories, marveling at his lifetime accomplishments and celebrating the privilege of knowing him.

Photo by Patricia Hamilton.

Red Skelton's summer visit to Yosemite, early 1950s, remembered by Bob Eckart: "I had the pleasure of meeting Red and shaking his hand. Not only funny, he seemed a very warm and sincere person. This photo was taken at a cocktail party held at George Oliver's house on the Ahwahnee Meadow. George was the company's PR and Sales director. Back row: unknown, unknown, Harold Ouimet (Personnel Director), Red Skelton, George Oliver, Henry Berrey. Front row: Jan Robertson, Muriel Ouimet, Hil Oehlmann, Else Oehlmann, unkown, unknown, Luggi Foeger, Director of Winter Sports." Courtesy of Bob and Nancy Eckart.

RED SKELTON (1913–1997)

Red Skelton was a frequent visitor to Yosemite. He and Ansel Adams became friends, and the two of them would tell jokes. Red Skelton had an affable personality and he enjoyed hanging around with Park employees.

Red Skelton was not simply a famous comic; he was a man of great personal wit. One evening he showed up for dinner at the Ahwahnee dining room not wearing the mandatory coat and tie. When the *maître d'* politely told him of the dress code, Red graciously agreed to comply with the rules, went to his room, and returned wearing the required coat and tie, but with no shirt. He was seated.

Red Skelton's heart was as big as his distinctive humor. When he learned that a local kid, George Murphy, was recuperating from an injury in a toboggan accident, Red showed up unannounced at George's front door and spent the morning entertaining him.

Red is mentioned as an icon because he was a famous person who greatly enjoyed Yosemite and visited frequently.

Mary and Don Tresidder.

DON (1894–1948) & MARY CURRY (1893–1970) TRESIDDER

Don Tresidder's name has been mentioned frequently in this book: as the man who took me for ride on his prized palomino pony, which I did not enjoy; as the man who played Santa Claus to me; as the man all the kids in Yosemite knew as "Uncle Don"; as the man who fired my father and caused our family to leave Yosemite; as the man who came to Camp Curry as a porter and married the boss's daughter; as the first president of the consolidated Yosemite Park & Curry Company; as a visionary who established Badger Pass as the first ski area in California and almost brought the Winter Olympics to Badger Pass; as the perennial Squire of the Bracebridge Dinner; as the president of Stanford University; as a close friend of my father's best friend and my stepfather Hil Oehlmann from their early working days for the Curry Camping Company. I have to acknowledge that I did not really know Don Tresidder. He was of a different generation. He died when I was only 14 years old. I have mentioned that my mother, Della, never forgave him for firing my father, although my father did. These conflicting views color my recollection.

I will defer to someone I did know to describe the man, Don Tresidder. Stuart Cross, who later became CEO of the Yosemite Park & Curry Company, described Don Tresidder in a publication of the Stanford Historical Society entitled "Sandstone and Tile" in 1982:

Don Tresidder.

"Don Tresidder, at this time, was a handsome, charming, laughing, cordial and yet extremely complex man who had the ability to make each person with whom he conversed feel an intense interest in him and his ideas. Articulate and graceful… , he was at home whether testifying before a congressional committee, negotiating with the secretary of the interior, with friends in the Bohemian Club, entertaining at the Ahwahnee, or on a camping trip in the High Country. *Time Magazine*, in its then-distinctive style, once referred to him as 'no greasy-thumbed innkeeper.' His enthusiasm for the out-of-doors was genuine, and his charm was felt by everyone who met him. With these attributes went exceptional administrative skill, a keen intelligence and the ability to draw from others' advice and counsel before reaching his final decision. It is not surprising that there were rumors and overtures toward a political career (which Mary dreaded)."

Stuart notes that despite these attributes a note of pessimism crept into him after battles with Harold Ickes about a government takeover of concessions, charges of profiteering by concessioners, which proved to be unfounded, conflicts and litigation within the Curry family that have been described and the takeover of the Ahwahnee by the Navy in World War II. He came to believe that the Yosemite Park & Curry Company would not make it financially.

A low point in the accusations about him came with an anonymous diatribe to Stanford faculty stating, "Dear Colleague, How much longer will we accept the former manager of Camp Curry—Uncle Don—as President? Is not Stanford worthy of a scholar rather than a resort manager as President? Let us stop merely expressing our disapproval and unite for action."

Don survived this blast of intellectual snobbery and went on to be respected for his accomplishments at Stanford. It is unfortunate that he did not live to see the Yosemite Park & Curry Company survive and prosper.

Don Tresidder earned a medical degree but never practiced medicine. He was once fired by David A. Curry for taking Mary on an unauthorized ascent of Half Dome before the cable. He played a lasting role in Yosemite history for a young man who came west from Indiana and made his first visit to Yosemite because a train was delayed in Bakersfield.

Unlike Don, Mary was present for a good part of my life. Also unlike Don, Mary grew up in Yosemite from the age of five and grew up with Camp Curry. She was Phi Beta Kappa at Yale, a highly educated and intelligent lady. After Don's death Mary returned to Yosemite and was president of the Yosemite Park and Curry Company for 22 years, giving it firm leadership and direction Mary was a private person who had a quiet elegance about her, not easy for one from a different generation to know, although I came in contact with her frequently.

She was gracious, generous and universally respected, and loved Yosemite passionately. She knew every corner of it, including every species of flora and fauna. Stuart Cross noted that she often startled Park Service employees, company guides and packers by taking them on long forgotten Army trails and unmarked passes to little known fishing lakes. Don and Mary built the Snow Creek cabin in the High Country and spent many days there with friends. She established Sunrise Camp, the last of the High Sierra Camps, where my son Vince worked.

Mary was provided a place to live at Stanford and also had quarters on the 6th floor of the Ahwahnee. She continued to participate in winter sports, take backpacking trips into the High Country, travel around the world and welcome Stanford friends, former students, family and Yosemite acquaintances.

Stuart Cross notes: "Her leadership skills were a combination of inspiration and quiet criticism, which was even more effective because of the gentle way it was offered. We simply wished never to disappoint her."

Mary left a lasting footprint in Yosemite in a manner far different from Don's. In many ways they complimented each other. Mary died in 1970 at a time when Yosemite was undergoing profound changes and the old order was making way for a new order in the concessions, under the direction of Ed Hardy.

Mary Curry Tresidder.

Stuart Cross

Stuart was the grandson of Rufus Green, who was on the first faculty at Stanford, a mathematics professor who was instrumental in assisting the Curry family in setting up the Curry Camping Company. Stuart's first assignment at Camp Curry, at age 12, was to assist Herbert Sonn, known as "the birdman," who gave lectures on birds and fashioned souvenirs out of pine cones. Stuart worked at Camp Curry in the 1950s when I did. He also taught history at Stanford when I was in law school. I would sneak away from law studies at times and visit with him about many subjects. Stuart had a wide range of interests.

Stuart elected to pursue a career with the Yosemite Park & Curry Company rather than an academic career, and rose in the management ranks. He became the handpicked successor of Mary Curry Tresidder to succeed Hil Oehlmann, Sr., as CEO of the Yosemite Park & Curry Company. He married Hil's daughter Lenore, one of my former babysitters. Stuart did succeed Hil as CEO and also as president of the National Park Concessioners Association. I worked with him in both capacities.

Stuart and Lenore divorced, and both remarried. Both couples and Hil remained friends. I handled the amicable divorce for Stuart. I recall once after Else had died and before Stuart remarried, the two company executives as single men occupied the two largest houses on The Row, two houses apart. When Shasta acquired the company, Stuart was a casualty, both as CEO and as president of the National Park Concessioners Association. Stuart went on to manage hotels for the Mormon Church, including the Hotel Utah in Salt Lake City. After that he founded a headhunting firm for resort hotel executives and was a frequent consultant on National Park matters. Stuart traveled to several foreign countries to consult on establishing national parks.

Stuart was quiet, scholarly and soft-spoken. He had a keen intellect and an inquiring mind. He could converse on many subjects and had an ability to absorb information and later call it up when there was an interest in it.

Shirley Sargent (1927–2004)

No discussion of Yosemite icons would be complete without mention of the late Shirley Sargent. I was privileged to know her as a classmate in the Yosemite Grammar School in 1941 for six months, meeting her several times over the years in Yosemite, reading many of her books on Yosemite, and being interviewed for her last book, *Children in Paradise,* which was introduced at the 1993 reunion of Yosemite Grammar School attendees.

Shirley was born in Southern California and introduced to Yosemite at the age of two, when she spent two summers in Tuolumne Meadows. Her father was a victim of the Great Depression, losing most of his wealth in 1929 and having to go to work on road crews, which is what he was doing when Shirley was living in Tuolumne Meadows. At the age of nine Shirley contracted a crippling neuromuscular disorder, dystopia, which converted an adventurous tomboy into a wheelchair-bound disabled person for most of her long life. Not only did this not destroy her indomitable spirit, it fortified it. Shirley became recognized as the foremost historian of people who influenced Yosemite. She wrote novels, children's books and numerous articles, as well.

For most of her life Shirley lived alone, confined to a wheelchair, taking care of her own needs with the help of many devoted friends and relatives. She managed to get around by driving a car and a three-wheeled bicycle, and even was able to ride a mule into the High Country that she loved. She could walk very little but often managed to crawl for short distances where she wished to go. She devoted her life to writing about Yosemite and exhaustively researching everything she wrote. If you wanted to know anything about the people who shaped Yosemite, Shirley was the most accurate source.

Shirley established a home in Foresta, known as Flying Spur. Foresta is an "in holding" (private property owned before the Park was established, usually a homestead) just outside of Yosemite, adjacent to a big meadow visible from Highway 120 between Merced Canyon and Crane Flat. She lived part of the time in Mariposa, but vastly preferred Flying Spur.

In 1990 her home and most of her belongings were tragically destroyed in the Arch Rock fire. She barely escaped with her life, after refusing offers to retrieve priceless research materials that were lost in the fire. She rebuilt Flying Spur and moved back, before finally having to live out her later years in Mariposa under constant care and in great pain. She hated doctors and hospitals and avoided them whenever possible.

Shirley was accurately described by her biographer, Fernando Penalosa, in a book simply entitled *Shirley Sargent: Yosemite Historian* as "a little bit crazy, adventurous, brave, conservative, courageous, daring, defiant, determined, exceptional, fearless, feisty, gallant, gifted, high-spirited, imaginative, independent, mean, perky, persistent, prickly, rebellious, sharp, spoiled, spunky, strong, stubborn, tolerant, tomboy, traditional, unafraid, wonderful, but most commonly as 'She's such an inspiration.' " She had many admirers, few detractors.

Shirley was honored at many events, including being Squire Bracebridge's honored guest at the Bracebridge Dinner. When she received the Yosemite Fund award in 1994, the citation read in part: "Shirley has devoted her life to the study of Yosemite, its history and its people. As an authority on the Park she has readily shared her knowledge with anyone who expressed an interest, and devoted thousands of hours of her time to participate in events, reunions, the Centennial Celebration and much more to represent the full spectrum of Yosemite's great past."

Martha Miller

Martha qualifies as icon. When Patti and I worked at Tuolumne Meadows Lodge in 1957, Martha worked there. She was still there when my son Martino started working there in 1978, having been manager in the interim. She can still be found there. She was also Special Events Coordinator at the Ahwahnee, and the Coordinator of the Bracebridge Dinner for many years. In the off season Martha is involved in opera. The water rushing over the rocks and pools of the Dana Fork of the Tuolumne River, immediately above Tuolumne Meadows Lodge, is appropriately named Miller Cascade.

Carl Sharsmith

Another icon of note is Carl Sharsmith, a ranger naturalist who has delighted thousands with talks and walks in the High Country.

My contact with Carl is brief but memorable. I have been on several nature walks with him, but the one I remember most is a venture up Erratic Dome in Tuolumne Meadows, with my son Martino when Martino was six years old. Erratics are large granite boulders deposited on the top of domes.

Carl had a gentle nature as a naturalist, despite an earlier career as a logger, and was a hiker of legendary prowess. This story, related by another ranger naturalist, is a good illustration of his character. While Carl was giving a talk along the Merced River in Yosemite Valley, a lady listener peeled an orange and threw the peels on the ground. Without a harsh reprimand, and without interrupting his talk, or saying a word about it, Carl gently picked up the orange peels and placed them in the lady's hand.

Ed Hardy and Don and Kay Pitts

These friends have been extensively portrayed in other chapters. Here I will simply note that they deserve the designation of icon.

Mike Tollefson

Mike Tollefson.

In 2009 the Yosemite Association and the Yosemite Fund were restored to a single association. Mike Tollefson was in charge of that important merger, which has helped to augment the activities that serve park visitors. He resigned in 2008 as park superintendent in order to assume that position.

My friend Bob Hansen spoke for all of us when he said concerning Tollefson's appointment:

"Mike is the perfect choice to lead the Yosemite Fund and work with the National Park Service, donors and many others to improve the Park in the years ahead. I have been fortunate to be associated with many of the Park's sung and unsung heroes and to hold the trust of individuals who care so deeply for this place that they would provide their personal gifts in its favor. The passion of those people for Yosemite, like Mike Tollefson and those at the Fund, will continue to achieve what John Muir exhorted us all to do: 'Make the mountains glad.'

The appointment of a retiring park superintendent as Yosemite Fund president serves to complete an ideal of public and private partnership, which should be a model for all national parks. Mike may rightly be called a developing icon.

Dave Mihalic

I first met Dave Mihalic when he was assigned to Yosemite as superintendent in October 1999, Dave was handpicked by Bruce Babbitt, secretary of the interior. This was due to Dave's reputation for knowing how to get things done. Dave had just completed the General Management Plan for Glacier National Park, where he was superintendent, in just three years, by engaging the public, environmentalists and other interest groups, the local communities and several American Indian tribes, who all came together to support the plan. The approval of the Yosemite Valley Plan (discussed in Chapter 18) was a high priority of the Clinton administration in its final days. Master plans had been either ignored or only partially implemented for 20 years.

Dave completed and delivered the job set forth by Bruce Babbitt. Dave's view on what followed is detailed in Chapters 18 and 19.

I became better acquainted with Dave as we both served on the board of A Christian Ministry in the National Parks (ACMNP), described in Chapter 16. Dave has creative ideas about national park policies, and is not afraid to express his opinions. He is not reticent about making waves or offending those who may disagree with his ideas. It has been refreshing to know a career employee of the federal government with this outlook. I will recognize him as an icon.

David is 1/4 Ogallala Sioux. He jokingly notes, "I don't look like an Indian. That is very hard to do with blue eyes and no hair." David is a graduate of Michigan State and the Kellogg School of Management at Northwestern University. He has worked for the Army Corps of Engineers and the Bureau of Land Management. He joined the Park Service as a ranger in Glacier National Park, then as the Old Faithful District Ranger in Yellowstone, then was named the first superintendent of the Yukon Charley Rivers National Preserve in Alaska. He has served the Park Service at the Great Smokies Mountains and Mammoth Cave National Parks and as chief of policy in Washington, D.C. Before coming to Yosemite he was superintendent in Glacier National Park.

David Mihalic has now retired from the Park Service and lives in Missoula, Montana, with his wife, Jeri, also a career National Park Service professional, and two children, Emily and Nicolas. Since retirement, he does business under the self-styled name "Mihalic Consulting" describing himself as a "Natural Resource Management Consultant and Professional Training Coach and Contractor."

His latest venture was to evaluate the nomination of beech forests in Germany for world heritage status. Since he has retired, Dave has done several world heritage evaluations and monitoring missions for the International Union for the Conservation of Nature, which is part of UNESCO. (Yosemite is one of 22 World Heritage Sites in the United States.) As a technical expert because of his long career in national parks management, Dave has engaged in missions for IUCN in Germany, Austria, the Slovak Republic and Ukraine, and on the Kamchatka Peninsula in the Russian Federation.

NATIVES AND LONG-TIME FRIENDS

This section describes people I know. They are like myself, with roots.

Mike and Jeanne Adams

Mike and I like to say we  are each other's oldest friends. We were in the Yosemite kindergarten and played in the rhythm band, as well as in the dirt outside our houses, in the meadows and in the river. We were in grammar school up to the fourth grade. Once in the third grade I had

Mike and Jeanne Adams. Courtesy of Adams Family Collection.

to step in as Mike's understudy in "The Frog Prince" because Mike experimented with cigarette smoking and got sick. We saw each other somewhat regularly until we both worked at Camp Curry in the 1950s. We both participated in the Bracebridge Dinner as lackeys. Mike was a bear one year, if I recall correctly. Mike commuted to Mariposa High School one year and then went to Wasatch Academy in Mount Pleasant, Utah, before we both met up again at Stanford. We roomed together one quarter in Stanford Village.

Outside the Adams home and the Ansel Adams Gallery there is a rock with potholes in which the Ahwahnechee ground acorn meal. We started a tradition known as the Pothole Party. We scrubbed out the potholes and assigned each guest a pothole in which they could mix their favorite beverage and drink it with a straw. We held several of these gatherings There has not been one recently. The potholes were no worse for the event, and cleaner.

Mike left in his junior year to join the Air Force. He flew in the Air Force reserve 40 years, attaining the rank of Major General. He returned to Yosemite after graduating from Fresno State and worked as a ski instructor and manager of several units. Mike is an expert skier and still skis. Mike visited Patti and me in Italy when I was stationed there. In the summers of 1958 through 1960 Mike managed Tuolumne Meadows Lodge. We share the experience of meeting and courting our respective wives in that special place. Mike and Jeanne were married in the Yosemite Valley Chapel in 1962. Mike went on to obtain a medical degree at Washington University in St. Louis and participated in a flight surgeon program in Germany before establishing a practice in internal medicine in Fresno.

Mike's family still operates the Ansel Adams Gallery. I am on the Board of Directors. Mike is now retired from medical practice and spends time in his home in Fresno and the home of Ansel and Virginia in Carmel Highlands and their A-frame in Yosemite West. Mike travels around the country and the world giving presentations on Ansel's work. Mike and I are on the board of ACMNP.

Being the son of a world-famous father is not always easy. Mike has handled it gracefully and is his own person. Ansel was once known to remark that two things he always wanted to do were to fly and to be a doctor. Mike fulfilled both those ambitions. Recently we were on a float trip on the Snake River in Jackson Hole. The guide, a pleasant young man, pointed out the spot where he said Ansel took his famous picture of the Tetons and Snake River. I asked him if he knew that Ansel's son was on board. While he was trying to figure out if we were putting him on, Mike said, "I was with him when he took it." Mike did not tell our pleasant river guide that he was wrong about where the picture was taken.

We have been on some notable trips, one a journey through Namibia. We traveled with a group, each of whom knew someone else in the group. When we added up the total years of acquaintance it came to 250 years. I also was on a memorable trip through the Greek Islands on the famous yacht the *Sea Cloud* with Mike's wife, Jeanne, and daughter, Sarah. This was usually a pricey trip, but we found out a Stanford trip had been cancelled and the price reduced by two thirds. We signed up in about 24 hours of hearing this. I look forward to more adventures with Mike and Jeanne (see Jeanne's bio on page 160).

Anne Adams Helms and Ken Helms

Anne is Ansel's daughter and Mike's sister. I am between Mike and Anne in age. Anne and I were in kindergarten together in the year in which I was held back from "the big school" due to bureaucracy. Anne attended Dominican High School in Marin County, California, and Stanford, when I was also at Stanford. She also attended Barnard College in New York one semester while I was at Cornell.

After graduation from Stanford Anne worked briefly in the Stanford business office. She worked for the California Tuberculosis Association in San Francisco and as a junior editor for Stanford Research Institute. She married Chuck Mayhew and had three daughters before Chuck was tragically killed in an accident. She was married to Ken Helms in 1971.

Anne ran the family publishing business, Museum Graphics, for 25 years until her daughter Alison took it over. Another daughter, Virginia, is a talented and recognized jazz musician in New York. Virginia crossed my path when she worked as a clinician at the Monterey Jazz Festival when my wife Patti was on the board, another example of how Yosemite people come in and out of my life. Anne's third daughter, Sylvia, is a Realtor® in Pleasanton, California. Anne has written extensively on the history of the Adams family and has done genealogical research.

Ken Helms has had a career that somehow defies description. Originally from Peoria, Illinois, he served as a Unitarian minister in Canada and Redwood City, California, where he met Anne. He left organized religion and converted to atheism and secular humanism. He completed an M.A. in psychology from San Jose State University in 1978.

His professional efforts have included drug education teaching and counseling at the high school level, director of a summer youth project, a Veterans Administration study associated with coronary bypass surgery, instruction in psychology at the community college level, private counseling, and several projects involved in creating greater self-awareness, pride and self-esteem in early adolescents. Ken has been an instructor in a wide variety of adult education courses including effective parenting and remedial memory training for seniors. Ken has been a guest lecturer on several major cruise lines on the topic "Memory: How it works, and why it sometimes doesn't."

Anne inherited Ansel's devotion to environmental causes. Anne and Ken have started a local humanist group that tries to help with local peace, social issues and conservation locally. Anne and Ken travel extensively throughout the world. They moved to Monterey County in California to be near Virginia after Ansel died in 1984 and now live about five minutes away from me in the area John Steinbeck described as "The Pastures of Heaven," in a home overlooking a tennis club which I helped found and still frequent. Anne just keeps coming in and out of my life, but I don't see her enough.

Dick Otter

I met Dick Otter when we were both children and playmates in Yosemite. Dick lived in Yosemite until his mother was killed in an automobile accident when Dick was in the first grade. After Dick moved to Berkeley to live with his grandmother, he spent a couple of summers with my family in Yosemite. We two only children were like brothers.

Dick's father, Wendell, started as a porter at Camp Curry. He then managed Yosemite Lodge for many years. Dick spent a summer with me on the Orme Ranch Summer Camp in Arizona. Dick and I frequently visited each other in Palo Alto and Berkeley during high school. I attended Stanford and he UC Berkeley. After college Dick joined the Marines and went on to become a stockbroker, investment advisor and prominent civic leader in San Francisco.

Dick met his wife, the former Ann Wiper, on a blind date on September 26, 1960 at the first Kennedy-Nixon debate in Washington. Dick was prominent in founding the Yosemite Fund when it split off from the Yosemite Association.

Gordon and Louise Hooley, Bart and Nancy Hooley

Bart and his late sister Nancy are twins, born in Yosemite. They were both in my kindergarten class with Anne Adams Helms. Bart's father, the late Gordon Hooley, came to Yosemite from Canada as a ski instructor. His mother, the late Louise Hooley, whom we called "Hoopee," studied art in Seattle with my mother Della before either of them came to Yosemite. The Hoss and Hooley families remained close friends as Gordon and Hoopee moved to various resorts that Gordon managed. Bart and Nancy left Yosemite after the first grade. They moved with their parents to Sugar Bowl, which Gordon and Hoopee managed in the late forties.

At Sugar Bowl, Bart and Nancy skied in the winter and went to school in summer, both becoming expert skiers. They both attended Wasatch Academy in Utah with Mike Adams and several other Yosemite kids. They both wound up at Stanford when I was there. Gordon and Hoopee moved on to manage hotels: Castle Hot Springs in Arizona, Rickey's in Palo Alto and the Casa Munras in Monterey before ending up in Reno, where Gordon managed the Mapes Hotel.

Adventures in Bart's company are related in Chapter 5 and Chapter 23. I could never match his mountain man skills. Bart graduated from Stanford as a civil engineer and worked on the linear accelerator five years before going into public works in Reno. While at Sugar Bowl Bart met and visited some sons and daughters of the rich and famous, but he remained his original self. When Bart retired, he and his wife, Diane, decided they would like to sail around the world and bought a sailboat and learned to sail. A three-year adventure turned into a six-year odyssey. Bart and Diane now live outside of Reno and raise horses. Bart

Max Hoffman and Mrs. Gordon (Louise) Hooley, at the Wawona Tunnel dedication, 1933. Courtesy of Yosemite Research Library.

never seems to change much as he pops in and out of my life.

Nancy was perky and fun and loved a good time. She was an erstwhile girlfriend, but she was too much like family. She used to kid me unmercifully about a romantic interlude in the linen closet at Camp Curry. We had lots of good times in Yosemite. When I think of Nancy I think of her imitating Eartha Kitt and doing renditions of Eartha's favorite songs, quite authentically. Nancy fought a long battle with cancer courageously and managed to be her old self a good part of it but finally succumbed.

Charlie Castro

Charlie grew up in the Indian village near Yosemite Lodge, which is no longer there. He attended Yosemite Grammar School. He is one of a handful of descendants of the original Indians in Yosemite Valley. Charlie attended Yosemite Grammar School when I did, then Mariposa High School, and one semester at Fresno State. As Charlie tells it, he was hanging around Yosemite Valley wondering what to do with his life when a ranger, Emil Ernst, asked him if he would like to work for the Park Service. When Charlie responded affirmatively, he was asked "Do you know anything about trees?" Charlie replied, "No, but I can learn."

Here are Charlie's comments on his career in the National Park Service:

"I started working seasonally in Yosemite in 1951–1953, with steady employment in 1953. Darla and I were married in the little Chapel in Yosemite in 1953. I started on the old Bilster Rust Control crews and wood-cutting crews in the beginning, and progressed into climbing and felling trees throughout Yosemite National Park. I became a professional tree climber fire fighter, which was highly beneficial for my NPS career. I moved to Sequoia and Kings Canyon National Park in 1964, where I started their first forestry crew. As time passed, I was recognized as the top NPS hazardous tree removal expert. After a few years of being involved in the NPS HazardousTree Mitigation Program, I was given the responsibility of managing the program throughout the Pacific Northwest Region, which included all NPS public and permanent facilities from Alaska to southern California, east to Arizona, and west to the Hawaiian Islands."By this time our kids had grown up, some married with their own children. Darla and I made our home in Three Rivers, California.

"Because of my exposure and acquaintance with rock climbing in Yosemite, tree climbing came easy. In 1967 I ascended the large California Tree in the Grant Grove area. I was labeled as the only man to climb a burning Sequoia tree to suppress a fire caused by lightning, and received recognition from the professional science research team that covered ecology of the Giant Sequoia trees in the Sierra Nevada. I work with that team, climbing the huge Sequoias for their entomology field research.

"In Kings Canyon National Park, there's a 'Castro Tree' in Redwood Canyon. It's the tree I climbed and attached an elevator basket to, 250 feet above ground."

Charlie learned to play drums by banging on pots and pans in the Indian Village. This led him to become a drummer with the High Sierra Jazz Band from Three Rivers, one of the most popular and sought-after traditional jazz bands. I became reacquainted with Charlie when he played with High Sierra in Monterey. Since then I have accompanied Charlie and Darla on cruises to the U.K., Ireland, Iceland and Portugal.

On a recent cruise, in May 2011, the High Sierra Jazz Band, with Charlie playing drums, performed before an audience of 10,000 Japanese near the famed Miho Museum. The concert started slowly and respectfully and ended with the audience on its feet dancing and cheering, with smiles everywhere. This is coming some distance from banging on pots and pans in the Indian Village in Yosemite Valley.

Charlie and Darla have ten grandchildren. One has graduated from Stanford and two attend Stanford. Another is attending Westmont College, and another has graduated from Columbia College.

IN AND OUT OF MY LIFE

The people in this section are not icons of Yosemite, family or natives. They are discussed here to illustrate how close friends from Yosemite have a way of coming back into my life in a quite remarkable way. The description of them is briefer than deserved.

Meredith Little

I knew Meredith Little at Stanford and Yosemite. She was an avid hiker and a fellow employee at the Tuolumne Meadows Lodge. She is one of the most fascinating and unconventional people I have ever met. She and a friend once hiked all 200 miles of the John Muir trail playing a recorder for food. At one point a Boy Scout Troup was generous in rewarding her for her performance.

The day I reported for duty at the Tuolumne Meadows Lodge I discovered that another new arrival was a set of steel drums that had been made in the

Virgin Islands, which Meredith had recently visited. Meredith wanted to add the drums to the list of instruments that she was able to play. The camp manager permitted her to practice, but insisted that she take the drums into the woods a sufficient distance that the sounds of her practice wouldn't offend the ears of the guests.

Meredith plays harp-sichord, recorder, piano and

Peter with Meredith Little.

guitar as well as several other instruments I may have forgotten. At Tioga Pass Resort, about ten miles from Tuolumne Meadows Lodge, there was an ancient, dysfunctional organ that no one except Meredith could play.

Her attention to music was no idle pastime. She obtained a Ph.D. in music from Stanford, specializing in obscure baroque music and giving numerous concerts on the harpsichord. She became friends with my parents during these years, as they followed and supported her varied endeavors.

Meredith married an equally brilliant and unconventional person who was pursuing a Ph.D. in biochemistry. They both eventually wound up teaching at the University of Arizona, where Meredith taught humanities as well as music.

In the middle of her academic pursuits Meredith switched careers, went to law school and became a practicing attorney. Meredith has a strong social conscience and has done a lot of pro bono work for the underprivileged.

I have followed the course of Meredith's career with great interest, watching to see what she will do next. She has been slowed down by a stroke, and turned the law practice over to her daughter. She carries on.

Rol Summit

Rol Summit and I were coworkers, tentmates and close friends for three summers. During one of them, he engaged in the unusual project of installing a drinking fountain in his '49 Ford.

He attended Pomona College and UCLA medical school. After graduation and residency he became a psychiatrist for Los Angeles County. He became an internationally recognized expert on child abuse. He developed a breakthrough theory about the blockage of memories by sexually abused children entitled "Child Sexual Abuse Accommodation Syndrome."

I lost track of Rol for about 20 years. Then I read in a newspaper article that he had been an expert witness in a much-publicized trial.

I discovered that he had developed the unusual hobby of buying, restoring and trading carousel horses, which turned out to be enjoyable and lucrative.

Rol invited me to participate in his retirement dinner. To celebrate in high style he wanted to produce a version of "This Is Your Life," featuring people from all the parts of his life. I covered the events of our working days in Yosemite. This part of his life was unknown to his later professional colleagues.

George McInnis

When George was in middle school in Oakland, California, in the late 1940s, his mother would take him and his older sisters to Yosemite, drop them off in a campground, and leave them on their own for a week and pick them up. They got along fine. It is hard to imagine doing something like that today. George worked in Yosemite in the early 1950s when we both worked at Camp Curry. We had many good times. He knew my wife, Patti, before I did. George went to law school at Boalt Hall. I lost track of him for about ten years. Then one day he showed up as a new deputy district attorney in Monterey County, later going into private practice in Salinas.

George and I have hiked all over the Sierras and the west for thirty years and see each other several times a week. He lives less than a half mile from me. We have had only one contested legal case in all this time. George's client tried to enjoin my client for going into a competing business and sued him for a million dollars. I countersued for two million. The case never got to a preliminary injunction.

George happened to be at Tuolumne Meadows at the time of a Celebration of Life for Patti. He conducted the celebration for her, attended by Nic Fiore, Sarah Adams, Don and Kay Pitts and Martha Miller, among others.

Harkjoon Paik

Harkjoon Paik has been identified as a companion on my first date with Patti. Our paths crossed in Monterey County, when he became the first public defender in Monterey County and later a Superior Court judge. I appeared before him on several occasions in his role as a judge.

Due to his distinctive style in getting to the core of the issue without a lot of dialogue, he was referred to by the attorneys who practiced before him as the "Oriental Express."

John Argue (1932–2002)

John came to Yosemite one summer while in college at USC. He was a good softball player. At that time there was intense competition in softball between teams coached by Fred Pierson and Earl Pierson, who were chefs at the Ahwahnee and Yosemite Lodge. John was invited to join the Ahwahnee team. When he excelled at softball, he was offered a job at the Ahwahnee. John and I worked at the Ahwahnee one Christmas. At that time John was practicing law with his father under the classic firm name "Argue and Argue, attorneys at law." On two occasions I had a need for an attorney in Los Angeles, once to help a serviceman while I was in Italy, and the second time to set up a trust on some oil-producing property in Los Angeles owned by an deceased aunt of Della, whose husband struck oil on her property. This led to a thirty-year relationship with John representing the trust. John became a very prominent attorney in Los Angeles, a prime mover in bringing the Olympics to Los Angeles and the drafter of what was then the largest television contract in history. John had contacts throughout Los Angeles who were invaluable.

Bob Righter

Bob has been mentioned as the writer of the leading historical book on Hetch Hetchy, and also as a co-tenant in the cabin in El Portal. I lost contact with Bob for over forty years, until he showed up at the Spring Forum of the Yosemite Association to talk about his book. We took up on where we left off, as if no time had intervened.

During those "silent years" Bob received his Ph.D. from University of California, Santa Barbara. He taught at universities in California, Wyoming and Texas. Although he was trained as an historian of the American West, he is specifically interested in environmental history. He has authored six books on national parks and wind energy.

I have lost touch with Bob again. I hope this book finds its way into his hands.

Tom Shepherd

Tom is the senior partner at Neumiller & Beardslee, a prominent law firm in Stockton, California. He played a very active role in the Yosemite Association, holding various positions and serving on the board of trustees. I never met him in these capacities. In 2006 on a trip to Australia his wife introduced them as "the good shepherds." We enjoyed the rest of the trip, finding that in addition to the Yosemite connection we had considerable other connections.

Sue Mathewson

Sue Mathewson lives in Chicago. We had adventures in Yosemite. She was at Stanford when I was in law school. After raising four children she returned to Yosemite to manage the May Lake High Sierra camp for one summer. Sue has hiked as far as the Mt. Everest base camp. She was on the trip to Namibia with Mike and Jean Adams and told us about the discount on the *Sea Cloud* sail.

Roger and Ann Hendrickson

Roger is responsible for the chapter on medical practice in Yosemite (see photo, page 154). I have run into Roger and Ann Hendrickson several times since he left Yosemite as a doctor. We have been on the Trans-Sierra Gourmet Ski Trip (see Chapter 24), and we have attended several traditional jazz festivals.

Backpacking, Peter Hoss style. Courtesy of Dick Mansfield.

CHAPTER 24

ADVENTURES & MISADVENTURES

DICK OTTER'S ICY INTERLUDE

Dick, Mike Adams and I were hiking above Mirror Lake. We were skinny-dipping. Mike and I got out and got dressed, leaving Dick in a very cold pool. A group of Girl Scouts came along. Mike and I engaged in extended conversation, while Dick modestly declined to get out of the pool. "Why isn't your friend getting out of the pool?" the girls asked.

Dick replied, his teeth chattering, "I really like it in here."

ASCENTS

I was not attracted to technical climbing, which can become a consuming passion to those who embrace it. However, I have been attracted to ascending peaks whose summits can be reached by walking. Over the years I have ascended most major peaks in Yosemite National Park, notably Half Dome (three times) Clouds Rest, North Dome, El Capitan (via the trail from the top of Yosemite Falls), Sentinel Peak, Mt. Hoffman, Mt. Dana, Mt. Conness, Mt. Clark, Cathedral Peak, Matterhorn Peak, Mt. Banner, Mt. Lyell, Vogelsang Peak, Forsyth Peak (at the north boundary of the park) Tenaya Peak, Ragged Peak, Gaylor Peak and a few lesser summits. I have never tired of drinking in the view from the summit of a Yosemite peak.

While working at Camp Curry a group of us ascended Mt. Whitney, the highest point in the continental U.S. This required a 200-mile drive over Tioga Pass and down Highway 395 to reach the trailhead. The group included my perennial hiking companion Bart Hooley. Also in the group was my close friend Rol Summit. Rol was saving money for medical school and was noted for his parsimony. He would take salad dressing from the cafeteria and buy lettuce at the grocery store for lunch. We resolved that we would each carry a can of beer to the summit. At the summit a hiker who had been in the backcountry three weeks offered Rol $5.00 for the beer, which would have amounted to about a 2000% recovery on his investment. Casting off parsimony, Rol declined the offer and offered the hiker only a sip.

On another occasion Bart Hooley and I attempted a climb of Mts. Banner and Ritter, on the east side of the Sierras near Mt. Lyell. We made it to the top of Mt. Banner at 5 p.m. and arrived back at the trailhead at 2 a.m. after walking in a rainstorm with a carbide lantern that expired. Bart and I also climbed Matterhorn Peak by the route described by Jack Kerouac at the beginning of his 1958 classic, *The Dharma Bums*.

I can claim one ascent of a previously unnamed peak near Emeric Lake where three fathers were camped. The fathers were Tony Royal, Joe Hancock and myself. In honor of ourselves we named the peak Royal Hosscock Mountain. Joe Hancock and I resolved to climb it and did so. Tony stayed at the lake to watch the boys. Near the summit we encountered a Sierra thunderstorm of major proportions and fortunately found a dry comfortable cave in the rocks from which to watch lightning dance off the peaks and thunder roar near us, a memorable experience. Tony was very relieved to see us return safely.

For thirty plus years, Eric Brazil, now a retired journalist, and I hiked all over the West, as well as the Sierras. Our first venture was with our sons, then aged 12 or 13. We hiked across the Sierras from one side to the other, starting at Florence Lake, on the west side, ending at Parchers Camp, on the east side, through Evolution Valley, over Muir Pass and into Dusy Basin. Two other hikers left a car on the other side and we traded keys, but they managed to meet us in a rainstorm. It rained every day, but it was a great adventure. We found out later that someone had been seeding clouds.

After this somewhat unprepared start, Eric and I explored the Trinity Alps in Northern California; the Three Sisters area in Oregon; the North Cascades in Washington; Boundary Peak, Arc Dome, Wheeler Peak and the Ruby Mountains in Nevada; the Green River by canoe, Dark Canyon and Paria Canyon in Utah; Organ Pipe Cactus National Monument and the Superstition Mountains in Arizona; Carlsbad Caverns in New Mexico; and Guadalupe Peak and Big Bend National Park in Texas.

Eric far surpassed me as an explorer of mountains and has visited about twice as many as I have. However, he finally got around to exploring Yosemite and asked me what my three favorite one-day hikes were in the Yosemite High Country. I told him Mt. Hoffman from May Lake, Waterwheel Falls from Tuolumne Meadows, and North Dome from Porcupine Flat. He did them on three successive days and confirmed my recommendations.

Through these and some lesser experiences I retain a vision of what the world looks like from atop a Yosemite peak. The frenzied anticipation of an ascent can be accurately described as a fit of peak, and conversation when the climb is complete as a summit conference.

BACKPACKING TREKS I HAVE KNOWN

Since my experience with mules at the age of 13, I have never attempted another backpacking adventure with these sturdy but stubborn beasts. I am not a fancier of horseback riding and consider it a rather uncomfortable means of transportation. Therefore, I have not ridden a horse into the backcountry since putting up and tearing down the High Sierra Camps in 1957. Some lovers of the backcountry prefer to go in style, to be spot-packed in and left at an idyllic spot with gourmet food, drink, camp chairs and other amenities. This was Hil's preference.

My style has been to load everything in a backpack, eat freeze-dried food and carry as little as possible. To me this style of backpacking is therapeutic because of the magnificent simplicity of it. Choices are reduced: how many miles, where to camp. When we see a lake, we jump in for a bracing swim. We stop when we feel like it. We don't need to look for pasture for mules or horses or round them up and pack them. There are concerns, such as whether it will rain or whether bears will get food, but they are solved by a good tent and a good tree in which to hang food.

There is a routine: find the campsite, swim, a cocktail hour with a precious supply of wine or bourbon, dinner (which always tastes good), an evening constitutional to the top of a promontory to watch alpenglow, a campfire (wood is generally plentiful), watch Venus and then the stars rise, good discussions, doze off, sometimes awake to moonlight, and awake to a usually glorious morning. The weather pattern in the Sierra is most often crystal clear mornings, clouds gathering in midday as the warm air hits the cold granite, and possible afternoon thundershowers clearing at dusk. There have been exceptions, mistakes, and a few miserable nights, but they are few, fade away and make good stories. After a few days or a week of this style of backpacking, one emerges refreshed, spiritually renewed, in good shape from the exercise, ready to face the stresses of work and the world, a new person. I have gone mostly with perennial companions, sometimes with family, once with Boy Scouts, once with a Sierra Club group, never alone, and never with strangers thrown together.

Traveling in this manner, I have seen most of the Yosemite High Country.

WHERE ARE MY FRIENDS?

I am indebted to Les Hilmer, a coworker in Yosemite in the 1950s for this story. I have long ago lost track of Les, but remember the story.

Les was hiking near Tuolumne Meadows and had seen few other hikers all day. He was several miles from the road head as twilight began to descend on the peaks. There were two, maybe three hours of daylight remaining. Along came a sole hiker carrying a very large pack. He sat down, and he and Les exchanged pleasantries as hikers do who meet in the mountains.

Les noticed the pack that the sole hiker was carrying contained nothing but beer. The sole hiker inquired, "Have you seen a couple of other guys recently?" Les said he had not seen anyone for a few hours. He sole hiker continued. "Well, we all started out. One of us took all the food. Another took all the tents and sleeping bags. I took all the beer. I seem to have lost track of them." Les said he was sorry he could not help.

The beer-laden backpacker trudged off into the gathering twilight. The end of the story is not known. I have often reflected on this question: Who would you rather be on a night in the Yosemite backcountry—the guy with the food, the guy with the tents and sleeping bags, or the guy with the beer?

A CLOSE CALL FOR BART

During the spring break of my senior year at Stanford, we were visiting our cabin. While there, a storm system passed through the Valley, turning our planned brief visit into an overnight stay due to heavy rain.

A group of cross-country skiers from the Stanford Alpine Club had ignored warnings about the impending storm and decided to ski across the Sierras from Mammoth Lakes to Yosemite Valley. One of the skiers was my aforementioned childhood friend Bart Hooley.

The weather turned savage. The skiers foundered in deep snow in the High Country. They were left stranded by one storm while another was bearing down on them. One of the skiers developed pulmonary edema. Bart and another skier, Max Allen, left their companions and skied 40 miles over passes and down the canyon of the Merced River, past Nevada Fall and down into Yosemite, making their way in white-out conditions, hardly able to see the snow at their feet. They navigated by a few visual references, their familiarity with the territory and a lot of skill. I don't know many other people who could have done it.

When the Park Service learned of the plight, a helicopter was dispatched to rescue the skiers left behind. The pilot somehow located the spot where the group had encamped, picked them up only minutes before the next blizzard hit, then flew them back to Yosemite Valley, where he made a landing on one of the roads into the Valley, leaning out the window and hollering at the traffic below to move aside and give him space to land.

The blizzard conditions in the High Country were only rainstorms on the Valley floor. We were able to watch the helicopter land and discharge the refugees from the relative comfort of our rain-drenched cabin. The skiers were told to leave all their equipment behind at the departure point. They knew they were fortunate to get out with their lives.

Once the weather cleared, in the spring, the Park Service ordered the skiers to hike back to the site to retrieve the skiers' equipment. They discovered that the skiers had actually camped on a lake. When the surface thawed, their gear sank to the bottom of the lake.

Bart wrote about the adventure in an outdoors magazine. He was pleased, of course, that he and the others survived the ordeal, but tended to be nonchalant about the incident, and referred to it as "not a big deal," just another of many adventures. His zeal for the mountains remained undiminished.

TRANS–SIERRA GOURMET SKI TRIP

During the winter of 1972 I had one of the great adventures of my life, spending four days cross-country skiing through the wilderness areas of Yosemite Park.

The Yosemite High Country in the winter is a completely different place frm the summertime version. Tourist facilities are closed. Hillsides and meadows are often covered with blankets of drifted snow to depths of 20 feet. Except for skiers, the region is deserted except for a couple of park rangers who have the place to themselves.

All of the Sierra High

Snow Canyon Creek cabin.

County is closed off to snowmobiles, so cross-country skiing or snowshoes provide the only practical way of wintertime access. Members of the Yosemite Winter Club have, in fact, been skiing into and through the area since the club's formation in 1928—long before skiing had become the popular pastime that it is now.

The Cross-Country Section of the Yosemite Winter Club has developed a unique adventure known as the Trans-Sierra Gourmet Ski Trip, which is dedicated to providing enjoyment of the wilderness in five-star style. The four-day, three-night trip crosses Yosemite National Park from the Tioga Pass entrance to Yosemite Valley—slightly less than the 70 miles by road. Preparations are made for the trip before the roads close. An advance group stocks the three overnight stops with food and spirits, so the trekkers need carry only clothing, sleeping bags and sundries in light daypacks.

The trip was a real adventure for me, because up to that point my skiing experience had been of the downhill variety. However, an associate in our law firm, Al Smith, talked me into going on the trip with him. He assured me that cross-country skiing would be no problem and that he would look after me. He proved to be true to his word.

We flew out of the tiny Pine Mountain Lake airport on a clear winter day. I was feeling a little creaky because Al and I had spent the night sleeping on the floor of the small waiting room, together with my new skis, poles, gaiters, wool knickers, light pack and socks, together with a bag of cookies and other goodies that Patti had provided.

The reality of what I was about to do began to dawn on me. It seemed to me that it might have been foolish of me to attempt such a daunting cross-country skiing trip in the absence of any cross-country skiing experience.

The flight across Hetch Hetchy Reservoir, Yosemite Valley, Half Dome, the Clark Range, Tenaya Lake, Mt. Hoffman, Tuolumne Meadows, Mt. Conness, Matterhorn Peak, the Sawtooth Ridge, Twin Lakes, Virginia Lake and Mono Lake was spectacular. It was familiar territory clothed in winter garb.

We landed at Lee Vining airport. We met people from two other flights. The 25 of us, mostly complete strangers, got into the back of pickup trucks and we started up the Tioga Road. The weather remained favorable as we assembled beneath a pinnacle that we once nicknamed "Nigel's Needle." We suited up, adjusted our packs, and applied sun block. The trip began with an easy uphill through truly spectacular scenery. We skied through a world that was completely silent except for the soft shushing sounds of our skis over the snow and the call of an occasional winter bird.

As we rounded the turn above Ellery Lake, the sunshine and the exercise began to make us warm. By that time some of us were skiing in shorts and shirtsleeves. We stopped at the Saddlebag Lake turnoff to enjoy a candy bar and the spectacular view. The Tioga Pass Resort was almost totally covered with snow and looked like a something in a Currier & Ives print.

We crossed the frozen Tioga Lake and made it to the top of the Tioga Pass by 1 p.m. We found the ranger station. An earlier blizzard had covered everything with a thick blanket of snow. An earlier party had thoughtfully shoveled a path to a bathroom window, which provided easier access to the ranger station than the front door that was buried beneath many feet of drifted snow.

The interior of the ranger station was gloomy because all the windows in the place, except for the one in the bathroom, were covered. We enjoyed the supply of beer that had been thoughtfully provided months earlier for our enjoyment. The ranger station was a picturesque place with a wood stove, bunks, a collection of signs, a fireplace, ranger materials, brochures, and news magazines that were three years old. We had some free time. One ambitious group set off to ski toward Mt. Dana, another group to ski to a nearby ghost town, called Bennettville. Others napped, read three-year-old news or sat around telling mountain stories.

As evening shadows fell, we turned on electric lights, boiled snow to make water, and partook of a delicious dinner complete with appropriate wine. Following dinner we joked, and sang folk songs, sea chanteys, and oldies-but-goodies from the 40s and 50s, including a song called the "Frozen Logger," which only Don Pitts and I knew. We were no longer strangers. We were comrades. By 10:30 p.m. we had sung all the songs we knew, so we spread our sleeping bags on whatever floor surface we could find and drifted off to sleep. Some of the more adventurous among us spent the night sleeping in snow caves they had excavated in the drifts that were piled up everywhere.

We woke the next morning to another cloudless day. Following a brisk breakfast of juice, eggs and cereal, we put on our skis. By 9 a.m. we were cruising down an easy eight-mile downhill run toward our destination at Tuolumne Meadows, passing a series of breathtaking vistas and overlooks for a series of mountain peaks including Dana, Gibbs, Mammoth, Lembert Dome, Unicorn and Cathedral. We skied down the road on a gentle grade, passing those scenes of snowy beauty in perfect weather.

We arrived at Tuolumne Meadows at about 12:30 p.m., unlocking the ranger cabin to find more treasures of beer and food. In addition, the Tuolumne Meadows Ranger Station came complete with actual rangers. We found that the cabin was much roomier than the one we had stayed at the day before. In addition, the facility had more of the trappings of civilization, including such things as curtains on the windows and working telephones.

That afternoon we explored Lyell Fork and Tuolumne Meadows Lodge. The Dana Fork of the Tuolumne River was completely buried in snow. I was intimately acquainted with the place, after having worked there one summer and visiting it on several occasions, but now—with snow up to the rafters and dumpsters barely visible above the drifted snow—the familiar scenery had an eerie air of unfamiliarity.

The ranger station took on a festive air that evening as we broke out champagne, prepared another delicious meal and ended with singing around the fireplace songs that we had forgotten about from the night before. There was much more sleeping space; each of us actually got his own bed.

Our luck with the weather held out, and the next day dawned bright and clear—mind-boggling in its beauty. We had coffee, juice and cereal and then put on our skis again and headed across the familiar bridge at Tuolumne Meadows. We viewed the frozen river and the snow-capped pinnacles of Cathedral Rocks, Unicorn Peak and Echo Peak. While skiing across the Meadows, I began to feel really at home on cross-country skis—the rhythmic gliding motion had become comfortable and felt graceful. We were skiing down a pleasant downhill to Tenaya Lake. The sunshine reflecting off the brilliant snow began to bother my eyes. We saw a few places of open water on Tenaya Lake, so we decided to ski the road rather than chance the lake's ice.

The afternoon skiing was uphill, difficult, and hot. The difficulty of the ascent was considerably ameliorated by two nurses who were handing out beer and backrubs. Later in the afternoon our course led through a deep forest and the trip began to grow pleasant once again. Mount Hoffman came into view and then the pleasant shade of the May Lake parking lot. We began looking for our nighttime destination, which was the snow survey cabin at Snow Flat. It was 4 p.m. and we were feeling the 12 miles that we had covered.

The old Tioga Road began to diminish, filling our minds with the unsettling surmise that we might have gone too far. We stopped to reconnoiter, and some of our party began a furtive search back along our trail to see if we had gone astray.

Some of the more mellow members of our party decided to imbibe a pleasing libation they had thoughtfully brought with them consisting of gin and lime juice—a gimlet. They offered me one. The exercise of the day, together with the gorgeous surroundings and pleasant company, made the drink one of the most refreshing drinks of my life. By the time we had finished our drinks, the searchers returned and said that we were actually at the junction of the very trail we had been looking for and that the cabin was only 100 yards from where we had been enjoying the drink. I learned a lesson from that experience. When you are in confusion and doubt, take a break! Have a gimlet! Things will work out.

The Snow Flat snow cabin, which was our destination, is an A-frame with a loft and a balcony, smaller than previous accommodations and with no electricity. We illuminated our evening with Coleman lanterns.

I climbed onto one of the upper bunks so I could get out of my gear, and wound up remaining in that bunk for five hours—though two beers, a nap, wine and dinner, all of which (except for the nap) were passed up to me. The evening songfest, which had by that time become a tradition, was greatly augmented by an extemporaneous talent show that included skits, songs, jokes and a memorable rope trick in which Al Smith roped himself to an appellate judge who was part of our expedition. By this time a great feeling of camaraderie had developed among us and we all felt as though we had been lifelong friends.

The illusion of my being a competent cross-country skier was dispelled by the difficulties that I faced when we left the Snow Flat cabin. The day started out with a reasonable course that wound through forests. We had lunch on a beautiful but windswept spot known as Serendipity Point, overlooking Tenaya Canyon with a spectacular view of Clouds Rest.

After lunch we began skiing down a relatively steep grade, which is the most difficult part of cross-country skiing, threading our way through a heavily wooded area. Cross-country skis are narrower than downhill skis and have no edges. The heels of cross-country boots are not attached to the skis. This helps walking movements on a flat or uphill level, but gives the skier little control when going downhill.

The most effective way for cross-country skiers to slow their progress downhill is by encountering an uphill grade, but that isn't always possible. Skiers are able to spread skis in a snowplow, but with difficulty if inexperienced, as I was. A skier can help further slow progress by dragging his pole between his legs, but that trick is not easy, nor was it effective for me. Downhill cross-country skiers have one weapon in their downhill arsenal. A descender is a sock-like device fastened to the rear of the ski by a rope that is crossed across the bottom of the ski and fastened to the front of the binding, in effect converting the ski to a narrow snowshoe. Descenders permit a downhill skier to walk straight down a hill. It is safe but laborious.

Downhill skiing with cross-country skis becomes even more difficult when boots get wet and begin to slip off the skis, which then turn sideways in the soft snow. At one point even side slipping down a steep slope became so ineffective that I finally removed my skis and simply trudged down the hill, sinking to my thighs with each step. I would sometimes think that I could ski the switchbacks and then put the descenders on, but I fell on every other turn, becoming increasingly aggravated and filling the uncaring trees around me with my expletives. Al remained sympathetic and helpful.

I clumsily shuffled the final two miles on descenders and finally reached the end of the snowline on the top of the switchbacks leading down Tenaya Canyon. At that point I had a beer, which tasted marvelous under the circumstances. I shared it with two Yosemite employees I encountered who were on their way to ski to June Lake, where they were going to register for unemployment.

It was a blessed relief to be out of the snow. We strapped our skis to our backs and started walking down the trail, watching with interest the snow falling off the face of Half Dome. I was grateful to be able to control my course again, but the walk grew tedious. It seemed that we would never arrive at the Valley floor, which we could see so clearly below us. We finally arrived on flat ground at Mirror Lake.

It was 6:30 and evening shadows were descending on the Valley when I came limping into camp in the company of Don Pitts and his then-fiancée, Kay. We discovered that the others had arrived only shortly before us, which made me feel somewhat less incompetent. The trail hadn't been easy for anyone.

We arrived home at 3:30 a.m., following one of the more eventful 21-hour days of my life. My calves and ankles were sore, but I was proud of the accomplishment, which had actually been somewhat foolhardy due to my lack of experience. If the weather had not been perfect, there could have been big-time trouble.

I never again went on a Trans–Sierra gourmet trip and never really mastered the niceties of cross-country skiing, but contented myself with downhill skiing.

However, I became an evangelist for the trip. I spoke so enthusiastically about my experience that several of my friends started taking the trip—going multiple times and calling themselves groupies of the experience, accepting me as a fellow groupie since I was the one who had first directed them to the event.

When he learned about my experience, my son Vince went on the trip ten years in a row and has now gone 12 times. He met his wife Wendy on one of the trips.

The trip continues, but the course has changed.

RIVER RATS

In 1969 a group of eight young couples went on a trip down Northern California's Klamath River. We had such a great time together that we formed a group, calling ourselves the "River Rats." We have continued doing some outdoor activity together as an annual event since 1969.

We knew that no trip would actually happen unless someone was in charge, a "dictator" responsible for selecting the location and other details. Later we changed to two dictators so that there would be backup. Every year we have drawn lots for the positions, selecting the two couples to be responsible for the subsequent year's trip.

We always conduct our annual event on the first weekend following Labor Day, from Thursday night through Sunday. At the beginning, when we were still young couples, we chose this weekend because it was the week when the kids went back to school. After five decades our children have all grown into adults, but we continue the tradition.

We have included Yosemite on a number of these occasions: Vogelsang High Sierra Camp, Tuolumne Meadows, Sunrise High Sierra Camp on two occasions, Evergreen Lodge near Hetch Hetchy, and Wawona.

The first trip to Vogelsang High Sierra Camp was our third River Rat trip. Half way up Vogelsang, a Lady Rat tried to hitch a ride with a mule train that happened by. We found excuses to laugh, as we always have. We climbed Vogelsang Peak, introducing the River Rats to the "glad tidings."

Two avid fishermen were embarrassed on that trip when another Lady Rat put lures on popsicle sticks and caught more fish than the fishermen did with their fancy poles and elaborate tackle. Another Lady Rat was having diarrhea and asked a Rat who was a medical doctor what she could do about it. The doctor was an orthopedist. He gave her a cork.

While we were on a trip to Sunrise High Sierra Camp, a Rat doctor celebrated his 40th birthday. We packed champagne and party supplies and had a high old time. There are three big rocks in a meadow near Sunrise camp, so we established a choir on each rock and sang rounds back and forth at each other.

On our second trip to Sunrise we had a great time hiking to the top of Clouds Rest, which is northeast of Half Dome and is higher than Half Dome. We assembled on the 9,000-foot summit and could see thunderheads massing in every direction except where we were.

The year we were scheduled to go to Tuolumne High Sierra Camp we sent announcements to the members:

CHIEF TENAYA INVITES YOU TO A NO-HOST COCKTAIL PARTY ON THE SHORES OF LAKE TENAYA. DRESS FORMAL.

Another River Rat played the role of Chief Tenaya in an Indian suit. Everyone else showed up in tattered and ripped Salvation Army hand-me-downs. We made our appearance at dinner dressed accordingly. Later another guest at Tuolumne Lodge recognized Patti as one of the participants, while both were in San Francisco.

I share these anecdotes to point out that part of the Yosemite experience has always been doing offbeat things, having fun, and shedding conventional roles and ordinary existence.

MARTINO AT TUOLUMNE MEADOWS

Mike and Jeanne Adams drove into the Tuolumne Meadows parking lot. They looked over into the area where employees lived. They saw a table set up with fine linen and table settings, with four young people sitting around it, enjoying a luxurious meal.

Mike remarked that it looked like something Peter Hoss would do. Sure enough, it was Martino and friends.

On another occasion Martino and Harkjoon Paik were chatting with the father of another Tuolumne Lodge employee, who had worked at Camp Curry as a porter. He was telling of the crazy adventures of a fellow Camp Curry porter, Peter Hoss.

Martino listened with rapt attention as he heard tales he had not heard before. Finally, as the conversation neared a close, and the yarns wound down, the former Camp Curry porter finished by saying, "I wonder what ever happened to him."

At this point Martino interjected, "I think I could tell you. He is my father."

BOY SCOUTS AND HELL'S ANGELS

One summer a former Yosemite employee and I took some Boy Scouts, including my son Vince, hiking in the Yosemite High Country. We were returning home on a warm afternoon and decided to visit Rainbow Pool, which had been a favorite spot for my buddies and me when working as Yosemite summer employees.

Rainbow Pool was a wonderful spot, an excellent swimming hole. We had a good time swimming, and diving off the surrounding rocks.

The roar of motorcycles suddenly disturbed the quiet serenity of the place, and a band of Hell's Angels, with their back-riding molls, arrived. They parked their bikes, drinking beer and acting as though they owned the place. They ignored us, but caused us to feel uneasy.

The invading bikers were all dressed in leather jackets. Some of them had stubs of arms and legs, most likely having lost the missing appendages in biking accidents.

Without a word being said, we decided to leave the place to the Hell's Angels. We changed back into our clothes in a nearby restroom and passed through the bikers as we walked to our car. We reached the car without incident.

After we had driven about five miles down the road one of the Scouts pulled something from his pocket, held it up for our inspection, and said, "Look what I found." He was holding a key to a Hell's Angels motorcycle.

"Where did you find that?" we asked.

"It was lying on the ground," he replied.

We had visions of a drunken biker storming around in a rage, searching for a key that he was never going to find. We decided not to return it.

We probably violated the *Boy Scout Manual.*

VINCE AT SUNRISE HIGH SIERRA CAMP—FAMILY REUNION

Sunrise High Sierra Camp was constructed on the site of one of Mary Curry Tresidder's favorite spots, a ledge overlooking a meadow, with mountain peaks in the distance and meadows in the foreground. Sunrise is the last of the High Sierra camps to be built, in 1961. Vince worked there three summers, managing it during the third.

Sunrise Camp may be reached either by climbing a steep four and a half mile trail from Tenaya Lake or by hiking a more leisurely but lengthy seven-mile trail from Tuolumne Meadows.

A crew of between six and ten young people operates each of the High Sierra camps.

The crewmembers at Sunrise Camp slept in tents. If the camp was overbooked, they would sometimes give their tent to a guest and sleep under the stars. On nice nights, they would move their mattresses to a place they called "Monk's Shelf," named for a monk who reportedly had spent three days there in meditation.

The members of the Sunrise Camp crew rotated among themselves the jobs of table servers, dishwashers, wood stackers, restroom cleaners and other miscellaneous handyman chores. When Vince worked there, the crew worked seven days a week, with some time off at midday. If crewmembers occasionally wanted a day off, the others would cover for them. Today, they have a day off.

The days at Sunrise were relatively unstructured for the guests. At 7 a.m. a crewmember struck a triangle, which announced to sleepers that breakfast would be served in half an hour. Following breakfast, the crew moved a table into the sunshine and handed box lunches to the guests. A cook named Julia turned out delicious meals from basic equipment in a kitchen in the permanent stone building. Guests applauded the meals. There was a good spirit among all the guests.

Vince told how he and most of the Sunrise crew once hiked eight miles each way to attend a party at the Merced Lake High Sierra Camp. They had a great time and then walked all the way back, arriving at Sunrise Camp by 4:30 in the morning, at which point they turned out a batch of blueberry muffins rather than going to bed. The story made me smile. It was just the sort of thing I would have done when I was their age.

Early photo of Sunrise Camp.

In 1984 we had a family reunion at Sunrise Camp. On the second day of our stay we awoke to a hearty breakfast. The meadows seemed particularly green that morning; the chipmunks seemed particularly merry as they scurried across the rocks. The clouds continually changed the appearance of the peaks of the distant Clark Range. The majestic scenery and beautiful weather collaborated to evoke a feeling of peace and serenity.

Later in the morning we climbed to the top of a large rock outcropping named "Bug Dome" and ate our bag lunches while sitting in the warm sunshine, trying to take in the panorama of mountain peaks that stretched away in every direction. A pair of large domes named by locals the "Jayne Mansfield domes" was clearly visible. The domes were prominent landmarks for cross-country hikers.

We observed a familiar summer Sierra weather pattern that began with a crystal clear morning, gathering clouds by midday and thunderstorms in the afternoon as warm breezes from the Central Valley encountered the cold granite in the Sierra. As the clouds gathered we hurried off Bug Dome and raced the storm back to our tent, where we had a peaceful nap lulled by the sound of rainwater on the top of the tent.

Still following the normal summer pattern, the weather cleared in time to enjoy one of Julia's incomparable meals while trading stories with other guests. In the evening we sat around a roaring campfire, heard a lecture about Yosemite Indians from a ranger naturalist and sang campfire songs together. We finally headed for our tents with the conviction that life just doesn't get much better.

The next day the couple of honor arrived, our son Martino accompanied by his fiancée Maura. We ran into some other guests and backpackers who had been camping in the adjoining campground. Two of the campers turned out to be Jack and Jill. He was actually Jack Stark, who was president of Claremont McKenna College.

We began talking about Martino and Maura's plan to get married and to take a backpacking honeymoon. Jack made the incredibly generous offer of the use of his cabin on Silver Lake, on the east side of the Sierras, for the honeymoon. It turned out, unfortunately, that Martino and Maura's car broke down and the newlyweds never arrived at the cabin.

As of this writing they have been married 27 years and have a daughter who has just graduated from high school and a son who has completed the sixth grade.

Two decades later I happened to run into Jack and Jill while having dinner at the Mono Inn. We remembered each other and had a friendly chat.

We spent a few pleasant hours rambling about the meadows and then watched the unforgettable sight of a helicopter depositing brand new portable toilets, called Jet-Johns, on the campsite, which caused me to reflect about what John Muir would have thought about the spectacle, if he had witnessed it.

The regularly scheduled afternoon thunderstorm chased us into our tents, where we played a game of Trivial Pursuit and then enjoyed another of Julia's magical meals followed by another evening around the campfire singing and enjoying the fellowship of new friends and old.

All too soon the experience came to an end. Vince had hiked out previously and moved our car to the Tenaya Lake trailhead so we could hike out by a different trail.

Following a swim in Sunrise Lakes, Patti, Martino, Maura and I

Martino and Vince on Cathedral Peak.

headed up Tenaya Peak for a spectacular view over a sheer drop down to Tenaya Lake far below us. The regular afternoon thunderstorm caught us out in the open. A small bolt of lightning, a miniature version of the full blast, hit Martino and sent a few arcs from him. We sought shelter beneath a spreading hemlock tree until the storm passed.

We descended the switchbacks to Tenaya Lake, carrying fond memories.

FAMILY ATTEMPTS MT. LYELL

One of our most memorable family adventures was an assault that we made on the 13,000-foot summit of Mt. Lyell. Martino was 19; Vince was 17.

The family assembled at Tuolumne Meadows, where Martino was working. It was late summer; we arrived in mid-morning. It was a 13-mile hike from Tuolumne Meadows to the upper base camp. We arrived at the base camp about 6 p.m. and spent the night there. Vince had driven from sea level and was at the 11,000-foot base camp in less than 10 hours. The abrupt change gave him a bad case of altitude sickness.

We were attempting to do in two days what would normally require three days. We were on the trail the next morning before 7 a.m. We had to cross the Lyell glacier, the largest in Yosemite. The glacier had over a mile of slippery footing across depressions called sun cups, which are ridged cavities up to two feet deep. We were heading for a rock and gravel saddle.

In early afternoon we arrived at the saddle, where we stopped for lunch. Vince didn't have anything to eat, as he was trying to recover. Martino urged him to keep going. I made an executive decision that the guys would go on, and Patti and I would stay. Patti was disappointed, but I persevered.

Martino and Vince reached the summit and returned. We reached the Upper Base Camp by 5 p.m. We still had a few hours of light, but a long way to go. The boys gave us their flashlights and went ahead since Martino had to get to work. Vince ran with Martino most of the way down to Tuolumne Meadows Lodge, where Martino had to work the dinner shift. There was no moon, our light went out, and we were stumbling along the trail through the darkness. My glasses got caught in a tree, which delayed us for a while as we groped for them in the dark. It was nearly midnight before we finally stumbled into Tuolumne Meadows Lodge from the wrong side of the river that flows past it.

Patti later made one more unsuccessful attempt at the climb with my cousin

Starting off on the Mt. Lyell climb. Left to right, Martino, Vince, Peter and Patti.

Byron Beach, Jr., and another friend, but they were halted by bad weather. I was forced to be content with my one and only ascent at the age of thirteen.

MOUNTAIN MEN'S MENTAL LAPSE

My son Vince and I decided to spend Father's Day in Yosemite.

On the way home we were seized with a sudden urge to hike the four miles to the top of Nevada Fall. The trail up the Merced River gorge is one of the most popular Yosemite hikes. The Merced flows over two spectacular waterfalls, one located above the other. The 300-foot Vernal Fall is the lower of the two, and the 500-foot Nevada Fall the higher. Above and below Vernal Fall the river splashes over rocks and creates foaming eddies along an almost continuous series of rapids, all of them visible from the trail.

We started up the trail at midday in bright warm sunshine. We saw a few thunderclouds far away in mountains but judged that we would be safe from rain. Summer thunderstorms occur frequently in the High Country, but not very often on the Valley floor. In our judgment, as experienced mountain men, there was no threat.

A trail passing beside the river is appropriately named the Mist Trail, since hikers are often drenched with the windblown spray from the falls—very refreshing to sweating climbers on warm days.

Vince and I climbed the Mist Trail to the top of Nevada Fall where we could see the river flowing toward the fall over smooth granite. From the top of Nevada Fall we hiked along a granite face and leaned over a railing to get a spectacular view of the cascading tumult of waters roaring over Nevada Fall, just below our feet.

Vince and I sat on some rocks enjoying the warm sunshine, feeling mellow and very pleased with our spontaneous adventure. We noticed that the sky up the river was growing darker, but the coulds were still too far away to disturb our reverie.

The very first whisper of what was going to occur came when Vince made the observation, "Up at Sunrise Camp when the weather looked like this we were often in for a real dump." Sitting there in the sunshine, Vince's memory seemed a mere abstract comment with no connection to our present situation. We thought nothing of it.

However, Vince's casual remark suddenly became prophecy as the wind blew the clouds in our direction, shutting out the sunshine and darkening the sky over our heads. In less than ten minutes the first raindrops began to fall, and before twenty minutes, we were in a real deluge, pounded upon by a driving rainstorm with lightning striking around us and thunder echoing in our ears.

We joined other dayhikers in scrambling toward the trail. We were forced to use the much longer horse trail. Those wiser souls who had thought to throw a rain jacket or poncho into their backpacks donned them and proceeded down the trail, able to appreciate the display of raw power in relative comfort.

Vince and I, clad in our shorts and light shirts, were not able to derive much excitement. From the beginning, we were wet and cold. We questioned our lack of foresight. We knew that Yosemite weather was unpredictable. We had actually noticed the thunder clouds piling up on the horizon. We had behaved like clueless city-bred tourists.

By the time we arrived at the car we couldn't have been more wet if we had fallen into the river. We got dry things out of the car and changed out of our soaking wet clothes in a nearby restroom. I was halfway home before I was warm.

We were reminded of a timeless observation attributed to Adlai Stevenson, "God chose to limit the intelligence of man, but not to limit his stupidity."

PART 4

Perspectives on Preservation and Enjoyment

*A summary of my opinions based on
75+ years of hands-on experience*

Peter, backpacking in the High Sierra. Courtesy of Dick Mansfield.

Chapter 25

What Is the Standard?

The mission of the National Park Service in Yosemite is defined in the Organic Act of August 25, 1916, creating the national parks, as follows:

"The service thus established shall promote and regulate the use of the federal areas known as national parks, monuments, and reservations hereinafter specified by such means and measures as conform to the fundamental purpose of the said parks, monuments, and reservations, which purpose is to conserve the scenery and the natural and historic objects and the wild life therein and to provide for the enjoyment of the same in such manner and by such means as will leave them unimpaired for the enjoyment of future generations."

The Academic Answer

In the early days of Yosemite the conflict was between the type of conservation and recreation defined in this law and commercial uses, such as mining, logging and sheep herding. John Muir actually operated a sawmill in Yosemite Valley for James Hutchings, and did not view this operation as an environmental threat at the time. Today there is a universal belief that commercial development unrelated to the uses defined the Act of 1916 does not belong in Yosemite or in any other national park.

In his book *Mountains Without Handrails* Joseph Sax addresses issues relating to national park management and the visitor experience. He analyzes the origins of the current divisive conflict between the preservationists and the recreational tourists, noting at the outset that this conflict did not always exist.

> For a good many years, this fragile coalition held together with only modest conflict. The preservationists (as they are now called), who always comprised the most active and interested constituency in favor of national parks, had little to complain about. The parks were there, but they were so little used and so little developed— Congress was so grudging with appropriations…That those who wanted to maintain the parks as they were, both for their own use and as a symbol of man's appropriate relationship to nature, had what they wanted.…In its early years, and particularly before the full

blossoming of the automobile era, the Park Service was able to take an actively promotional posture, encouraging increasing tourism, road building and hotel development without losing the support of its preservationist constituency. It was then in everyone's interest to create greater public support for the parks…. even the most ardent wilderness advocate complained little about the Park Service as a promotional agency. The adverse effects tourism might have were long viewed as trivial.

However, Sax notes, as recreational use of the national parks in general, and Yosemite in particular, increased, all of this changed. The change was accelerated by easy access to Yosemite by automobile. The hardy visitors of earlier days had to endure long, uncomfortable stagecoach rides, risking occasional armed robberies. They had to stay in primitive accommodations in order to see Yosemite. They were supplanted by a new breed of recreational tourist who could jump into a car or recreational vehicle, load it with the comforts of civilization, drive to Yosemite, and enjoy amenities similar to those at a conventional resort.

The recreational explosion of recent years has unraveled that alliance (i.e., between the preservationist and the recreational tourist) and brought to the fore questions we have not previously had to answer: For whom and for what are the parks most important? Which of the faithful national park constituencies will have to be disappointed so that parks can serve their "true" purpose? The adverse impact on natural resources generated by increased numbers is the most visible sign of a cleavage that goes much deeper. The preservationist constituency is disturbed not only—and not even most importantly—by the physical deterioration of the parks, but by a sense that the style of modern tourism is depriving the parks of their central symbolism, their message about the relationship of man and nature, and man and industrial society.

Sax sees the preservationists not as elitists who want all the space in Yosemite for themselves, but rather as moralists, wishing to convert visitors to their own viewpoint on how to enjoy Yosemite without planned entertainments and the customary activities and amenities found at conventional resorts. He sees the preservationist as an evangelist for a secular religion rooted in nature worship. He notes:

> Many of those who are most opposed to the claimed over-development of (Yosemite) Valley do not themselves use it much. Wilderness lovers go into the wilderness, and Yosemite, like most national parks, has an abundance of undeveloped wilderness. What offends is not the unavailability of the Valley as wild country, but the meaning national parks come to have when they are represented by places like Yosemite City, as the Valley has been unkindly called.

Sax describes the views of Edward Abbey, a preservationist of this stamp, as follows:

> His complaint is of quite a different kind. Industrial tourism debases the significance that national parks have for him, and he is troubled to see people using the parks as they use Disneyland, simply as places to be entertained while they are on vacation.

Recreational tourists have no counterargument to preservationists and few vocal advocates; they are basically consumers. If Yosemite comes to be a place where they cannot enjoy themselves, either because there are too many people, or too little entertainment, or too few amenities, they will move on to another place. Perhaps they are only interested in seeing Yosemite once. Most recreational tourists do not have the fervor to "save" Yosemite that the preservationists have.

There are other categories of visitors to Yosemite which Sax omits to mention: neither preservationist nor recreational tourist. I have preferred to call myself a privileged visitor who has played many different roles in Yosemite, but never the role of a manager.

Some preservationists believe that the National Park Service should actively discourage people from visiting Yosemite, and that Yosemite should not be publicized or "marketed." The late Galen Rowell was a well-known photographer, mountaineer and writer. In my opinion he was the Ansel Adams of color photography and an explorer of the far corners of the earth. Rowell would meet most definitions of a preservationist. However, he encountered a problem in connection with an adventurous climb of Half Dome. A group of preservationists attempted to discourage him from publicizing the climb. He later commented:

> The … reason for mentioning the Half Dome incident is that it is a classic example of the chasm between two philosophies of environmental preservation. Some people believe that the way to preserve wild lands is to leave them alone and not publicize them or the adventures that take place in them. They believe the stories in books and magazines bring additional people, who harm the environment and detract from the wilderness experience. And that is what the group of Yosemite activists was trying to prevent by thwarting our climb. The other school, to which John Muir clearly belongs, believes that the salvation of wild places is rooted in public awareness. Muir wrote book after book, article after article, which brought new people into the wilds, but which also helped create an informed electorate which greatly increased awareness of conflicts over natural values.

This discussion of the parting of the ways between recreational tourists and preservationists—plus the schism between preservationists who want to encourage visitation and those who want to discourage visitation—illustrates why it is so difficult to arrive at decisions about national park management. Some preservationists feel that any compromise would be a betrayal of their principles. Some recreational tourists argue that preservationists, who are a minority, should not be able to impose their will on the majority with regard to the use of public property. There are a number of visitors who do not fall into either of these categories, and I am one of them.

There is no indication that Yosemite will ever cease to be attractive to visitors. There will be more, not fewer, who wish to visit. The debate between preservation and recreational tourism will likely intensify. While the debate rages, someone must manage Yosemite and make day-to-day decisions attempting to balance preservation and enjoyment, with someone certain to be unhappy. The National Park Service is charged with making those decisions.

Concessioners are caught between attempting to observe the maxim of the hospitality industry—that the guest is always right—and the regulations that the

National Park Service must impose to protect the integrity of Yosemite.

All other players, nonprofits and other organizations having an interest in Yosemite—as well as the surrounding communities that depend upon tourists visiting Yosemite—will be caught in the crossfire.

Dennis J. Herman, who identifies himself as a disciple of Sax, is another commentator who has attempted a scholarly discussion of the conflict between preservation and enjoyment in national parks in general and in Yosemite in particular, making recommendations to address the issue. Herman was a 1992 graduate of Stanford Law School. He wrote a thought-provoking article in the 1992 *Stanford Environmental Law Journal* that contained some additional insights that build on the conclusions of Sax.

Herman began with an observation with which I wholeheartedly agree:

> Visitors' tolerance to overcrowding varies widely according to their initial expectations for their visit. There is no objective standard by which to measure overcrowding: It is a subjective judgment that will vary from person to person, and is dependent on factors ranging from the number of people encountered to the individual's perception of how those people have impacted the environment. The more disturbance to the environment that is perceived, the more likely a visitor is to complain that the area is overcrowded ....
>
> Thus, visitors may continue to report that they are "satisfied" with their park experience without first considering what type of experience they really would have preferred. Reality becomes the measure of their expectation, and personal values and goals become subverted to the lowest common denominator. A visitor heading for Yosemite Valley in the middle of summer, knowing that it will be crowded, may be more likely to expect to socialize on a vacation than to seek a nature-oriented experience characterized by solitude, self-reliance and aesthetic enjoyment. When he or she encounters the expected crowds and urban-like attractions, he or she will be less likely to be disappointed.

Herman proceeds from this accurate observation to a conclusion that sounds good intellectually but which has not, in my observation, played out in the real world:

> Park managers, therefore, must be cautious in reaching planning decisions based on what visitors want, or how satisfied visitors are believed to be. Rather, the National Park Service must first determine the best strategy for preserving park resources and creating quality visitor experiences, and craft its policies and concession decisions accordingly. All too often, the Park Service takes the opposite approach: first determining desires, then deciding how to accommodate preservation goals.

He begins to sound like Alfred Runte and his followers, who believe that preservation, according to their definition, is the only reason for national parks and that enjoyment is secondary and must be severely limited or proscribed.

Herman frames the issue in these words, as he sees it:

> The national parks are a powerful symbol of our nation's respect for the natural environment. Our commitment to preserving and protecting the natural world must be strongest in our national parks, for if we do not have the will to aggressively seek preservation of these areas, how will we marshal the strength to protect the less unique features of our natural world? The national parks are integral to our efforts to instill respect and appreciation for the environment, and must be managed in a manner consistent with their importance as educational, inspirational and scientific resources.
>
> Preservation has been a guiding mandate for the National Park System from the moment Yosemite and Yellowstone were set aside for the enjoyment of future generations of park visitors. The mission of the parks is to provide visitors with a natural experience in a natural setting, to challenge people to meet nature on its own terms and come away with an appreciation of the importance of the natural world. In carrying out this mission, the National Park Service must refuse the whims and desires of popular demand and instead exert

a strong hand in shaping both the type and scale of development to create an experience worthy of this mandate.

Sax, Herman and Runte suggest that the Park Service has a power that I question, that is, the power of a government agency in a democratic society to dictate how visitors must enjoy Yosemite.

Herman does acknowledge that it may be too late to alter development drastically in places like Yosemite and Yellowstone. This suggests that his ideas are prospective and addressed to other wilderness areas, not yet developed. This makes him more a realist and less of a radical than Runte.

I took time to locate Dennis Herman, have lunch with him, and bring him up to date on what has happened in Yosemite in the ten-plus years since he wrote his article. He had not been tracking it, or visiting Yosemite.

We had a friendly and lively discussion. We agree, I believe, that the issue of enjoyment vs. preservation is by no means easily addressed, and it is not likely to be resolved to the satisfaction of all concerned. We continue to approach the issue from a different perspective—Dennis Herman from an academic viewpoint, and I from the perspective of a privileged visitor.

Even if the Park Service had the authority which Sax, Herman and Runte believe it has, it is doubtful that the Park Service would exercise that authority in a way that Sax, Herman and Runte would like to see. The Park Service is a large bureaucracy operated by managers who make decisions or, in some cases, fail to make decisions for a number of reasons, including political pressure, lack of creative energy and avoidance of controversy. Many Park Service managers lack the temperament required to make the strong and potentially unpopular decisions that implementing Herman's and Runte's ideals would require. The political climate of this age differs from that in which strong personalities like Stephen Mather and Horace Albright were able to chart the direction of the national parks as they did.

A report on the premature retirement of Dave Mihalic from the Park Service by Dean E. Murphy of the *New York Times* provides a graphic illustration of this observation. Mr. Murphy describes what happened to Dave Mihalic after he skillfully completed his assignment of implementing the 2000 YVP plan.

After 30 years with the Park Service, Mr. Mihalic is at the top of his career in a high-visibility assignment, a member of the federal government's prestigious Senior Executive Service, and recently picked by the Bush administration as the next superintendent of Great Smoky Mountains National Park, the nation's most visited national park.

But Mr. Mihalic is saying good bye to it all. On January 3 (2003) he will retire to Missoula, Montana, where he plans to take up fly-fishing, tobacco chewing and watercolor painting.

"I have nothing lined up, other than buying a can of Copenhagen and a jackknife," Mr. Mihalic said.

Mr. Mihalic said the Bush administration wanted him to push through two contentious proposals at Great Smoky. The proposals, a land swap and a road project, had long been opposed by the National Park Service because of environmental concerns but had been backed by some influential Republicans in North Carolina and Tennessee.

A National Park Service spokesman said no decision had been made to allow the two proposals to go forward and that Mr. Mihalic's transfer to Great Smoky was not related to the proposals.

When Mr. Mihalic refused the Great Smoky assignment and asked for another, he said, he was told there would be none. When he asked for a meeting with Fran P. Mainella, the Park Service Director, he was told there was not time on her schedule, he said. Finally, when he submitted his retirement papers, they were accepted without a word from his superiors, he said.

With this type of example out there, where do Sax, Herman and Runte expect to find Park Service officials who are willing to promote their visitor-unfriendly and unpopular agenda in an aggressive fashion?

This is not a bad thing, in my judgment. Most Park Service personnel cannot be accurately described as bureaucrats. They have a difficult job, often under pressure. They are underpaid for what they are expected to do. Most of them are dedicated and truly believe in what they are doing. Most of them love the national parks they work in. They have been good stewards of the public property that has been entrusted to them. They deserve praise and recognition for the many good things that happen in our park system.

I agree with Herman's conclusion that it is too late to alter the course of development in Yosemite Valley. I do not think, however, that this should become a cause for pessimism or drastic action. It is simply not realistic to tear out the entire infrastructure in Yosemite Valley, abandon it and start over again from scratch. Those who think this should happen need to realize that politically, it never will.

I find an inconsistency between what academics like Sax and Herman would like to see and what the Organic Act of 1916 provides. To test this, I invite the reader to examine both.

PRAGMATIC ANSWER

The most simplistic, pragmatic viewpoint is that Yosemite is a public trust. It is for all of the public to enjoy as they see fit. Don't tamper with it by telling visitors how they must enjoy it. Let them find their own way. The only role of the Park Service should be to regulate so that no one desecrates Yosemite. The role of the concessioner is to provide the amenities the public wants, including entertainment found in other resorts. The mantra of the pragmatist to those who disparage current conditions is, "If you don't like it, go somewhere else." The pragmatist sees master planning as a gigantic waste of time and energy. The pragmatist does not recognize the academic answer as a moral crusade and looks upon environmental purists as elitists who want Yosemite for themselves only and want to exclude others.

MY ANSWER

Like most visitors, I am part pragmatist, part academic. It varies with my mood and my age. I go to Yosemite for different reasons and in different moods. I tend to avoid Yosemite Valley during the summer and go to the High Country instead. I have the luxury of visiting Yosemite pretty much whenever I want to visit. I usually go with a specific purpose in mind. I have a good idea of what to expect. As I grow older it becomes more enjoyable to sit and drink in a beautiful scene, instead of seeing how far I can hike in a day or how many peaks I can bag. I am no longer motivated to party on beaches. I am flooded with memories that sustain my image of Yosemite. However, I continue to be resistant to anyone telling me or others how Yosemite must be enjoyed. I am resistant to the idea that the visitors are the enemy and that keeping visitors out should be a management goal. It is highly unlikely that visitors will stop wanting to visit Yosemite. What is the point of "preserving" Yosemite if no one, or fewer visitors, can enjoy it and drink in the glad tidings?

The fondest memories of some will be the pristine beauty of the backcountry and the spiritual uplift of just being there. The fondest memories of others will be the fire fall, the Bracebridge dinner, or other man-made entertainment and good times, or just sipping a beer with one's feet in the cool Merced River.

So far, the pragmatic visitors have by far outnumbered the academics pressing for change, despite the trend being toward preservation. Don Neubacher, the current and recently appointed superintendent of Yosemite National Park, did not waste time declaring preservation a priority, while also declaring making Yosemite available to youth a priority. I suspect he is passing on the priorities of the current administration and the current top management of the Park Service. There is a little bit of a disconnect there. It remains to be seen how it will play out. There has been remarkably little change in the natural environment in Yosemite during my lifetime, despite the great influx of visitors and the changing attitudes toward enjoyment and preservation.

The federal government owns the infrastructure in Yosemite. The public owns the cliffs, domes, waterfalls, meadows, trees and rivers. The visitor owns his or her experience in Yosemite.

Yosemite is not for everyone, although Yosemite is held in trust for everyone. Some people prefer man-made attractions to natural attractions. There are plenty of places for visitors to enjoy man-made attractions without transporting them to Yosemite en masse. What is a man-made attraction and what is an experience to enhance enjoyment of a natural attraction will be the subject of endless debate.

To some, a Yosemite experience means drive in, shoot some pictures, have a hamburger at a crowded facility, send some postcards and drive out. Having done that, such a visitor can say, "I've seen it. Check it off the list of places to visit. Been there, done that." In my view such people should be pitied rather than censured. They would probably receive a headier dose of the glad tidings by looking at Ansel Adams' photographs or reading John Muir's eloquent prose. However, if these folks are not excluded from visiting Yosemite, it is just possible that something unexpected could rub off from a visit.

The great silent majority of visitors have a pragmatic viewpoint. They are likely to accept rather uncritically what the Park Service deems to be appropriate, whether it makes sense to them or not, and also to accept what the concessioner offers for amenities. There are, of course, those who will complain about anything, anywhere. The present situation is not perfect, but it is more than acceptable to millions. Programs geared toward the historical Yosemite continue to be popular, including the traditional ranger talks, presentations like Lee Stetson's one-man shows on John Muir, and Shelton Jackson's portrayal of a buffalo soldier. Descendants of the original Ahwahneechees still give demonstrations of basket weaving and grinding acorn meal, and their lifestyle can be viewed for those who are interested.

PRESERVATION: WHAT?

Preservation has become the leading buzzword of the environmental purists and the academics above quoted. To them, preservation means "restoring" Yosemite Valley to something it never was—a wilderness.

The word "preserve" does not appear in the Organic Act of 1916 creating the national parks. The word "conserve" is used instead, and historical traditions and wildlife protection are mentioned as well as scenery. The act speaks in terms of "providing for the enjoyment of the same in such manner and by such means as will leave them unimpaired for the enjoyment of future generations." This is not limited to scenery. Arguably, eliminating a historical tradition in the interest of preserving scenery or protecting wildlife is a violation of the spirit of the law as well as the letter of the law. What is called for is a balance.

A meaning of preservation more consistent with the law is that preservation should be interpreted to mean preservation of the Yosemite experience, which includes all the historical traditions and subculture that have developed in Yosemite. Some traditions unrelated to natural scenery have been preserved, notably the Bracebridge Dinner and Badger Pass. Others, notably the fire fall, have not.

Speaking for environmental purists, Alfred Runte in *Yosemite: The Embattled Wilderness* (see my critique of this book in Chapter 22) makes an impassioned argument that visitors are destroying Yosemite Valley by their mere presence.

Runte attempts to apply a theory developed by Garrett Hardin, an ecology professor, entitled "the tragedy of the commons" to visitation, largely in Yosemite Valley. He starts with this remarkable quote from Professor Hardin: "Any resource open to everyone is eventually destroyed."

He continues. "Extending the thesis (the tragedy of the commons) to Yosemite, Professor Hardin argued that perhaps access should be denied to anyone unwilling to walk the prerequisite distance for ensuring that the Park would not be overused or overdeveloped. Although labeled as elitist, the idea did have broad appeal among preservationists, who considered resource conservation the only legitimate purpose of national parks. Development in any form was therefore illegitimate.... Further, bearing on Professor Hardin's thesis, setting priorities for conservation required every interested party, from government officials and visitors to park concessioners, give up insisting that access standards should be self-determined."

When I first read Professor Hardin's comment, without understanding its true context, my immediate reaction was that this is Murphy's Law applied to ecology. I equated "commons" as a derogatory reference to the clueless tourists we used to call "peasants." Later I came to understand the real meaning of "the tragedy of the commons." "Commons" as used in the theory refers to common ground held by different users who have an equal right to use it. If they all exercise their common right, they will destroy the resource. A notable example is grazing on common ground, in which case overuse by those having equal rights will deplete the grass and destroy the resource. Another example is that if a body of water is overfished, that use will lead to no fish for anyone. In this context, the theory makes sense.

The tragedy of the commons theory makes no sense when applied to visitation of Yosemite Valley. By merely viewing the majesty of the natural scenery of Yosemite Valley, an infinite number of viewers will not consume the resource, as is the case in the examples noted above.

Nevertheless, commentators continue to draw an invalid conclusion from a misapplication of the theory of the tragedy of the commons. Jan van Wagtendonk, identified by Mr. Runte as "a Yosemite research scientist," put a further spin on the tragedy of the commons theme, as applied to visitation in Yosemite Valley, as follows: "A reasonable interpretation of the Organic Act indicates that Congress intended that the secretary of the interior protect natural conditions in parks, as an absolute duty, and to only allow use consistent with that protection. It is questionable whether the Park Service should determine public desires and attempt to accommodate them."

Runte explains his concept of preservation as follows: "People seeking organized recreation would be asked to head elsewhere. Similarly, every duality in the management structure would be fully eradicated, allowing no business to compete for attention with the natural environment. The few necessities of any visitor's experience, namely food, lodging and camping equipment, could be provided by nonprofit foundations operating strictly as adjuncts of the National Park Service. The criterion of every product or service would be compatibility with the goals of preservation. The purposes of Yosemite, as an uncommon resource, would remain strictly educational, scientific and protective."

In other words, what Runte and his camp followers are saying is, "Visit Yosemite our way, or be banished and excluded. Our way or the highway."

In my view, the argument that too many visitors viewing nature will inevitably detract from an appreciation of nature is conclusively disproven by considering nature appreciation in Japan, a scenic but overcrowded country, where the opposite can be readily seen by any visitor. In Japan a veneration of nature has been elevated to a national religion, Shinto, embraced by over 90% of the population.

PRESERVATION: WHY?

The basic purpose for which Yosemite was set aside as a national park, enjoyment of the public, is what the law provides, whether environmental purists like it or not. The arguments of Runte, Hardin and Van Wagtendonk are not only elitist, they are at variance with the core principles of American democracy. If the false premises of the above-quoted environmental purists are combined and reasoned logically, one reaches the conclusion that the visitor to Yosemite Valley must depart or be severally restricted in enjoying Yosemite, which is totally contrary to the spirit of the law, if not the letter of the law, as well as historical tradition.

In short, the only purpose of preservation is to guarantee continued enjoyment. The Park Service is in Yosemite National Park to enforce this requirement, and to educate the public in doing so, and for no other purpose. The concessioner is in Yosemite to serve the needs of the visitor and for no other purpose. The nonprofits are in Yosemite to enhance the visitor experience in a way the other players cannot, due to financial limitations, and for no other purpose. This notion of preservation is clearly what the law establishing Yosemite as a national park contemplates.

A concessioner in financial difficulty will provide inferior service to visitors. I have seen this happen in places other than Yosemite. Therefore, a concessioner must be allowed to make a reasonable profit. If concessioners are required to be open year-round, as they are in Yosemite, to serve visitors, they need to be allowed to offer some inducements to attract visitation in the off season. Most importantly, the concessioner is in Yosemite permanently and provides continuity, whereas superintendents tend to be there a short time, sometimes hardly long enough to learn what needs to be done to manage.

Hil Oehlmann answered the accusation that concessioners are only interested in profit as follows: "Probably what troubles me most is the apparent unqualified assumption that the people who operate concessions in the national parks would subscribe to any form of desecration of these areas for the sake of additional profit."

Hil stated the case for the concessioner succinctly as follows: "I am opposed to the philosophy that all human pursuits beyond eating, sleeping and enjoying nature should be interdicted if only because they can be followed somewhere outside a national park."

Ed Hardy, chief operating officer under MCA, stated it this way: "Our first responsibility is to our guests. Additionally, there is the responsibility for a private business in a national park to operate in support of the National Park Service goal to provide for the use and enjoyment of the Park while protecting the Park resource for future generations.... The guest is our reason for being here, and quality guest service is critical."

Ansel Adams was often critical of management decisions by the concessioner and the Park Service. However, he never equated excluding or restricting visitors with preservation, which he championed so ardently. He said it this way in 1971: "Any attempt to reduce visitors would be futile, socially or politically, and would be a real disservice to people at large. The maximum number of people should see Yosemite and should experience its incredible quality. To shut that off from the world would be somewhat similar to closing St. Paul's Cathedral for the sake of the architecture."

In 1979 Ansel wrote to William Whalen, director of the Park Service, "However, in spite of all of this development, the Valley itself is more beautiful than when I first came; it is clean, well managed by the service, free from dust of earlier days, and the services are surely superior. It should be made clear that what has been done, inappropriate as much of it is, has been done quite well...."

I am in agreement with Ansel. Yosemite Valley now is more beautiful than it was when I worked there in the 1950s, despite the millions who have visited since. I categorically reject the argument that the people are the enemy.

Therefore, in my judgment, preservation does not mean exclusion. Moreover, the only reason for preservation is to insure future enjoyment. Enjoyment, not preservation, is the only justification for national parks, precisely the opposite of what the environmental purists say.

I have offered an academic view, a pragmatic view and my own view about preservation. There is conflict in my own thinking as well as in practice. There are certainly times when I am in Yosemite that I wish there were not so many people there. However, Yosemite is not my private property. I have to realize that all those other people have as much of a right to be there as I do.

Planning efforts mandated by the settlement in the recent litigation over the Merced River seem to be headed in the direction of preservation trumping enjoyment. However, the planning is a three-year process in its beginning phases. The planners have classified all of Yosemite Valley as recreational under WSRA, which arguably should allow recreational uses to continue and make enjoyment primary in Yosemite Valley. The catch is that WSRA requires designation of certain areas as ORVs (Outstanding Recreational Values). The Park Service could adopt the viewpoint that if a recreational use conflicts with what has been designated as an ORV, the recreational use must go. ORVs have not yet been clearly defined.

The Park Service has not yet been confronted with making this type of decision under its management authority. To consider some extreme examples, if it were determined that swimming in the river, a traditional recreational activity, adversely affected water quality, would the Park Service be obligated to ban swimming in the river? If it were determined that campgrounds or tourist facilities located near the river were adversely affecting the river, would they have to be moved or dismantled in order to "preserve" the river? If it is determined that historic bridges, traditionally a feature of the Yosemite scene, interfered with the natural flow of the river, would the Park Service be obligated to remove and rebuild them? How is an adverse effect on the river to be determined? These are unanswered questions as the planning process proceeds. It is unclear to me if any approach has been mandated by a court. A further question arises as to whether the basic approach can come from a court, or whether it must be mandated by Congress. These questions are blowing in the wind of Yosemite.

PRESERVATION: HOW?

Preservation should mean "preserving the Yosemite experience for future generations," not just preserving scenery. Setting aside land for public enjoyment was revolutionary when first proposed. It was an experiment. If you accept Ken Burns' recent pronouncement, it was our most noble experiment, our best idea.

My own experience in Yosemite would not be nearly as complete or enjoyable without memories of the people with whom I have shared Yosemite and my adventures with them, some of which have been described in this book. Admittedly, my situation is unique. Yosemite is roots to me. Tearing it out and starting over in the name of preservation would be taking away my roots. I would strenuously object to that, as would anyone in my situation.

For many, a visit to Yosemite is about more than looking at scenery. The happiest memories of some visitors are from man-made attractions that environmental purists denounce and want to eliminate for the sake of preservation, such as the Bracebridge Dinner and Badger Pass.

In these cases, enjoying the spectacle outweighs the damage, in my opinion. I have denounced events that harm the environment, such as bear feeding under the lights and creating a tourist attraction by defacing a Giant Sequoia so cars can drive through. The Park Service is in Yosemite to make this kind of judgment call.

Yosemite Valley is full of roped-off areas in which natural habitat is being restored and visitors are forbidden to tread. I support these efforts. They outweigh any argument that visitors should be able to walk wherever they please or camp wherever they please, as they used to do.

If preservation means that the total Yosemite experience be preserved, this would mean allowing traditional man-made attractions that do not damage the environment. This could mean reinstating the fire fall, which I would not oppose, perhaps not every night, but for special occasions. The matter of "how often" would be a judgment call for the Park Service. To me, the enjoyment of the event outweighs problems of traffic congestion and trampling meadows, which can be dealt with. I have seen the fire fall hundreds of times, so restoring it would not be very meaningful for me. However, it might be meaningful for the present and future generations who have been denied the opportunity to enjoy a Yosemite tradition. On this issue I part company with Ansel Adams, who vocally criticized the fire fall and applauded its demise.

My concept of preservation means that visitors should enjoy some amenities to make their visits more pleasant. One of these is the sale of alcoholic beverages, which some environmental purists deplore. David A. and Jennie Curry joined them on this issue, strange bedfellows. I see nothing wrong with a refreshing beer or glass of wine, particularly after a long hike. This approach should be extended to many activities, such as rafting the river, which used to be illegal. Rafting is a great way to view Yosemite Valley.

On the other hand, Yosemite should not be made into a theme park, or dominated by recreational activates that can be enjoyed elsewhere. The Park Service is there to prevent that. It is an ongoing judgment call to determine what activities are appropriate for visitors. Public tastes change. There always has been and always will be disagreement. I have not agreed with all decisions of the Park Service, but I accept them.

The use of automobiles within Yosemite Valley has been the subject of debate since they were introduced. Automobiles are needed to reach Yosemite Valley. They are less needed once the visitor is in Yosemite Valley. Walking, bicycles, and shuttle buses are sufficient to get most places, but autos are much more convenient for carrying items for picnics and children. I still believe that the usefulness of the automobile outweighs the inconvenience of traffic congestion, except at times of peak usage. However, I also believe that visitors should be strongly encouraged to use an automobile around and within Yosemite Valley as little as possible. The Park Service could enhance this objective by restoring some of the parking places that they precipitously removed.

In summary, I believe the human footprint on Yosemite has enhanced the visitor experience, not detracted from it. Perhaps the greatest need of visitors is to be saved from the saviors.

USER CAPACITY

A new buzzword is emerging with the introduction of WSRA. That is "user capacity." The Park Service has never been forced to consider whether there is some magic number that represents too many visitors in Yosemite Valley. Now the U.S. Ninth Circuit Court of Appeals has ruled that the Park Service must do this. The opinion is not totally clear to me on this point, but perception is reality. It has been reported that the experts appointed to advise the planners realize that user capacity varies widely with the time of year, and that only at peak times is it a present problem.

The Park Service has chosen to retain consultants who are supposed experts on user capacity. As of this writing I have not examined their credentials or heard what they have to say. Therefore, I will only say that if truly impartial experts, not dominated by environmental purists or concessioners or pro development advocates, come up with a formula for determining user capacity, I am willing to accept it, whether I agree with it or not, if it will avoid more litigation, end the debate, silence the critics and allow the Park Service to move on with their primary responsibility of managing Yosemite, in cooperation with the concessioner and the nonprofits. I fear this is a Utopian hope, based on past experience.

If the Park Service determines that there needs to be a limit on the number of motorists allowed to be in Yosemite Valley at one time, who enter Yosemite Valley by automobile, the least expensive and fairest way to enforce such a requirement is by a reservation system, which so far the Park Service has been unwilling to recommend. There are obvious problems with this, but I don't think they are insoluble.

VISITORS ARE NOT THE COMPLAINERS

For years I have had the perception that it is not the visitors who are complaining about management of Yosemite. It is some writers in the media and a small but loud and strident minority of environmental purists. This perception has been reinforced by countless glowing accounts of visits to Yosemite by friends and others who told me how much they enjoyed visiting Yosemite. I asked superintendents and CEOs of concessioners about the subject, and they reinforced my perception uniformly.

Finally, I was able to test the perception by looking at an actual survey of visitors. Don Neubacher, present superintendent of Yosemite, reported to me the amazing statistic that 99% of visitors to Yosemite had indicated overall satisfaction with appropriate facilities, services and recreational opportunities in a survey conducted by the University of Idaho Park Studies Unit at the request of the government in August 2010. I asked to see the survey in order to discern how it was conducted.

We live in an age in which decisions are influenced by polls, which have varying degrees of reliability. For more information about the survey, contact the superintendent of Yosemite.

For me the survey is a reinforcement of everything I have observed, heard and seen with my own eyes. In short, Yosemite is not broken and does not need to be fixed by drastic measures. To be sure, there are existing problems, but they are manageable. The survey is also a tribute to all the dedicated people who have worked hard to make the Yosemite experience meaningful to those who visit. The survey is a massive rejection of the rhetoric of the dueling environmentalists, naysayers, purists and chronic complainers whom I have become so tired of hearing. The glad tidings are in good hands, and the prospects for their continuing to inspire visitors look promising.

ADVICE TO VISITORS

In conclusion, I offer the following advice to potential visitors interested in the Yosemite experience:

If your idea of an ideal vacation is to enjoy man-made attractions, golf courses, spas, shopping, urban entertainment and related activities, Yosemite will be a disappointment. There are plenty of alternatives that will better suit you. Although Yosemite has been set aside for enjoyment of all the public, Yosemite will not be enjoyed by everyone.

If you have never been to Yosemite, be prepared to experience the glad tidings without preconceived notions, particularly based on what you may have read in the media or in books by environmental purist writers who tell you in eloquent rhetoric that Yosemite has been ruined by overdevelopment and is not worth visiting. I do not accept this, nor do the other 3,000,000 annual visitors, many of whom who regularly return to the Park.

If traffic congestion and perceived overcrowding bother you, visit Yosemite at times other than the peak summer months. I avoid Yosemite Valley in the summer and head to the High Country. On the other hand, the warm days and nights of the summer are pleasant for family camping. Every season has its particular charm.

If all you want to do is drive in, buy a postcard or souvenir, drive out and say you have been there, that is your prerogative as a beneficiary of a public trust. But you have missed the main reason for going. You might just as well buy a video or read a picture book.

If, like me, you want to go back to Yosemite time and time again and never get tired of it, and if you derive some form of spiritual uplift just from being there, accept Yosemite for what it is, and do not brood about what it is not or what it might be. Don't do anything to degrade it. Yosemite will endure.